Working Girl
Behind the Cellar Door

An Entrepreneur's Journey from a Bankrupt Winery to Gold Medals

By Kathy Charlton

Foreword by Leslie Sbrocco
A small business memoir by Kathy Charlton

Copyright © 2017 by Kathy Charlton
Published by Kathy Charlton

All rights reserved. No part of this publication may be reproduced, distributed, or transmitted in any form or by any means, including photocopying, recording, or other electronic or mechanical methods, without the prior written permission of the publisher, except in the case of brief quotations embodied in critical reviews and certain other noncommercial uses permitted by copyright law. For permission requests, write to the publisher, addressed "Attention: Permissions Coordinator," at the address below.

Kathy Charlton
Sequim, WA 98382

Acknowledgements

My story would be really short without you, *Our Olympic Cellars' Customers*. Your support and feedback over the years contributed to the winery's success. I consider each of you a part of the winery family. You took the time to visit us, attend our events, read my emails, drive out of your way or order on-line to purchase wine. Your hard-earned dollars spent at the winery allowed us to contribute to local non-profits supporting women and families. Thank you from the bottom of my heart.

I wish I could reach out and personally thank and hug all the *Winery Volunteers*. You invested your valuable time . . . from harvest, to bottling, pouring wine, working events . . . you did it all. The partnerships we formed with you and our local non-profits are priceless, each invested in each other's success. Your Cause became our Cause.

The Olympic Cellars Team. I could write another book chronicling how each of you helped rebuild our winery. Molly, Libby, Lisa, Kathy K, Randi. . . you exemplified what it meant to us to be a Working Girl. Michael and Ralph (my husband and coach) you are our beloved Handymen. Sara, Benoit, Virginie and now Greg . . . without your amazing wines there would be no business. I hope I told our story with love and compassion for all you've done.

And now the *Book Team*. As I mentioned in this book, if you don't have the needed skills, hire them. Jim Williams, a friend and teacher of "Start Your Own Business", gave me the wake-up call. Kathy, "This book is impossible to read, it jumps around, repeats itself. I gave up." So, on that input I found an editor, Helen Page. Her input, "It needs significant rework". She guided me with constant encouragement, made editing suggestions, but I had to do the work. Nine months later I handed the manuscript over to Marina Shipova, a teacher of computer graphics and publishing and an accomplished artist and illustrator. My book came to life in her hands. Without this team, you wouldn't be reading this book.

Foreword

Working Girl: Behind the Cellar Door, is more than a tome about what it took to revive a failed winery…although that's a great story in itself. There is so much more in this poignant, personal, and practical book. It takes you on the journey of a hard working woman who risked much, faced fears, and ultimately created a successful business against all odds. It's an insightful, funny, and thought-provoking read that keeps you wondering . . . what is that Working Girl going to do next?

I first met Kathy Charlton back in April 2004 at the Hotel Vintage Park while in Seattle for the Taste of Washington, the largest single-region wine and food event. The Hotel honors the Washington wine country and features a winemaker or winery owner during their evening wine hour. It was a perfect place to talk about my first book, *Wine for Women, A Guide to Buying, Pairing and Sharing Wine (Harper Collins)*.

And that evening offered up the perfect book and wine pairing. Kathy, the owner of Olympic Cellars Winery, poured her Working Girl Wines for the guests. After I talked about my book, Kathy's Working Girl persona revealed itself as she entertained us with funny anecdotes and an engaging, non-intimidating description of the wines. I knew then I wanted to know her better.

Kathy and I both came to the wine industry and to marketing wine to women from totally different paths. I had combined my love of theater into a production company and my consuming passion for wine into a business as a wine communicator, educator, speaker and television host.

Kathy inherited a bankrupt winery with little recognition and parlayed it into an award-winning operation with gold medals to prove it. By her own account, she had no background in wine, having spent 25 years in the semi-conductor industry. Not the most natural career path. But what she had was a strong business background and an innate sense of marketing that led her down the same path, capitalizing on an underserved market in the most non-traditional way. That's what got the attention of our industry, media, and the people she values most, her customers.

As I was running WineToday.com in 2000, the internet site about wine owned by The New York Times Company, I became aware of research that stated that the majority of wine consumers were women. I noticed as I was speaking at wine events that I would often get different questions about wine from men and women. That's when I got the idea to write a book geared specifically towards women.

Kathy was also realizing the importance of reaching out to women at about the same time. My book was published in 2003 and Working Girl Wines were launched in 2003 . (Great minds think in the same channel as my mother always says.)

Both of us took some criticism early on. Some said my approach of focusing on female consumers was "condescending." Nothing was further from the truth. I wanted to educate women to feel comfortable knowing more about the wines they enjoyed. My book actually won the Georges Dubouef Wine Book of the Year and was highlighted in national magazines as groundbreaking. Kathy was chided for offering up a lot of "red neck" clichés like Working Girl Wines; Created by Women for Women. What was left out was the important part of her tag line, the winery's moral code, In Support of Women. Both of us focused on empowering women to enjoy wine as part of their lifestyle. And, we both shared a career highlight of being honored by Margrit Mondavi and Women for WineSense with the Rising Star Award. I am proud of our contributions in shining the light on women and wine.

As you read Kathy's book you'll find that an integral part of her success was combining a strong focus on business basics while developing a unique partnership (and financial support) with non-profit organizations and volunteers in her community. Then add in her off-the-wall marketing approach and you find her schlepping wine one day and the next she's skydiving into Washington Wine Country to promote winery tourism. These in-the-trenches lessons from the front lines are interspersed with her unique marketing email-stories throughout and will keep you reading, spawning ideas, and like me, sometimes laughing out loud.

I especially related to Kathy's marketing mantra; Out of Sight, Out of Mind, Out of Business. You know . . . it's so true. But she wrapped that mantra into a communication style that evolved into a two-way dialogue that focused on earning, not buying her customers' attention. A quote from Kathy that got my attention, "I've said it before, but I'll say it again: I just knew in my heart that my customers needed to know I valued them. I needed to reach out in a personal way and show the love." And, that's exactly what she did.

Working Girl takes you Behind the Cellar Door and shares what it takes to run a business while being a wife, a mother, a grandmother, a team member and a leader.

As Kathy is so fond of saying, "Pour yourself a glass of wine, I have a story to tell."

It's a story that captivated me. And regardless of why you chose to read this book, it will captivate you as well.

Leslie Sbrocco

An award-winning author, speaker, consultant, and television host, Leslie Sbrocco is known for her entertaining approach to wine and food, as well as inspiring others to live a life of passion. Voted as one of the Top 100 most influential people in the American wine business, Sbrocco's engaging personality, humor, and ability to connect with the audience – whether on screen or on stage – are her trademarks.

Table of Contents

PART ONE
Behind the Cellar Doors

1. I Am A Working Girl 1
2. The QUESTION That Changed My Life 4
3. What Do You Mean It's Closed Down? 8
4. Can We Really Fix aAnything But Death? 14
5. Kathy, We Won! 19
6. Work On – Or – Work In 23
7. Women, Wine and the Working Girls 29
8. The French Influence 36
9. Cellar Rats 47
10. California, Here We Come! 56

PART TWO
Running Your Own Business – Advice from The Front Lines

11. Marketing and Chardonnay 64
12. Marketing: Out of Sight, Out of Mind, Out of Business ... 68
13. What's In It For You 71
14. Social Responsibility: The Heart of the Winery 74
15. Attract More Customers With Events 83
16. Shake it Up, A Non-Traditional Approach 98

17. The Business - Some Basic Marketing Strategies 104

18. Advertising vs. Public Relations.. 114

19. The Team Is No. 1... 122

20. One With Your Community... 132

21. Marketing with Emails 138

22. Holidays – It's Not All About Sales 154

23. Your Pet Is Part of the Marketing Team 161

24. Humor and Marketing 166

25. Show the Love for Your Customers..................................... 175

PART THREE
The Rest of the Story

26. Meanwhile Life Happens 180

27. Sometimes You Just Have to Take a Stand 181

28. Fight for What is Right... 189

29. Women Supporting Women... 194

30. Managing Business Downturns... 200

31. Life Doesn't Stop Just Because You Own Your Business ... 205

32. Times Are A Changing 209

33. The Circle Is Still Unbroken 215

Part One
Behind the Cellar Doors

Chapter 1
I am a Working Girl

That's who I am ... and I'm damn proud of it!

Well, that is what I said when I was promoting my winery and our Working Girl Wines.

But to be perfectly frank, that's not how I felt raising my kids. See, I grew up with a stay-at-home-mom in the 50s. Dinner was always on the table at 5:30 p.m., laundry put away, and my clothes ironed for the following day.

I was lucky to get my two kids picked up at day care on time, fighting Dallas traffic while working a full-time job, much less dinner on the table. Each night when we pulled up to the house and the garage door was closing I headed to the bathroom and closed the door. I needed just fifteen minutes of my alone time as I regrouped to deal with the evening chores.

When my kids were older they would greet me with a smile on their faces and a glass of wine as the garage door closed, silently signaling that there were going to be some hiccups to deal with that evening. That glass of wine was known as Mommy's Little Helper. Again, off to the bathroom I went to regroup and have a few minutes of my alone time.

One night when homework was done and my kids were watching the Wizard of Oz, I heard Dorothy in the background say, "There's no place like home."

I started chanting ... "There's no place like home. There's no place like work. There's no place like home. There's no place like work!" *And, no I hadn't had another glass of wine!*

See, when I graduated college in 1977 and landed a job at Texas Instruments (TI) I had finally found my Happy Place. This was me. I loved my job and literally grew up at TI. Although the 'entrepreneur' word wasn't even in my vocabulary then, the concept was in my genes and unbeknownst to me it had started to grow.

What I struggled at was being *The Mom*. As many of you will remember, this was the era when women could do and were expected to *Do It All and Love It*.

Not me. I sort of sucked at it. My cooking left a lot to be desired, so I settled on a seven-day menu that I replicated week after week. To this day my kids hate goulash, tuna fish salad, and salmon patties made from a can.

Also, I was a dork at even the simple motherly duties, like doing hair. But that wasn't my fault. I always wore my hair short (well, maybe because I couldn't do hair). So, one day after struggling with the brush and blow dryer and getting frustrated because we were going to be late for school, my daughter exploded. "Mom. You. Can't. Do. Hair." And then she took the hair brush away - forever. She was in second grade.

My kids are eight years apart in age because it took that long for me to forget the pain of childbirth. Okay, not really. That was just the time it took to put my first husband through school, then save enough money so I could get my degree in accounting and him his Master's in Engineering.

There were more ups than downs, and memories of my kids' childhood are rich and many. One that stands out and always warms my heart is my eight-year-old daughter rocking and singing to her baby brother each day after work while I regrouped in the bathroom . . . with the door open so not to miss a single minute of our circle of love.

Well, we all survived my cooking, and now my kids, Tamara and Kiah, have kids. Tamara is a pediatric physical therapist and Kiah is an Army Vet and now a fireman. Plus, I'm a grandmother seven times over. I'm known as the cool Grandma because I have five tattoos . . . I got my first one to celebrate my 60th birthday.

So maybe I didn't follow the Mother's Guide to Raising Children and that's okay. What I did learn was there is more than one way to do anything and everything in life. You don't have to follow a rulebook.

I retired from a successful 25-year career at TI and went on to buy a small bankrupt winery on the Olympic Peninsula in Washington State. Again, I didn't follow the rulebook and that entrepreneurial gene of mine went on steroids.

It wasn't an easy transition from corporate life to owning a small business, moving from a big city to a small town or running every facet of the business without a corporate machine behind me. Communicating with customers face-to-face who just walked in the door was way easier than learning how to connect outside the winery doors – that's when I discovered marketing was my middle name.

Over the years, friends and colleagues have commented that they loved my marketing, especially my emails to winery customers. I learned very early on that I needed to nurture a lasting connection with my customers if I was going to save and grow the winery. How I did it? Well, that's where the fun began.

You might want to pour yourself a glass of wine and put your feet up. I'm a Working Girl and have a story to tell you from *Behind the Cellar Door*.

CHAPTER 2

The QUESTION That Changed My Life

It's spring, - my children are married. Tamara and her husband, Rodney, live in Lubbock, Texas, and my son, Kiah and his wife Sabrina, live in Cupertino, California. And I have one grandson, Danny. I remarried in 1993 to Ralph Charlton, although I didn't change my last name at work until Ralph got tired of being called Mr. Harper. Ralph has his own marketing business and I still work for Texas Instruments. Life is good.

While I've been at TI for twenty-two years, I've been fortunate to work different assignments in widely diverse sectors of the company. Not realizing it at the time, these various jobs have provided me with a boatload of knowledge and the confidence to tackle new assignments even if I didn't have any background in those departments.

I started off as a supervisor in an accounting department at age twenty-seven with ladies twice my age reporting to me. Let's just say they taught me a lot. Then I was moved to the corporate profit sharing, pension, and employee stock option department. Managing the department a few years later and reporting to TI's CFO, I outsourced the entire department. Then on to Human Resources (HR) where my title of "outsourcing queen" was my middle name and we designed and implemented a centralized Human Resources Service Center.

After that, I think my boss thought I needed a mental break and maybe some fun and, would you believe, I was given a yellow hard hat? Yep, construction ... responsible for the construction of a 68,000-square foot, state of the art, fitness, aquatic, and sports center.

Then my favorite assignment of all, I moved into one of the business sectors of TI as the Human Relations (HR) manager for the international ASIC (application-specific integrated circuit) business at TI. I've always worked in administrative and support departments, i.e. overhead. These departments didn't make any money. They were just allocated a budget each year and could be "out sourced" if it made good business sense.

In April 1999 I was on a business trip in Bangalore, India, where ASIC had a software design center.

Ralph called one evening and we chitchatted for a while about this and that, then he nonchalantly asked, "Remember the winery we went to when we visited my Mom?" Stumbling over the words, he added, "It's for sale. How would you like to buy a winery?"

"Well, that would make good dinner conversation!" I laughingly retorted, not taking the question seriously. I then proceeded to tell him about my day.

I was really excited about this business trip because I got to see my family's house where we used to live in Bangalore. We moved there for three years when I was seven while my father conducted classes on working with hot line tools on high power electrical lines. We all know time changes things, but I wasn't prepared for my childhood home to now be a Honda Moped dealership.

It was still painted white with the tall cement wall around the yard. Rabid monkeys used to perch on the wall just waiting for a chance to raid the kitchen. I stood by the door remembering the cow that its owner led to the front steps each day for milking. We had to boil the milk so we wouldn't get sick and it tasted bad even with added vanilla and sugar. To this day, I can't drink milk. Closing my eyes, I can see and hear my mom screaming when she opened the door and was sometimes greeted by very, very large tarantulas and the occasional poisonous snake.

Well, Ralph seemed a bit distracted and wasn't in to my Bangalore memories. He came back to THE QUESTION.

"Honey, I'm serious about the winery. My mom not only invested in this winery but co-signed the loan and it's about to go bankrupt. There is a family connection to Mom but I don't know who they are. She used her retirement funds and is about to lose it all."

I remember muttering how sorry I was but asked why would we want to buy a bankrupt winery.

His answer: "We either buy the winery and she gets her investment back or we will need to support her because the rest of her retirement funds will run out."

Either way there was a cost to this decision.

His mother was very upset. She'd always been self-sufficient, not dependent on her kids. Knowing she would run out of money and have to ask us for support wasn't how she wanted to live.

So, Ralph called Dan Caudill, who owned the winery with his wife Sharon. We didn't know Dan, but he had the story behind the bankruptcy. Sharon was Ralph's Mom's family friend and her connection to the winery.

Here's what Dan told Ralph. Called Olympic Cellars, the winery was located in Sequim, Washington, on the North Olympic Peninsula. Dan was also the winemaker, which meant he supervised the entire process from contracting for the grapes, harvest, overseeing the production and bottling.

Originally named Neuharth Winery, Gene Neuharth, a winemaker from California founded Olympic Cellars in 1979. It was the fifteenth winery opened in Washington State and the first winery on the Olympic Peninsula.

And, now this historic winery was on the verge of bankruptcy.

When Gene passed away, Dan bought his winery and changed the name to Olympic Cellars. All was well for this small Sequim winery until the State decided to build a Highway 101 bypass around the town, and the bypass, unfortunately, went right through the barn that housed the winery.

So, Dan had to up and move in early 1998. Again, more history. He looked for another barn and found what is now the oldest standing barn on the Peninsula, built in 1890 in Port Angeles, just nine miles outside of Sequim, Washington. Many of the barns between 80 to 100 years old carry the names of pioneer families. The barn Dan moved to was the Willis Chambers barn and once part of the Wayside Farm.

Well you can imagine the work ahead?

And, a barn built in 1890 had to be brought up to current building codes. In fact, once the renovation started, the surprises ate up all the construction funding. Add in that Dan was also trying to make wine while not missing a harvest. It was a disaster waiting to happen.

So back in Dallas, Ralph and I sat hunched over his computer with this elaborate excel spreadsheet. Dan's winery records left a lot to be desired. Sales and financial reports were slim, some handwritten, and of course no QuickBooks. Imagine what this looked like to someone with an accounting background. And we were trying to forecast our future.

As it turned out, we had a couple of weeks to make a decision that would impact our lives for years to come.

Forecasting a business you don't know, with no accurate records from the past, and buying a winery that was just payables shouldn't have given us a green light. Right?

But, there was land, over fifteen acres, on Highway 101 frontage in what looked like God's country. Seattle was just two hours away and the Olympic Peninsula was known as Seattle's playground.

So, all was not lost, right? Didn't I just say that? Add in Ralph's MBA in finance and my degree in accounting, and oh, by the way, we would run the business from Dallas.

But this was Family. So, we labored over that dang excel spreadsheet – sales, payables, and expenses. It looked like we could do it. But we needed to sell a LOT of wine. And according to the inventory Dan gave us, we had it to sell.

We signed the papers, wrote a check, took out a personal loan (gulp) and Olympic Cellars Winery was now ours!

A couple of weeks later I had to go on another business trip and Ralph flew to Seattle and rented a car. In two hours, he would be walking through the winery doors.

What we didn't know was what was . . . *Behind the Cellar Door!*

Chapter 3

What Do You Mean It's Closed Down?

Ralph called me from the car as he drove from Seattle to the Olympic Peninsula. "It is beyond beautiful. There are massive green fir, cedar, and spruce trees as far as you can see, and the Olympic Mountains still have snow on them. It's still a bit cool. Glad I brought my jacket. Traffic is light. So, how's the weather in Dallas?"

Yeah, right. I could almost hear the smirk in his voice. He knew perfectly well what the weather was in Dallas. He hadn't left all that long ago. It was May; it was already hot and humid. Well, let's not discuss traffic. If you live in a huge metropolis you don't want to talk about it, either.

I'd done my research. Weather is generally mild on the Peninsula. A hot summer day was around 75 degrees and apparently, there weren't many of those. There are two major cities, Sequim and Port Angeles. Sequim is sometimes referred to as the Blue Hole because it sits in the rain shadow of the Olympics. Average rainfall is the same as Los Angeles, less than fifteen inches annually.

From sea to mountaintops, hiking, biking, kayaking – did I mention this was the playground of Seattle? At the end of fun-filled day wouldn't a glass of wine from a local winery be just what you needed? I had one in mind!

Ralph had had to wait a couple of weeks after we signed the papers before he could fly to Seattle. He'd told Dan his plans, so he didn't bother to call ahead that day because he would arrive during business hours when Dan covered the tasting room. Unlike many French wineries, most winemakers in the United States and elsewhere have a tasting room open to the public where they offer samples of their wares. Depending upon the winery, some tasting rooms are quite elaborate. While he was no longer the owner, Dan was our interim winemaker. Because winemaking is cyclical, many winemakers also work their tasting rooms. Who better to talk about and sell their wines but the winemaker?

Ralph never got past the Cellar Door. In fact, he didn't get past the front door.

When Ralph drove up to the winery he noted a couple of things. First, there were no cars in the parking lot . . . that meant no customers. And, second, a bright yellow notice was stapled to the locked barrel-shaped front doors. So, what was up?

First thing he did was read that yellow notice dated the day before. It said the winery was shut down for business.

Ralph walked around the barn and saw a truck parked in the back. He let himself in through an unlocked door on the side of the barn and saw Dan there, topping the wine barrels. Per Dan, a Clallam County inspector had come to the winery for one last inspection for the new winery business license, which had gotten delayed. While the winery had a Port Angeles address, it was actually located between Sequim and Port Angeles in Clallam County. The winery had been OK'd to be open for business and the inspector expected to see a brand new septic system installed, which had been required for the business license. But what he discovered was the old septic tank full to overflowing and leaking a small amount of sewage on the ground some distance behind the barn.

I've already mentioned that the construction cost was way over budget on this barn built back in 1890 and the new septic system just sort of fell through the cracks. The inspector shut the winery down until the septic system was replaced.

Ralph called me with the news. I started pummeling him with questions. "What do you mean the winery is closed down? What did you say about septic, uh? Why didn't we know about this?" The missing new septic system never came up in previous discussions with Dan or in any of the paperwork we received. But just as important, we hadn't done our homework. I could tell by listening to Ralph's voice that the discussion he had with Dan had not gone well and things were pretty tense.

Talk about getting off to a bad start . . . but just you wait!

Ralph planned to stay a few weeks to understand more of the business. On Sunday he went to Sunny Farms, a local grocery (heated by a wood stove), to get some food. He parked in front close to the newspaper stands. He casually looked over and saw a picture of our winery barn on the front page of the local paper. And, the headline read:

Winery Closed Due to Leaking Sewage

The story ran two weeks in a row on Sunday, on the front page, above the fold and with a picture of the barn.

No one could miss it. The actual details didn't matter because we were doomed from the start. The local perception was that our wine was tainted and the cleanliness required for making wine was indeed questionable.

I could practically hear people on the street declaring, "I'll never drink anything that comes from that winery again." I know because that's what I thought, because I had no idea how a septic system works (totally grew up in the city). And what or where the drainage fields were located... which weren't anywhere near the barn, it turns out.

Well, there went our Excel forecast. After $19K and a new septic system, the doors were back open. But in reality, it cost us a WHOLE lot more. Public sentiment and word of mouth are critical. When you're a small business, you *are* your business.

At this point Dan was running the winery for us when Ralph wasn't there. Still working at TI and traveling extensively, I had very little involvement.

While we still had tourists visit the winery and buy wine during the summer, we had no local business during the fall and holidays. Cash flow got pretty bleak the rest of the year, especially with the loans and bills.

I promised you a peek at what we found behind the cellar doors. Normally, it isn't all that exciting unless you're checking the wine barrels, which requires periodic tasting (yum). The cellar is where the work is done and is a place that must be kept very clean, which means mopping the floors regularly. Wine barrels (full and empty), tanks, harvest equipment and bottled wine inventory on pallets are usually stored in the cellar.

What we found though was missing inventory! That's wine in the bottle.

At the end of 1999 (our first year), Ralph was trying to complete some Federal and State wine usage reports and nothing was adding up. He was a newbie, of course, the first year he'd had to tackle them, and he thought he was doing something wrong. It looked like we were missing inventory. He went back in to the cellar and counted the inventory again. Adding it up – beginning inventory, less sales and tasting room bottle usage each month, should total ending inventory. Right? We hadn't bottled in 1999, so it was pretty simple math. But we were way short. I mean waaaay short.

Ralph got Dan to look over the reports and kept asking questions. Turns out the beginning inventory was off. Why this wasn't caught at 1998 year-end is the question, but records and reporting were not Dan's strong suit. The number of cases per pallet used in the calculation of the beginning inventory balance we purchased was wrong. See, wine pallets are stacked in a specific order and count. Usually 56 or 75 cases per pallet. In this case, all the pallets were calculated at 75 cases, when, in fact, most held 56 cases. That means when we calculated our inventory we were 19 cases short per pallet. That's 228 bottles of wine per pallet that could have generated income. And we're talking more than 14 pallets.

The cha-ching from the cash register would be deathly quiet missing the income of over 3,192 bottles of wine.

We didn't have a retail management system with inventory control. All we had was your basic cash register. And we didn't do monthly inventory. So, another hard and very costly lesson learned.

And we would run low and run out of some of the wine before the next scheduled bottling. Remember, I said we had to sell A LOT of wine to meet our monthly forecast.

It wasn't long before more of our savings started flowing into the winery and by the end of 2000 Ralph had spent half his time working at the winery, letting his marketing consulting business suffer.

I was traveling quite a bit for TI, leaving me no time to help Ralph out with the winery. Time zone changes and me just don't get along, add in the financial stress of the winery, working non-stop and no down time with Ralph, and it felt like life was spiraling out of control.

I took most of January 2001 off from my job and spent the time working at the winery trying to figure out what to do. While I learned how to run the tasting room and actually poured wine for our guests, I didn't have any profound ah-ah's.

As I look back, I think that stubbornness is why I stayed in the wine industry. The deck was stacked against us from the very beginning. All logic said to throw in the towel. I felt we hadn't really given it a chance, but I was Monday morning quarterbacking and I didn't do anything to help those first two years.

During this January visit, Ralph and I met with the owners of a sister winery and were told out in the parking lot as we left that frankly, "We couldn't do it." Jeez, sometimes in the middle of the night when I have a "worry attack" I wish she hadn't said that, because she threw down the gauntlet. Don't tell me I can't do something!

I went back to work and a couple of months later we had a very unexpected opportunity. I guess you call it good news for Ralph and me. The semiconductor market goes through cycles and late 2000 into 2001 was one of the down periods. Not good for the stock price but TI offered early retirement packages. With my age at 50 and my years of service I qualified by two weeks. Part of the retirement package was my salary for a year.

Given that we had a year to figure this out and fast running out of options, we decided to up and move to Sequim, nine miles from our money-losing little winery. Although we didn't really have a solid plan, we just knew that together we would figure it out.

We sold our house, and packed it all up, left Dallas on a 110-degree day and drove 2200 miles in four straight days. We arrived on July 31 and the temperature in the evening was around 55 degrees. A long sigh escaped me and I immediately felt at home. We were together and believed we could do it.

I needed to take the lead on the winery because we couldn't figure out a way to clone Ralph. He realized he simply had to step away from Olympic Cellars to focus on his own marketing business, which he had neglected since 1999 while working half time at the winery. We had learned some hard lessons in the last couple of years. I'm sure you could list them with me. But, this wasn't the time to beat ourselves up.

Turns out in early 2002 Ralph got a call from Tim Larkin who worked for a client of Ralph's. Tim had just launched his new self-defense business and wanted Ralph to do the marketing and join him as a partner. Here we both were, working to grow two businesses, only mine had a few more issues.

It was the time to follow my own advice. When I worked at TI and one of my employees would come to me with a problem that had to be fixed, I would start off by saying, "We can fix anything but death."

After a while, they'd say, "I know, we can fix anything but death." And laugh.

Then together we would address my three questions: What exactly happened? How do we make it right? What do we put in place so it doesn't happen again?"

Then throw in a bit of laughter, praise, and a 'You Can Do It' high five and on to the next task of the day.

WINE BITES

Since you're still reading, you might enjoy doing what I've been doing as I've worked on this book – a glass of wine at day's end.

If you like my suggestion, most wine lovers I know don't need their arms twisted – just saying – here are some of my favorite pourings. These are the wines I reached for depending on my mood as I worked on this book.

For example, now I'm deep in thought because this next chapter had me really thinking about my life, corporate career and one top-of-the-list-question.

I worked all my life for a big company. Do I even know how to run a small business? So, maybe I'll pour a Portuguese Douro Port. Sip slowly, savor, and think. It's my dessert tonight.

Chapter 4

Can We Really Fix Anything But Death?

I retired technically, unemployed in the traditional sense, and was now living in Washington State. Deep breaths, Kathy, I kept telling myself.

We rented a house in Sequim. The movers unloaded on Wednesday, August 1, and I did a real fast unpacking job. I had scheduled myself to start working the tasting room that weekend so I had three days to get our home life in order.

What I realized six months before in January when I took some time off from TI to spend it at the winery, I was totally burned out. You don't realize it until you step off the treadmill you're on. I thought by spending time at the winery, getting to know the business a little, seeing it from an outsider's point of view, that maybe answers would unveil themselves. Well what I found out was that I didn't have the mental energy to even come up with new ideas, much less implement them. I'd lost my passion to make things happen, which is what I built my reputation on at TI. I always made things happen and this was how I measured myself. I just never realized how important it was to my core.

Now, while facing the daunting job of turning our winery into a profitable business, at least it was my only focus, be it a large one, and I finally felt emotionally ready to tackle it.

But boy was I nervous. What did I know about running a small business, much less a winery?

But as I took stock, I realized something. Many of my well-intentioned incidents at TI where I didn't follow the rules got my hands slapped multiple times and nearly fired twice. Thank goodness, I had managers that would give me enough rope and not let me hang myself. I guess you could say I went rogue sometimes, but I got the job done. That said, I learned something valuable inside TI that prepared me for this next chapter in my life and it was this: sometimes circumventing corporate procedures to make something happen was worth the risk. Yeah, I had that down. So maybe I did have the necessary entrepreneurial gene.

Now going forward, though, I realized every decision I would make would impact the winery's future. No corporate dollars to back up a bad decision.

So back to "we can fix anything but death." What got us here and how do I fix it? Of course, I didn't have the answers yet. That insight, however, gave me the confidence to take the next deep breath and look to the future. First, though, I needed to get my butt to the winery and pour wine for customers and make some money.

My first day at my new job. It was a Saturday. I swept the floor, checked the bathrooms – plenty of toilet paper. Put cash in the register, wiped down the bar and uncorked the wine for tasting. Unlocked the doors and I was ready.

I also dressed like I lived in Dallas with totally inappropriate shoes for standing all day behind the bar on a cement floor and hauling wine from the cellar. Didn't think about wine stains and blisters, but I learned fast. Moved my corporate garb to the back of my closet and welcomed my new fleece and Birkenstocks.

Switching from semi-conductors to grapes is not the most obvious career path. When asked "How did you come to own a winery? Did you have any background in the wine industry?" I'd laugh and reply, "No – unless drinking wine counts."

I did drink wine though, and knew what I liked and didn't like, and, early on, I wasn't all that curious. Price had a lot to do with my decision on what wine to buy. BOC – Before Olympic Cellars, I would order my red wine to be served cold, which I'm sure elicited an eye roll or a half-hidden snicker from a waiter but I didn't notice.

Back in 1978, working for TI, my first assignment was in Lubbock in far West Texas where they grew a lot of cotton. Some of the land was being switched over to vineyards and I can remember tasting one of the first vintages from Llano Estacado, the first winery in Lubbock. Thinking back, I now realize that was my first taste of *terroir*, the unique flavor and aroma of the wine imparted by the region, soil, and climate in which the grapes are grown. Who would have guessed what my future would be?

Well … I'm digressing waiting for my first customer to walk through the door.

But working the tasting room every day (no money to hire help), pouring our wine, listening, and watching the body language of my customers, started me down the path of "what do I do" to turn this winery around.

I knew the wine industry intimidated a lot of people. I noticed that sometimes folks entering the tasting room didn't seem all that comfortable. Others, well they knew exactly what they wanted and that was wine. Pour it on.

Gradually, I narrowed my focus down to two types of customers: the Belly-Up-To-The-Bar crowd (which is self-explanatory), and those whom I came to refer to as my MerLOT customers, who were new to the winery scene. What's in a name . . . Merlow, MerLot, Mer-LOW? I never corrected a customer. Usually I found an opportunity in our conversation and mentioned, "You know, in France the grape is sometimes pronounced Merlot."

I began to really think about how to provide an UN-intimidating experience that would translate to sales and Customers for Life. (That's from my dog-eared copy of a book by Carl Sewell, with notes in the margin. I learned a lot from this book, which was required reading by one of my TI bosses).

Also, I discovered that, depending on where a customer was on his or her wine journey, their tastes in wine were different. White. Red. Rosé. Oak. No oak. Dry. Slightly sweet and sweet.

So, if I hoped to sell wine to every customer that came into the winery, I needed a variety of wines to offer. Now we all know you can't please everyone and you need to focus on what you do best.

But I didn't know what we did best. Heck, we were just starting. Or starting over.

I started flipping through business magazines, reading, talking with Ralph and jotting down notes. I found this formula for a small business/entrepreneur somewhere.

Entrepreneur + Capital = Products + Customers = Business

Well maybe I was an entrepreneur. I was definitely taking a big risk. But, I had very little capital, which for me is the cash over and beyond what you need in monthly expenses and loan payments to invest in your business.

Products? I just mentioned I thought I needed a bunch of different wines for customers. Again, you need capital to acquire them or produce them. Where to start?

Customers. Well we had the tourists, but remember we lost the locals when the leaking septic tank was the talk of the town. *Do I start here? Seems like a good place.*

Which equals my Business . . . that's what I want to save.

Back to my formula. I need to increase Capital, i.e. CASH. That means I need SALES from more CUSTOMERS.

Let's turn that around. CUSTOMERS are the key to SALES. Looking back, this was my first marketing lesson. Each day I found myself focusing more on the folks standing across the bar from me than on the dollars they might spend. I wanted my customers to know I cared that they took time to visit my winery.

As I mentioned earlier I began to realize how intimidating just walking into a winery could be. I can't tell you how many times a customer mentioned, apologetically, I'm not a wine connoisseur. That first summer when I was the only one working the bar, seven days a week during the tourist window, I watched and talked to hundreds of visitors. On a busy Saturday there could be 20+ customers lining our tasting bar with glass in hand.

Many would walk through the door and "Belly-Up-To-The-Bar" and others would open the door, not look me in the eye, with shoulders slightly hunched and walk over to our gift area. I would have to personally coax them over, asking a series of non-pushy kinds of questions to get them over to sample a wine. I can't tell you how many times I heard their timid statements, such as, "I don't know anything about wine," or "I'm not a wine aficionado," (or some word like that).

One day my bar was full mostly with the Belly-Up-To-The-Bar customers. They were easy, talked amongst themselves. I talked about the wines and kept their tasting glasses full . . . working toward a sale. Then this young couple came in and I could tell immediately they were not comfortable. I greeted them and guided them to an open space at the end of the bar.

I started off with a little info about Olympic Cellars and asked a few questions about the style of wine they enjoyed. The young man introduced me to his girlfriend and said this was the first winery they had ever visited. (I probably should have carded them but, jeez, that would have embarrassed them even more).

So, we started with the white wines and I kept working the bar from one end to the other. I remember looking down the bar, smiled and my young man spouted, "We would like to try the MerLOT now."

Well, you can only imagine. The Belly-Up-to-the-Bar crowd starts snickering and a few laughed out loud pronouncing, not too quietly, that the wine was a MerLOWWW. My young man turned beat red. I quickly made my way down to him, leaned in and whispered in his ear, "You are exactly right! It is pronounced MerLOT. They don't know what they're talking about."

The young man visibly relaxed and his girlfriend gave him an adoring smile. Down the road when he found out the correct pronunciation I hope he forgave me.

You never want a customer embarrassed in person or online. Showing you care, that you listened, asking un-intimidating questions builds trust. Then the customer is open to listening to you. I could start spouting Stephen Covey because his books are among my favorite in my dog-eared, highlighted, note-filled pages that have made sense to me both in business and personal life. Trust is the operative word. *Trust* is the glue of life. It's the most essential ingredient in effective communication. It's the foundational principle that holds all relationships.

Well, another day is done and I put the tasting room in order for the next day. Looking at the tasting bottles that were open I wondered what wine should I sip tonight? I think I better start tasting Olympic Cellars wine; after all I'm selling them now.

WINE BITES

It's wine time. Tonight I picked a Lemberger, in the bottle and a sample of our 2015 vintage still in the barrel.

This wine was new to me back when we first bought the winery. When I first heard the name all I could think of was Limburger cheese, which is notorious for its smell. Turns out the Lemberger grape was one of the first commercially planted grapes back in the late 70's in Eastern Washington, where 95% of the grapes are grown. It's an 'Old World' grape with origins in Austria and Germany.

Remember Gene Neuharth, the founder of the winery? He started making wine from this grape in the early 80's and we still do today. It's part of our heritage. This wine has won over twenty medals for us, including multiple Golds and a Double Gold.

Chapter 5

Kathy, We Won!

Ralph had managed the winery until we moved to Washington. Then I drove up to the barn, the new boss of one part-time employee.

Sara Gagnon had worked in limbo at the winery for the last couple of months. She was hired back in 2000 by Ralph as a part-time apprentice to Dan Caudill, the former owner and winemaker. Dan had left the winery for another job in the spring of 2001. Since then, Sara cared for the wines and worked the tasting room when Ralph wasn't there.

The big question ... Do I hire Sara as winemaker or advertise the job?

Sara and I sat down in the tasting room. The conversation started awkwardly. I knew Sara's lifelong dream was to be a winemaker.

I glanced down as we talked and noticed Sara's wine-stained notebook in her lap. Just then I remembered Ralph telling me about Sara's first days as an apprentice. Excited, always asking questions, doing every task she could while scribbling like crazy in her notebook.

As I looked at her notebook, I made my decision. Sara was the perfect choice. Not because she had a strong background in winemaking. Not because she had a degree in enology, the science of winemaking.

Eastern Washington, where the vast majority of wineries and vineyards are located, is the heart of Washington wine country. Winemakers wanted to be near their grapes and the camaraderie of others in their industry. That's where the opportunities were. And, winemakers from Eastern Washington weren't lining up for a part-time job to work at Olympic Cellars, my struggling winery on the state's West Coast.

Later, I was asked why I had hired Sara instead of a full-fledged winemaker. It's a simple answer. She was probably the only person who would take the job. It was part-time, and because we were a very small winery located in far Western Washington, we couldn't pay much money. One of my best decisions, as it turned out, because she wanted to break into the business so she jumped in with both feet and learned fast.

At the time, it worked out for both of us. You could say we both took a chance on each other.

So Sara and I divided up the work. I'm not a winemaker, but under her tutelage I also helped in all phases of making wine from harvest, crushing, fermentation, racking, aging and finally bottling. Of course, my favorite is tasting the wine as it ages in the barrel and noting how it evolves over time.

Then I oversaw the operations side of making wine, which means everything needs to run like clockwork. I orchestrated delivering the grape bins to the vineyards and arranging for the trucks to drive the grapes ASAP after picking to Port Angeles. Barrels had to be ordered in advance. Rearranging the cellar to handle the fermenting tanks. But oh the smell of fermenting grapes. It envelops you and the smell is alive and warm. Once you've smelled the grapes you'll never forget it. (I wonder if there is fermenting grape perfume?)

The 2001 fall harvest was pretty skimpy. In fact, we only crushed two varieties of grapes that year. You may not know this but a winery makes wines from grapes they grow on their own vines, or from grapes they buy in bulk from other growers. Sara loaned the winery the money to buy Syrah grapes from Sagemoor Vineyards in Pasco, which were her favorite. The second purchase was Lemberger from Champoux Vineyards. Both vineyards were in Eastern Washington. We carried forth the Dungeness Brand started by Gene Neuharth and the Lemberger was used to make Dungeness Red and Dungeness Rosé wines. Rumor has it the Dungeness name was an idea that was floated during one of the weekly poker games at Gene's house. In the late 70's wine labels referenced the winery name, the vineyard, vintage, and grape variety. Giving the wine a 'fanciful' name or brand in this case was breaking new ground.

Also, the name Dungeness has a lot of history here on the Olympic Peninsula. There is the New Dungeness Lighthouse located on the Dungeness Spit in the Dungeness National Wildlife Refuge near Sequim. And you could also wade in the Dungeness River or go crabbing for some Dungeness crabs in the Straits of Juan de Fuca or buy them locally like I do.

Paul Champoux bought the vineyard that he formally managed in 1996. The vineyard became a legend under his ownership. Paul was instrumental in helping Washington earn its first 100-point wine from Wine Advocate and famed critic, Robert Parker, for a 2002 Cabernet Sauvignon, using Champoux grapes. According to Robert Parker's rating system a 100-point wine has the ability to evolve and improve with age and is the very best produced of their type.

Today 75% of his vineyard is planted in Cabernet Sauvignon, but Paul had a love for the Lemberger grape and kept a small number of vines that we contracted for each year. Just having Champoux Vineyards on your label meant quality.

Wine Has the Power to Sucker and Seduce was one of my favorite one-liners when I was promoting my wines. And I realized it was true.

Turns out the 2001 Lemberger grapes we crushed and bottled the following year won a gold medal. The path to a so-so or great wine all starts with harvest and for us rested on Sara's decision on when to pick the grapes. The moment the grapes are picked determines the acidity, sweetness, and flavor of the wine.

Sara really babysat those few barrels. And we tasted them frequently to gauge the aging. Lemberger wine didn't have to age as long as say a Cabernet. Sara decided it was ready and we bottled the wine in the fall of 2002 and entered it in the Washington Tri-Cities Wine Festival and Competition held in November. Sara attended the event, which was about a six-hour drive to Kennewick in the heart of Washington wine country.

The Tri-Cities are a group of three closely-tied cities (Kennewick, Pasco, and Richland) located at the confluence of the Yakima, Snake, and Columbia rivers in Southeastern Washington. Besides vineyards, 75% of the nations' hops are also grown here, which means microbreweries along with an abundant amount of corn, hay, wheat, and potatoes because of the plentiful water supply from the rivers. It's a great place to visit and known as the French Fry Capital of the World, which got my attention.

Sara called later in the evening after the judging, and I could hear the excitement in her voice as she almost shouted into the phone, "Kathy, we won a gold medal!" At that time, I had no idea that we had won one of only seven gold medals awarded that night out of 189 wines submitted.

Winning a medal in a Northwest centric Wine Competition and the recognition that came with it for me was a game changer. I was an amateur in the wine business. But it was like winning a $2 bet on racehorse and you think you know the horses. I spouted frequently, "Olympic Cellars is making Gold Medal Wine." I think I was getting cocky.

Over the years our Dungeness Red label changed featuring Olympic Peninsula and Dungeness iconic pictures. In the fall of 2008, local photographer Christopher Enges sat alongside the Sol Duc River for hours to capture the perfect picture of a Coho Salmon swimming upstream. We haven't changed the label since.

Chapter 6

Work On – Or – Work In

Until we won that medal I hadn't realized that in my deep subconscious maybe I didn't think the winery would make it. It had been a year since I took over the reins and I worked every day in the tasting room. But looking back I hadn't even laid out a written plan.

I did realize, though, I had to work 'on' my business and not 'in' my business. We were one of the few businesses on the Peninsula open every day, including Sunday, which got me extra customer traffic. The winery was only closed on Easter, Thanksgiving, Christmas, and New Years' Day. Even so, with no major changes it would take forever to pay off everyone we owed. And, I wasn't going to default or declare bankruptcy in my new hometown.

I sat down one night and listed everything I was doing. Then I divided all those tasks in another list under two categories: Work On My Business and Work In My Business. I needed to focus on the first and hire the second.

To work 'on' my business I needed to hire part-time help for the tasting room. To do this I looked at every expense to see if I could eek out enough cash to hire help, knowing that if I wasn't pouring wine behind the bar I might be able to increase business through other avenues.

Next, I listed the character traits and the skills of the person I was looking to hire. I needed someone who would take responsibility for the tasting room as if it were hers, be able to make decisions, possess a work ethic equal to mine, who would speak her mind and genuinely care for people.

I never had to advertise for the job because I knew exactly who could do the job.

Molly Rivard joined Sara and me in July 2002.

Shortly after I moved here, I picked up a flyer that advertised "cooking classes with local, organic ingredients." I don't really like to cook. In Dallas there was a salad bar on every corner and then along came the Whole Foods deli. Why should I learn now? Well, it was either learn or starve. There were no salad bars, no delis with the kind of food I liked and fewer restaurants. Most people ate off the land. They had gardens, canned, fished, and hunted. So maybe I should give this cooking class a shot.

The teacher was, who else, Molly. She had recently retired as head of the Sequim school district lunch program. She was hands-on responsible for, and supervised the preparation of, over 1,200 lunches a day, along with ordering the food, managing the staff and lunchrooms in the elementary, junior high, and high schools.

I attended a six-week class and at the end Molly brought in her "famous" chocolate sauce for the cream puffs we made that night. Well . . . I told Molly she needed to sell her chocolate sauce and maybe add a bit of wine to it, you know, like a Cabernet Chocolate sauce.

Long story short . . . she sold her Chocolate Sauce exclusively at the winery, decided cooking classes were not her calling, and I offered her the job.

Finally, I could sleep at night knowing Molly was at the helm and Sara was busy making wine.

Now, I told myself I'm ready to kick ass. So, winning the gold medal did have the POWER to Sucker and Seduce me right off my duff. Still didn't have all that much experience, but now I had a Gold Medal, so obviously I knew what I was doing, right?

I mentally crossed the line and in December 2002, I put the beginnings of a multi-year plan together, my vision of which was more of a challenge and initial priorities. The corporate annual process coming back strong. I went back to my finance roots . . . Small Business is all about Cash Flow. When you purchase your raw materials one to three years before the wine is put on the shelf, you better have a plan. Also, a rainy-day fund when sales influenced by weather and tourists visiting the Peninsula don't go as planned.

My overarching vision was to reinvent the winery, who we were and what we stood for. The challenge: how do we stand out in the crowd? My initial priorities included: increase quality of the grapes and wine, upgrade our curb appeal, and bring back the locals.

I knew we couldn't go head to head, Merlot to Merlot so to speak, with other Washington wineries. We just didn't have the experience, resources, or reputation. The Washington's wine industry was flourishing in Eastern WA. I had local competition, also. There were five other wineries, all small like us on the Peninsula. Sorensen Cellars and Fairwinds in Port Townsend. Lost Mountain Winery in Sequim. Camaraderie and Black Diamond in Port Angeles. All were husband and wife owned and the husband was the winemaker. Already they had a cost advantage over me. I had to hire a winemaker, so guess who didn't get paid?

The local wineries formed a winery association and our membership fees went to promoting association wine events and our wineries on the Peninsula. When we had association meetings, each winery would bring a bottle of wine to share at our luncheon. Olympic Cellars wine was usually left untouched. Once I even watched one of the winemakers pouring some of our wine in his glass (guess he did this because I was watching) then he casually strolled into the kitchen (I sort of followed) and he poured it down the drain (it was the Gold Medal Wine). He hadn't even tasted it. That hurts to this day.

Well, that gauntlet was thrown down again when he poured the wine down the drain. The first time - when we bought the winery and the sister winery said we couldn't do it, our reputation still beyond repair. My resolve was unwavering - I'm the lady who said we can fix anything but death.

Back to my priorities.

First Priority: If I learned one thing at TI it was Quality First and Foremost. We bought grapes from well-known vineyards, which of course were more expensive. I added to my debt by paying for the grapes on time.

Since we couldn't buy all the grapes we needed to have a variety of wine to sell, we bought bulk wine from other wineries. We would request samples if the winery would sell in smaller quantities, like 375 (size of our tanks) or 750 gallons. We tasted, blended if needed with our own or other bulk wine we purchased and then bottled under our label. I had the start of white and red wines and a lightly sweet Riesling for sale in the tasting room.

Second Priority: Re-do the tasting room. The winery needed a cool 'curb appeal' inside and out. Perception is everything. We completed that project by the summer of 2003.

When you visit the Olympic Peninsula, there is only one major road, Highway 101, and you have to pass the winery going East or West. You can't miss it and at night the cupolas and the barn are lit. The barn in and of itself is its own advertising billboard. If you love old barns and/or you love wine, we're the perfect place for a visit. During the summer tourist season we greet 10,000 to 12,000 visitors to the winery.

The tasting room, remember, was an old barn that the previous owner, had turned into the commercial space for plumbing supplies. To say the décor resembled a big storage locker is probably unfair to storage lockers.

The tasting room walls were painted white and mostly bare of pictures or anything interesting. The tasting room, such as it was, comprised the wine bar and selection of wines for sale, and was situated at the far end of a long narrow room at the front of the barn. In the middle of the room we had a hodge-podge of old barrels and mismatched merchandize shelving with "stuff" for sale. Most of it was on consignment and had no real theme. Some of the items, though, were from local artists needing the money as much as I did. Painted gourds, stained glass, carved wood. An old wood bookcase holding post cards blocked off the very end of the tasting room. Behind the bookcase was an old gray government-style metal desk and file cabinet – my office. When you stood at the front door and looked in, it resembled an old, sort of run down antique shop, except nothing was antique.

It's amazing what just a modest investment in paint can do on the walls and on some display pieces. After the makeover, a welcoming warmth greeted you. Picture rich Tuscan colors, earthy red, pale terra cotta, and a deep yellow on separate walls. A comfortable seating area with nice lighting replaced my office.

The back-bar clutter of old bottles (antique?) was replaced with colorful

pottery and other items of interest with a story that we shared with customers. The back bar then popped. The bar's claim to fame was that it was almost as old as the barn, which would take it back to the late 1890's. In the 70's the barn used to be a dancehall. Folks from both Sequim and Port Angeles would go there, especially after a high school football game (the barn is located half-way between both cities). When the dancehall folded, the back bar was left in the barn, turned around and leaned against a back wall. Set under the open cupolas on the roof, over time it was slowly covered up with pigeon poop. At some point, the front bar was burned for firewood, a tragedy. When Dan started to restore the barn, they found the back bar, restored it and built a front bar to match out of fir.

Customers drove up to what looked like a century-old barn on the outside, and walked in to *barn nouveau* with a century-old bar. The tasting room has evolved over time but kept its warmth and welcoming spirit.

Third Priority: Change the local's perception of the winery. I started with the business community. No one really knew me. First step, in 2003 I joined the Chamber of Commerce and invited the members to an evening wine tasting. Lots of folks showed, I'm sure mostly out of curiosity – but I got the result I wanted. I had cracked the proverbial cellar door open.

Now it was time to get involved in my community and volunteer. Also, come up with ideas/events that would draw locals and maybe get coverage in the community newspapers.

Early on we would invite women, organizations, etc. to meet at the winery at no cost. We catered to these groups. Sometimes we'd even offer a wine tasting. One of those nights, Molly, Sara and I were sitting side by side at the table and someone remarked that we were the "Olympic Women In Wine."

That phrase wouldn't leave my head and I started researching Women and Wine. At the time (2002-2003 ish) there were few female winemakers and especially not many women who owned wineries.

Had I found my niche?

Fourth Priority: While I usually only think in three's there was a lot to do, so another priority was on my list. Start communicating with my customers beyond the tasting room. I had done local press releases and a few print ads, but needed to reach out to customers that weren't local. Under consideration: regular emails, a blog, website and/or point of sales system with online order capability. Now if a customer wanted to order wine they had to call during business hours or leave a message. We lost a lot of sales when folks reconsidered or we played phone tag.

Wine Bites

There's a lot to do and I'm tired so no heavy red wine tonight. I need something light and zippy, I'm thinking a Sauvignon Blanc. It's a popular choice in the Pacific Northwest because it pairs well with oysters, crab and scallops.

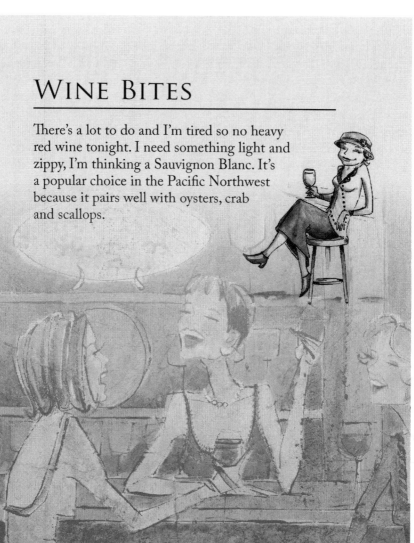

CHAPTER 7

Women, Wine and the Working Girls

Had I found my niche? Was Women and Wine the platform to reinvent my winery?

GOOGLE IT became my favorite phase!

I started researching Women and Wine and hit on an artist's website, Kathy Womack. She had a series of paintings under the name, you guessed it – "Women and Wine!" And, she lived in Texas. This was a sign in itself.

Kathy Womack's tag line, "Inside every woman lies the secret desire to be a lady of leisure and live . . . La Dolce Vida." Aah, The Sweet Life. I wouldn't mind a life of leisure. At first, though, I thought she spelled 'Vida' wrong. In Italian it's 'Vita.' which is what you normally see. But remember, she's from Texas and La Dolce Vida in Italian-Spanish is The Sweet Life. It was what we wanted at day's end . . . friendship, fun, good wine, nice clothes (not black fleece, a sore back and stained hands from cleaning wine barrels). To me it pictured success. We did it!

Either way, I could relate. I bought the first painting in her Women and Wine series, which Kathy Womack used as her website's homepage graphic – a painting of three women, all dressed up, at a party, sitting on a red velvet couch chatting away with wine in hand. While purchases like this were not in my 'approved expenses' forecast, I bought it anyway on my personal credit card. My gut said, do it. We hung the painting on the wall at the end of the wine tasting bar.

As I mentioned earlier, someone had casually tagged Molly, Sara and me as the Olympic Women In Wine. Now the Women in Wine painting became a topic of conversation with our customers as we told the story of how the three of us came together. Our winery persona started to evolve with this picture.

The branding of Olympic Cellars as a women-owned-and-operated winery continued when the first local article written about the winery appeared in the Peninsula Daily News Weekend Insert, appropriately titled "Sisters Through the Grape"... Sara Gagnon, Molly Rivard and Kathy Charlton, locally known as the 'Olympic Women In Wine.'

And like so many sisters, we were nothing alike. Different personalities, different backgrounds, and born in different decades! But we definitely agreed on one thing: we wanted to make great wine, have fun doing it, and find the time to enjoy the hard work ahead of us.

While the Olympic Women in Wine and a few strategically placed copies of the article in the winery generated lively conversations at the bar, they didn't sell the wine. We still needed wines with a variety of style and price, as I mentioned earlier, for customers who were at different places in their wine journey. I wanted the opportunity to sell wine to every customer who walked through the door. White, Red. Dry, Sweet. Oak, No Oak. Big and Bold, Easy Drinking.

But we didn't have a lot of choices from the wines in our cellar. We were looking to make a slightly sweet white and a very soft, easy drinking, soft red blend.

So, one evening Molly, Sara and I sat around a table blending and tasting . . . and tasting . . . and tasting. Our blending notes were becoming fuzzy and we were really enjoying ourselves. I remember leaning back on the back two legs of my chair and sighing, "This working girl has got to go home."

With a loud clunk, the front chair legs hit the floor and I said none too quietly, "That's it . . . Working Girl. Working Girl Wines. That's who we are!" Well, all three of us started talking at once. Sara pulled me back to earth when she rattled off a bunch of questions about the wines/blends for our new Working Girl brand.

We needed to finish our blending trials so Sara could actually blend and filter the wines for bottling. We needed to design a label for approval by the Federal Alcohol and Tobacco Tax and Trade Bureau (TTB) and the Washington State Liquor Control Board because you can't just throw down a new line of wine without going through the bureaucracy. Then order bottles, corks, capsules and other supplies so we could set a bottling date.

We completed our lists and were ready to head home when Molly, always thinking about our customers, asked, "Do you think we're going to get flack with this name? You know Working Girl has a whole other meaning."

We all paused and thought for about a nanosecond. Consensus: Yep, we'll probably get some flippant comments, but we can handle that. And, of course, we did, which became the catalyst for two of my emails appropriately titled: A Little Male Humor and From Ladies of the Night to Working Girls.

And for me, Working Girl was way more than a wine brand. It's who we were and what we stood for as women, mothers, and friends. It reminded me of what it was like when I started my career back in the 70's, having to prove myself over and over. We worked our butts off, making personal sacrifices to get the same recognition as our male colleagues. But as Working Girls, we persevered.

So, on a gorgeous, sun-filled, 2003 Labor Day Weekend, we released our Working Girl Wines: Working Girl White (a blend of Chardonnay and Riesling) and Go Girl Red (blend of Merlot and Lemberger). I wrote a press release to get attention and hopefully get it printed in the newspaper without cost, then took out a local ad to advertise our first wine release party.

> New *Working Girl* Wine Series will Ease the Crankiness and Stress
> of a Long, Sweltering Day in Pantyhose and Pumps
> "Olympic Women In Wine" Introduces Their New
> *Working Girl White* and *Go Girl Red*
> *Labor Day Weekend at Olympic Cellars Winery*

We even sprang for a Seattle-based band and hired an all-women Cajun band, Les Femmes d'Enfer – The Women of Hell, who kept the crowd on their feet. Dancing was non-stop. During one song, one of the ladies in the band turned around and pulled something over her head. When she turned back a roar of laughter erupted ... she had donned what looked like a cut-out of a fringe-edged hour glass shaped dress with super big, pointed copper metal breasts. I can't remember the song her outfit went with but I do know that from then on, the Working Girls were known for throwing a great party.

Molly and I were always fond of saying, "It's a Sign," when something unforetold happened. Well the Working Girl Wines were "a sign" of good things to come. The wines sold, the press was great and we started rebuilding the winery. There was still much to accomplish; the lists were a mile long. To this day we still exclaim "it's a sign" as that invisible rainbow shelters the winery once again and shows us the path as we work through problems, mechanical breakdowns, or just the aches and pains of cellar work.

Our finances also got better with income increasing 31% in 2003 and another 41% in 2004. My worry attacks in the middle of the night lessened and while there were still bills, I didn't have to watch every cent as closely as before.

The next summer we released Rosé the Riveter, affectionately known as Rosie. Now there was a character for each of the Working Girls. From left to right, Rosie – Sara, Working Girl – me, and Go Girl – Molly.

Stephanie Mallon, an artist and friend of Sara's, created the Working Girl characters.

Rosie became my inspirational icon. The "We Can Do It" headline on the WWII poster we all recognize became my personal mantra, although I changed it up to "We Can Do It, Too!"

In August 2004 Sara was in a tragic plane crash in the Olympic Mountains. The pilot died and Sara and her friend, Tammy, spent a harrowing night until they were found the next day. Sara needed to step back from winemaking to heal but left her very special mark on all of us and the winery. While it saddened us that she was not at the barn on a daily basis, we knew that she would still pursue the two loves of her life, kayaking and wine. And, she will always be one of the founding members of the *Olympic Women In Wine*. A year later she opened Harbinger Winery. She's created a very special place along with award winning wines.

Wine Bites

I'm having a hard time picking the wine for sipping tonight. Obviously with this chapter it should be one of the Working Girl Wines, but which one? WG White is a sassy little number, a blend of Chardonnay and Riesling. Go Girl Red is a lush Merlot blend that has the power to turn a gunnysack into velvet. And Rosie, well she just rocks, a semi-dry Lemberger Rosé. You pick tonight.

A Little Male Humor...

Last Saturday we were serving a full bar. One gentleman (let's call him Bill) told us, and everyone at the bar that he and his wife had friends visit the weekend before. As the story goes their friends drove around Sequim (with map in hand) and visited Olympic Cellars on their way into Port Angeles. (Sequim has some very unusual street names. I've never asked the history of the names, as you will soon understand why.)

Bill continues with this story, stating that all weekend long his friend kept saying "I visited the Working Girl Winery, down from Hooker Road, around the corner from Kitchen-Dick and just west of Woodcock."

Hah, Hah. Our retort ... he must have gotten lost on Jimmy Come Lately Road!

Yes, these are all legitimate roads! And now I have added a new road sign up to the winery.

Working Girl Lane

From Ladies of the Night to Working Girls

You might be wondering where this is heading, but bear with me.

Ralph and I are on "working vacation" in Cabo. Both of us with laptops at the pool (and towels over our heads so we can see our monitors). But we do take time out for fun ... we walk the beach and discuss everything under the sun. Literally!

The hotel's beachfront isn't all that long because of a huge rock outcropping at one end. I wanted to climb over the rocks and see what was on the other side, but it would take some climbing gear.

Instead, I just looked at the rocks and it seemed a sculptor had been at work, though I knew it was none other than Mother Nature wielding wind, waves and sand to carve a form into the sandstone. I tried to imagine the figure hidden in the boulders. At first, I saw a whale, breaching in the Straits of Juan de Fuca where I live. Then the whale appeared to have that carved, indigenous Northwest Indian art style. The natural formation intrigued me and I returned to it each day.

One day Ralph and I stood there so long staring at this monolith that we began to draw a crowd. People wondering what we were looking at and why I was taking so many pictures. Conversation started ... folks from Chicago, Montana, and Columbia, Missouri. One young boy thought it looked   like some animated monster from a movie I'd never heard of.

What I quickly realized was that each of us looked at this huge hunk of rock from a different perspective . . . sort of through our own personal photo lens.

Anyway, it got me thinking. And, I realized Working Girl Wines and this "rock sculpture" had a lot in common.

Our wine labels are seen through each individual's set of experiences. And often the labels start conversations. People definitely have different opinions and also judge the potential of the wine by its label. The old cliché,'you can't judge a book by its cover' applies here.

Sometimes our wines get stuck near all the other labels that are considered "sarcastic and irreverent," like Fat Bastard, Bitch, and Frog's Piss (yuk!). Yet some of these wines have earned prestigious awards just like our Working Girl wines.

By now you know the story of how our wine brand got named Working Girl . . . very much tied to the three working women who are in their second careers and now own and operate Olympic Cellars Winery. Our ages are spread across multiple decades giving us quite different perspectives and breadth of experience . . . a good combination for running a business.

When we look at our Working Girl wine labels we see a strong, diverse woman working each day to make a living for herself and her family.

But there are times as we pour the wine in our tasting room or at wine events, when we hear the same old "trying to be funny" comments or snide remarks about the real "Working Girls." You know, the *Ladies of the Night*. We often keep our replies light or launch right into the description of the wine, ignoring these derogatory comments.

But as I think about this, why should we let anyone else control us by their bad behavior? We always tell people it's about taking the name and image of the *Working Girl* BACK. Maybe in the past 'working girl' referred to prostitution, but not anymore. Back then it was the only job many women were paid for. But not now.

And, as I so often say . . . I am Woman, Here Me Pour!!!!

Chapter 8

The French Influence

I put out the word via emails to a long list of Washington wineries that Olympic Cellars was desperately in need of a winemaker after Sara's accident in August. Harvest was just a couple of months away. Sara told us she might be able to consult part-time, which was tremendous news about her recovery, given her injuries, but she was not capable of any physical labor.

Claar Cellars, located in Eastern Washington, contacted me about an intern from France. They had hired him through Experience International, a non-profit educational organization that offers professionals the opportunity to share and enhance their existing skills and knowledge abroad. The head winemaker at Claar felt he had enough staff for the harvest and offered the intern to us for the remaining twelve months on the J-1 Trainee-Program visa. If this worked out it would get me through harvest and bottling with time to find a new winemaker.

His name was Benoit Murat from Toulouse, France. He looked like he could still be in high school but he brought with him eight years' winemaking experience. We both interviewed each other. Benoit wanted to make wine in the U.S. and Washington's reputation was growing exponentially.

Eastern Washington grape country is way different from France's wine regions. It is semi-arid, stark open country and Italian immigrants planted the oldest vineyards in the Walla Walla region in the 50's and 60's. The 70's is when Washington grapes and wine started making news.

Contrast that with France. For example, wine production in the Burgundy and the Bordeaux wine regions in France began sometime after 43 AD, during the Roman occupation. Today the vineyard landscapes are dotted with historic castles, churches, and chateaus. Long family histories and cultural traditions in the wine business go back centuries.

For Benoit, it wasn't what he was used to. While the beauty of the Olympic Peninsula helped seal the deal to work at Olympic Cellars, it was the fact that he would totally oversee the wine production from grape to bottle. All his previous work experience was in large wineries where he was responsible for only a certain facet of the wine production. This arrangement didn't allow him to see and taste the final "fruits of his labor."

We shook hands and I completed the mountain of paperwork needed to transfer him just in time for harvest.

Benoit became interested in making wine while helping with the 1996/1997 harvest in Saint-Emilion, a medieval town in the Bordeaux region of France. His experience – pulling and trellising vines, racking tanks and barrels, and bottling – motivated him to enroll at La Tour Blanche School of Viticulture and Enology, located south of Bordeaux in the heart of the Sauternes Appellation. He apprenticed while taking classes, and gained experience in all aspects of vineyard and cellar operations. After earning an undergraduate diploma in viticulture and enology, he went to work as a winemaker for Chateau La Fleur Cravignac in Saint Emilion.

After completing an additional apprenticeship in marketing and estate management and working for two cooperative wineries in France, Murat came to Washington State and ultimately to Olympic Cellars.

Benoit barely made it through his first harvest alive. We had this old, bladder-style press designed and built by Gene Neuharth back in the 80's. Gene had purchased thirteen stainless steel milk tanks from a local dairy. At the bottom of the tanks there was a screw-off spout. The top of tank had a lid about eighteen inches wide and weighed at least twenty-five pounds. The tanks ranged from 6.5 to 7.5 feet in height and approximately four feet wide and weighed 1000 pounds each. To put the lid on the tank you had to stand on the tank and position the lid just so that it would drop onto bolts sticking out of the top of the tank so you could screw the nuts down. Every lid was different, so you couldn't get them mixed up because it would be quite a lot of work to find the right lid for each tank.

Of course, Benoit had never used this press before, because when it was built Benoit was just a toddler. The bladder was also old and patched probably a few too many times.

To press the juice off the pomace (the crushed skins, seeds and stems of grapes) after fermentation the bladder had to be stuffed down the top of tank. It was attached to a hose and air compressor. The lid was loosely bolted down and the bladder inflated up to about fifteen pounds of pressure. Air was continually added to the bladder for more pressure as the volume of juice and pomace went down.

I happened to be in the tasting room and heard a huge explosion. Benoit came staggering in to the tasting room . . . "Kathyeee, I think I blew up the press and I think I'm hurt." He raised his shirt and the heavy stainless steel lid which blew off the tank had grazed his chest . . . he still carries that scar. Honestly, it could have killed him.

When harvest was over and the tanks and barrels of wine in the cellar were put to bed for the winter, Benoit went back to France for a few weeks to visit family. About a month or so after he returned, he called me and asked if we could talk. He caught me in my car on the way to a Port Angeles Chamber of Commerce meeting. I said yes and told him I would be there in a few minutes. I made a U-turn and headed back to the winery. My heart was beating so hard. I thought Benoit was going to say it wasn't working out and he was cutting his internship short. After all, he was used to a higher standard of winery equipment and facilities and cellar rats to help him (the folks that do the grunt work) for all the laborious cellar jobs, like cleaning, shoveling grapes, stacking wine cases. Here he was a one-man show. And, my bad, I hadn't even begun to look for another winemaker.

But that was not the case. When I drove up I could see Benoit sitting on the forklift with lunch in hand just staring at the snow-capped Olympic Mountains. I watched him pick up his lunchtime glass of wine and take a sip. It was rare that he didn't have a small tasting glass of wine with food. He told me it was the French way.

The sun was shining and he turned around and smiled at me. He jumped down and got right to the point. Thank goodness because I was on pins and needles. "Kathyeee, I would like to stay and work here as an employee, the winemaker. Would you have me?" I think I said none to quietly "YES!" and hugged him, which I know made him uncomfortable, but I was excited and relieved.

So together we tackled another mountain of paper work for the submission of a 'H-1B Visa Petition by Olympic Cellars on behalf of Benoit Murat for an intended three-year period of employment.' What a mouthful. All the paperwork was sent to the U.S. Department of Homeland Security Citizenship and Immigration Services. I think you can imagine how long this took. In the end, Benoit was our winemaker for six years before returning to live in France.

He did have a few conditions if he stayed. He presented me with a long, very detailed list of what he wanted and needed in the cellar. Molly, Benoit, and I sat down and talked about what we needed in sales, how we would get there and how much this new equipment would cost. But remember my priority: quality of product starts in the cellar.

One of our first major purchases for the 2005 harvest was a beautiful Italian press. It was to arrive in the summer so Benoit could check it out before the grapes arrived. But there was a major delay on delivery because it got "red tagged" in New York by Homeland Security and the Port Authority. I can assure you unequivocally that there was no terrorist hiding in our press!

We knew our old press was on its last legs. I lost count of the number of patches on the bladder. As luck would have it, the old bladder could not take any more pressure and blew to smithereens just when we needed to press the Rosé. Another winery loaned us their old hand-cranked basket press, which you can find on eBay under Vintage Wine presses for $100-$200. Its capacity was small and physically draining to do one small batch of grapes after another. I think it would have been faster to use our feet and stomp the grapes, which was the original form of grape crushing.

Let me tell you, that press put a new meaning into *hand-crafted* wines. I thought about changing Rosie's arm in the Rosé the Riveter label to better reflect our bulging biceps!

2005 was a defining year for the winery and Benoit had his hands full, not only with increased production but also with us Working Girls. Libby Sweetser joined in the tasting room and was responsible for events and our gift shop. So poor guy, he was dealing with three women daily.

And, us Working Girls with Benoit - The Only Rooster in our Hen House.

Yep, I used that phrase in a press release for a Barrel Tasting Event showcasing our new French winemaker. Obviously, he was one good sport.

To me he was very French and opinionated. We soon found out that Benoit did not have the gift of gab with customers at the bar. Molly and I would start a conversation with our customers who began by asking questions about the different wines and eventually we were on to providing information about the Peninsula, telling stories about kids, grandkids, and pets. Laughter and a comfortable wine tasting experience.

Now Benoit would sort of slap down the wine tasting sheet, quickly point out the wines that were open that day, and pour the first one. Didn't even ask if they wanted that wine or even question if they'd like the style. Then lean against the back bar not saying much, just waiting to pour the next wine. And, God forbid, if someone walked into the winery trailing a heavy scent of perfume. Not that the perfume was bad, but it overshadows the nose (smell of the wine), which is part of the traditional tasting etiquette. Look, swirl, smell, taste. He just couldn't handle it.

But, if somehow our customer connected with him because they recognized his accent, spoke French, talked about their international travels or, the customer knew a lot about wine, then he would talk and talk and forget about the others at the bar. So, his tasting room duty was limited.

He was all about the wine and that's the way it should be. He ruled the cellar. In an interview, he was asked about his unique wine style. He replied, "I think I have a French heritage making wine in two distinct regions in France, Bordeaux and Languedoc, plus U.S. techniques. Now I make wines with American grapes for American people using a mix of what I've learned in both France and U.S. Syrah grapes are one of my favorites. I also try to make wine I like, really ripe to over ripe grapes, lots of fruits, flavors of berries, jam, not too oaky but strong fruit tannins mixed with oak tannins. A dark wine, strong but drinkable young."

He would just roll his eyes and not say much when it came to the Working Girl Wines and all the off the wall marketing that went along with the brand and the ladies. He knew, though, those wines funded his cellar and the ability to get the grapes he wanted for the wines he wanted to make. It was a silent compromise.

There were a couple of times I thought maybe I had pushed his French winemaking heritage over the edge. I had a couple of ideas for new blends that I knew would sell. We, the Working Girls, knew what the majority of our winery customers liked in their wines. A reasonable cost. Easy drinking. Something different. Local grapes. And, a little sweet.

While they loved to taste Benoit's big, bold and beautiful red wines, these were the wines that sold the slowest, even with multiple medals. If we had a special on four or six wines, the customer would buy one expensive and the rest at $15 or less.

So, I put my big girl panties on and approached Benoit with only one idea. I held the other for a later date. To say he didn't take it well was an understatement. He stormed into the cellar and would have slammed the door but the pneumatic door closer is set for slow. He didn't come back out to the tasting room and in fact he didn't even talk to me for a few days.

I really should have thought my approach through. Remember his favorite grape was Syrah. Well, I asked him to make a *sweet* Syrah. That was kin to sacrilegious because Syrah wine is usually dry.

When I came in later that week he walked into the tasting room and handed me a small glass of wine. I wondered if this was a peace offering because it wasn't lunchtime. While this wasn't unusual for Benoit to bring us wine for tasting and our opinion, I just didn't expect it after our little row.

I took a small sip and paused. Took another and broke into a smile. Benoit had just served me a very soft, a very smooth and slightly sweet Syrah.

"Kathyeee," he said, "I got to thinking. In France we normally blend a little Viognier with Syrah. This softens the tannins. So I tried blending Riesling with our Syrah. I think it works, although we will need a late harvest Riesling."

We bought a small amount of bulk late harvest Riesling and did a small test bottling of this new wine we dubbed, My Sweet Syrah.

We didn't have a label graphic and needed to do one fast for government approval. Libby and I talked Molly into dressing up in this great red dress (we called it her Marilyn Monroe dress), did her hair and makeup, poised her sitting on a barrel in front of the winery's barrel-shaped doors. She was a great sport; it was getting cold and we kept taking pictures. But we promised – her label was only on that test bottling.

I will probably get hit by Molly with a handful of grapes smooched all over my face for telling you that this first bottling was known as the bedroom wine. The tagline for the wine so perfect . . . The Sweetness of The Wine Lingers on The Lips Like Your First Kiss.

The rest is history. The wine was a hit and we changed the label to a commissioned painting, Wine Tasting, of the Working Girls by Kathy Womack.

As the wine's reputation traveled, we poured the wine at events. Winery owners and winemakers were quite curious about its popularity. One day Benoit charged in to my office and demanded that I trademark his blend that other wineries were copying. Wish I could've, but Benoit had a right to be proud . . . again we pushed tradition.

His reputation and the winery's grew as Benoit's wine earned prestigious medals. He was invited to New Zealand by Cloudy Bay, that country's most famous winery, to work the harvest for six weeks (our summer), observing different winemaking styles and learning techniques used Down Under.

"This will be my first harvest in the southern hemisphere," he said in the press release I wrote "and I'm eager for the experience. The wine industry is still young in New Zealand – only about 20 years old, similar to Washington. I look forward to learning from the winemakers at Cloudy Bay and sharing with them the experience and expertise I've gained working at wineries in France and the U.S."

Benoit met his wife, Joy, in Port Angeles. She was a chef and owned her own restaurant named Joy's. Benoit started hanging out at the restaurant and helping in the evenings. It wasn't long before they were married.

But before we leave Benoit and talk about a day in the life of a Working Girl and sometimes a cellar rat, I want to tell you the story of the Battle for the Cellar.

WINE BITES

As you're catching on, I sometimes end a chapter with a wine suggestion from the *wine pairing and your moods list*. Don't know why Syrah didn't make the list but I think it is only appropriate to raise a glass of Syrah or Sweet Syrah, your choice, to Benoit and Joy. And think, big-Bold-BEAUTIFUL!

The Battle for The Cellar
Moakie (Our Winery Cat) vs. Benoit (Our Winemaker)

Our small, black cat is as much a part of the heritage of Olympic Cellars as the historic barn, which is our winery home. When the winery first began it was housed in a dairy barn in Sequim. Our current home is also a huge, historic former dairy barn built in 1890 between Sequim and Port Angeles.

Moakie was born sometime in the early 90's. Her Mom was the FIRST Olympic Cellars Winery Cat and reigned over the winery barn in Sequim.

As the story goes, Moakie's mom went out prowling one night and never came home, forcing Moakie to take over her duties at a tender, young age.

A winery cat's job description is extensive, and includes, but certainly isn't limited, to the following (after all, we all know cats do whatever they please regardless of the rules):

1. Keep the mice out of the barn and oversee the cellar day and night.

2. Meow in that irritatingly loud cat-voice the moment our car pulls up at the winery reminding us we only have minutes to get the winery open for business (no, we're not late, just dang close).

3. Greet guests by softly drawing their attention for a head-pat by rubbing around their legs (I've told Moakie many times, no tripping).

4. Sun herself on the patio encouraging guests to stop and enjoy the sunshine, spectacular scenery . . . and maybe a glass of wine.

5. Pose at all the picturesque places in the winery for guest photos (what a ham).

6. Check out every barrel, regardless how high it is, to make sure the bungs (those are the things that plug the hole in the barrel) are secure. (Well, maybe not really so much check the bungs as to leave an occasional hairball on the highest barrel just to test our obsessive cleanliness.

7. Improve our hide-and-seek skills by hiding in every impossible-to-find spot in the tasting room right before closing so you can't set the alarm 'til the cat is found.

8. And, of course, score double job points when delivering her "ultimate present" on the floor right behind our guests at the bar. "What present?" you ask. All of us who work at the winery know the sound of that meow, and more importantly the crowd gasps of "Ugh" and "Yuk!" We've practiced our sprint from behind the bar, pulling off a wad of paper towels without breaking stride, diving to cover up the headless mouse while praising Moakie in a crowd-calming tone, softly telling all, "This is really a good thing." After all, see rule #1.

I met Moakie in 2001 when we moved from Texas and I took over the winery operations. She definitely was a barn cat, aloof and arrogant. She had a *don't mess with me attitude* and only submitted herself for petting when she wanted something . . . to get out, to get in, more food, whatever.

Her meow could stop a boisterous and happy wine tasting crowd dead in their tracks, all heads turning because Moakie was speaking.

I've never been a cat person. I grew up with dogs so there was much to learn. Like the changing seasons, Moakie's habits change.

Summer sun brings out the frisky side while cold weather brings out her more loving side. Cuddled up on the couch, she dares me to put her out in the cold of night. Of course, Ralph and I cave . . . usually finding a warm spot in the cellar just for her.

Winery life happily went along until Benoit, our VERY French Winemaker, joined the team in 2004.

Then a test of will was sparked and it came to a standoff between Moakie and Benoit . . .

Who Owns the Cellar...
The Winemaker or The Cat?

Benoit is pretty dang particular. And like a lion guarding his den, the Cellar is his domain ... or so he thought.

Benoit didn't like having a cat perched on whatever barrel suited her fancy, taking a nap on top of his wine tanks, or yes, leaving those unwanted hair balls.

It didn't take long before we noticed an abrupt change in Moakie's demeanor. Most obvious, she would leave the room when Benoit entered.

Then the proverbial *cat poop* hit the fan.

Trailing the sound of very loud French cursing, Benoit enters the tasting room. "Kathyeee," he says, "Moakie has got to go. She *sheeeit* in zee middle of my cellar. I will not have thiessss." (You have to practice your French accent here!)

Now, I may have grown up with dogs, but I've come to know that cats are very smart and understand exactly what they're doing.

Molly, Libby and I were all in the winery that day and almost simultaneously we ask, "Benoit, what did you do to Moakie?"

"Nothing," he says, still bristling with anger.

Sensing we haven't heard everything, we press on, "Are you sure?"

"Well," he says, "I just make a face, hiss and hold my hands up like a mad cat every time I see Moakie," demonstrating this action. Voila! (We are learning a few words of French.)

We explain to Benoit that Moakie has left him a *present* on purpose, just to get back at him.

Although he didn't believe us then, we know he tested our theory because miraculously, Moakie went back to her cat box almost overnight!

The cellar is now quiet ... AND CLEAN.

There's an unspoken truce between Benoit and Moakie. She does seem to spend more time in the cellar when Benoit is playing French music ... so maybe they're getting along. Or maybe she's just trying to understand the French culture.

Yesterday I hung the pictures you see of Benoit and Moakie in the cellar to remind them ...

The Cellar IS
Big Enough for Two!

Chapter 9

Cellar Rats

People often ask what's it like to own a winery.

From the outside looking in it looks like lots of fun, even a little glamorous. What can be so difficult about pouring wine for folks all in a good mood? Talking and sharing stories. Going to wine festivals, great dinners, and events where you pour more of your wines and share your experiences. And, you're dressed up with a cool looking pouring station that draws attention from across the room.

I did most of the promotion at events, stores and festivals. What I soon learned is that before the event even got started I was exhausted. First: load the car with cases of wine and stuff to decorate pouring station. Second: drive to the event, which could be hours away. Third: haul heavy wine cases (40 pounds each) out of trunk in a parking lot, put on dolly and trudge into the event site. Fourth: hope for a good table in the midst of all the other wineries, not at the very end with little traffic. Put wine under pouring station and then decorate it. Fifth: check out your competition. Sixth: Stand and pour your wine for hours at a time.

My job above all . . . to be remembered. Convince people to buy Olympic Cellars wines by the end of the evening, look up our website, place an order or stop by the winery.

Seventh: Oh yeah, look fresh and in style, too. I blew that in Las Vegas. We had a wine tasting event in a huge ballroom at one of the casinos on the strip. I was dressed professionally, but stylishly, or so I thought. All the pouring stations were set up, but I saw very few people behind them. That concerned me because time was drawing near for the event to begin. Then the doors opened wide and dozens of sexy, beautiful women in tiny, short, black dresses swayed into the room on very tall spike heels. All hired by distributors to pour their wine. My station was one of a few wineries staffed by the actual owner or winemaker. Well, all I can say . . . it was an interesting night. I did meet a lot of women but poured for very few men!

Probably my least favorite gig was in a grocery or spirits store. I can't tell you how many times I was placed near a refrigerated case of some sort. At the end of the pouring my legs would be frozen stiff and I couldn't bend my knees. But if I got customers to pick up a bottle of wine, put it in their basket, and I went through a couple of cases, I proved to the store manager I could sell. That got me better placement the next time.

Don't know when I started always wearing hats. Remember, I took on the persona of Working Girl White and the label depicts a character wearing a hat. People started remembering me and my hats, and you know I can't do hair, so I was all for it. And, I have a lot of hats because like shoes, the hat must go with the outfit. Someday I may auction them all off for charity.

Back at the winery the wardrobe changes depending if you're working the tasting room or out in the cellar. The cellar was definitely jeans or fleece and nothing you cared about because your cellar wardrobe was embellished with wine stains.

I don't know which was my favorite season, fall or spring, harvest or bottling. Summer was all about events, tourists, local festivals and selling wine.

Harvest was the most physical. Benoit handled the forklift, crusher and press, while his most loyal cellar rats, Libby, Michael and me, took turns and shoveled the grapes. Thank goodness the grapes didn't ripen all at the same time. Our harvest averaged 35-50 tons each year.

Benoit would stay in touch with the vineyard managers, talking to them each day along with receiving a daily lab report detailing sugar, acidity and pH. Together they would decide on when to pick. I can't go into any more detail here. I would just ask Benoit. "Are the numbers good? Are they in balance? Are you pleased?" We even had grapes mailed overnight in a temperature-controlled box so Benoit could taste them. I stuck dang close to Benoit because if he thought we were getting close to picking I had to work with the trucking firm. And the right number of bins had to be at the vineyard prior to picking. Calculation: approximately 650 pounds of

grapes to a bin. 2000 pounds to a ton. I did the math. So, trucks went east to vineyards with empty grape bins and back West with grapes.

I knew that the truck could hold 12,000 pounds or 6 tons but depending on the truck height there could be an issue in stacking the bins (47 inches x 27 inches tall). I always tried to get as close to capacity as I could so I wouldn't have to share the truck with other freight, which meant additional stops. I drove the trucking firm a bit crazy because there could be no delay in delivery and I was always checking status.

The grapes were picked on harvest day. The trucker couldn't be late or the grapes would sit outside in hot Eastern Washington. Rarely did I get a truck that would drive from Eastern Washington straight to Port Angeles. Usually the first truck made it to Seattle where the grapes and any other freight going toward the Peninsula were loaded on another truck. Then that truck went to Bremerton and trucks were switched again. I knew the dock guys (day and night crew) at all three stops and had their cell numbers. Also, I knew the schedule for delivery at each city and set my alarm at night to check in and make sure my grapes were on the way. Scheduled arrival at Olympic Cellars was between 8– 9 a.m. the following morning. We treated the truck drivers very well, sending them along their way with a few bottles to pass out on the return. I wanted them to feel part of our harvest's success.

The day grapes arrived Benoit would have the crusher set-up, along with hoses, pump and whatever else he needed. Libby, Michael, and I would arrive with coffee in hand and a bag of food and snacks to keep us going. What I will never forget is Benoit coming out of the barn clapping his hands yelling, "Libbeee, Kathyeee, time to shovel." He'd jump on the forklift, move a bin with around 650 pounds of grapes close to the conveyor belt and we'd all take turns shoveling and sorting out any bad grapes. Four to ten tons later (12-30 bins of grapes) that day's crush was over. We would get extra help as we could, but us cellar rats were always on duty.

It sucks to shovel grapes in the rain. We prayed for decent weather because all the work was done outside with no cover if it rained. The grapes got the prime, dry spot under the patio roof. One year a local musician even played his guitar and serenaded us as we worked.

Then morning and night the tanks had to be punched down. This meant, when the wine started fermenting in the tanks the grape seeds and skins would form a hard crust on top. It needed to be broken up and the wine stirred morning and night. We would climb a ladder and stand on top of a tank and use a long stainless steel "potato masher" looking tool and start pushing it in to the wine. Each tank would take about fifteen minutes. Our arm muscles burned and we were wet with sweat regardless of the temperature. But we had buns of steel.

Now bottling for me was exciting because we could finally sell the wines. For Benoit, all his hard work paid off and the fruits of his labor could be enjoyed bottle after bottle.

The day before bottling a huge semi-truck would back into the winery with a complete bottling line inside. I almost kiss the ground the truck is parked on because bottling can be done all in one or two days with a high-tech bottling line.

Picture this. The back door of the semi-truck is totally open and the doors are secured. The forklift hoists up a pallet of empty bottles for two volunteers to dump topside up on the conveyor belt. The empty bottles travel down the conveyor belt. A hose attached to our tank outside the truck fills them with wine, sending them a little further down the belt for a cork. Two volunteers carefully drop a metal capsule on top of the bottle where, at the next stop, the next machine secures the capsule neatly around the rim of the bottle. Then the front and back labels are applied. Just imagine hundreds of bottles going around inside the truck all day long on the conveyor belt, finally to be picked up manually two at a time by two volunteers and put into wine boxes. Once they are twelve bottles full, the volunteer pushes the wine case under a tape dispenser for sealing and the wine rolls downs another conveyor belt to another two waiting volunteers for stacking 56 or 75 cases to a pallet.

The volunteer crew totals eight or ten. We fed them well and sent them home with a Love Box full of wine they bottled. In total, twenty-five thousand to thirty thousand bottles passed through our volunteers' hands and traveled around the truck every harvest. Using volunteers for harvest and bottling is common practice for small wineries.

We didn't always have the luxury of a bottling truck. The winery used to have a very small bottling system that filled twelve bottles, one at a time. We would stack cases of empty wine bottles on the table to the left of the filler. One person would pick up an empty bottle and put it under a filling spout. Another person would take the bottles off as they were filled and put them on the corking station. Once corked, the bottle of wine traveled down a conveyor and had to be hand wiped because wine would trickle down the bottles as they filled. Then the last person on the line would take the dry bottles and put them back into the wine boxes. Later we would open the boxes, pull out the bottles, hand label one bottle at a time and finally tape the boxes shut.

During bottling we gravity-fed the wine to the bottling machine with the help of nitrogen pumped into the tank that had been hoisted as high as the forklift would go. Well, during one bottling Sara accidently added to much nitrogen to the tank (sound familiar) and blew the lid, which created a Merlot geyser that hit the top of the inside of the barn. It created a monumental mess. Picture in your mind drilling for oil and hitting a gusher, resulting in oil gushing out of the ground. The only good side of our Merlot geyser . . . as it dripped off the ceiling you could stick your tongue out and taste the wine.

I don't know who started it but we started humming then singing . . . It's Raining Men, Halleluiah, No It's Raining WINE, Halleluiah over and over.

Between harvest and bottling, the wines were aged, racked, lab tested, and tasted. Before bottling a bottle sample of all the wines were pulled from the barrels and tanks and tasted again to determine the final blend. For example: We tasted the Merlot. Then tasted it with 5% Cabernet Sauvignon added, or maybe 10% of Cab Franc. The real power of blending lies in the potential for adding complexity to the final wine — multiple flavors and aromas. And everything was in the pursuit of balance — that happy marriage of fruit, acid, tannin, alcohol, color and (sometimes) oak that makes great wines sing.

Benoit would get especially frustrated with me when we tasted wines for blending because it wouldn't take long and I would either want to sleep or giggle. (I'm a lightweight when it comes to alcohol.) Benoit had to teach me how to taste, analyze the wine, then spit. "Kathyeee, do not swallow, taste, spit."

He didn't care where he spit either. Molly and I would be at the bar serving customers and he'd come in with a barrel sample of wine for us to try. (We would all drink out of the same glass. I guess alcohol kills all germs.) He would take a mouthful, lean up against the back bar, swishing the wine around in his mouth, thinking about the wine, then boom he'd spit across the walkway into the sink. Splat!

The customers would jump back in surprise. We'd quickly introduce Benoit and ask him to tell us all about the wine. Our customers would usually go home with a story to tell about Olympic Cellars' French winemaker.

You know after bottling the last thing I wanted to drink was wine. I had my favorite porter and India Pale Ale, a hoppy style beer, in the fridge. When we had finished all the cleaning we enjoyed a cold beer together.

I've described briefly working the winery. It is demanding, physical and never ending. There is no 9-5 work schedule, but you must find your down time. I wrote the *Pile of White Rocks* email after one of my more grueling days.

     And, our Team grew. Let me introduce you.

Pam Erickson joined us to help re-do the tasting room from ceiling to floor. I mentioned before we needed cool curb appeal inside and out. Pam also took our "gifts section" to new heights and taught us the importance of merchandising, keeping the gift section fresh and always updated.

Michael Smith had worked at Neuharth Winery as needed and lived on our winery property for a while. He was a jeweler and rented an office in the back of the barn. More important, he was a black belt and worked late into the evening. He was there when we were alone in the tasting room and made sure the winery was locked up each night. Michael is our beloved "Handyman." Whatever was happening —bottling, harvest, concerts, breakdowns — he was there to help.

Libby joined our team in 2004, worked in the tasting room and did all the merchandizing of our gift shop that continued to grow. She was our event coordinator extraordinaire. She played the drums, was super creative, an artist, and my fellow cellar rat. She was with us 'til 2009 when she ventured on a new career at 7 Cedar Casino.

Kathy Kidwell, KK for short, to distinguish between the two Kathy's. She joined our team in October 2005. She worked both the winery and my husband's business juggling their diverse needs with ease. We worked in tandem away from the winery. She had the website and graphic design expertise and I wrote website content, emails, ads, and press releases. We created the website, Facebook design, graphics and if that wasn't enough, she also did all the financial books and reporting when I started traveling and promoting the Working Girl Wines. She ruled the home office.

Cathe Muller (now there were three) joined the team in 2007 as our gardener extraordinaire when we re-did our landscaping around the winery. Like me, she took early retirement after 25 years from the Aerospace Industry, traveled for a while then relocated to Sequim starting her own landscape business.

Lisa joined us in 2009 and had a broad knowledge about wine and food pairing that had come with time, patience, and travel in the US and abroad. Lisa's studies began with chemistry and ended with a degree in Public Relations, which were a great combination for the winery. Early in her career she worked for an environmental consultant. As part of that job, she transported samples and equipment around Seattle in large bread trucks. When talking about this job, Lisa said you haven't lived 'til you had to parallel park a bread truck on a hill in the rain in Seattle traffic! Now I know why she can drive a forklift so effortlessly!

A Pile of White Rocks

Last night I got home from the Winery pretty late. I walked into the kitchen, poured myself a glass of wine and stood at the counter sipping. My mind was still in high gear, reviewing the events of the day and making a mental list of what I still needed to do before bed.

I don't know how long I stood there in that slump-shouldered, weary stance (I'm sure you can relate ... we've all been there too often). But all of a sudden I noticed ... my glass was empty!

I didn't even remember drinking the wine and, worse ... hadn't even TASTED it!

That was it!

I changed clothes, stomped downstairs to our combined home offices, handed my husband his tennis shoes and bellowed, "We're going for a walk!"

Whether coming home from work or working out of your home, too often we just transition from one job to another, never stopping even if just for thirty minutes.

Quality over quantity: that's my new motto right now. I'm committed to making it work. No more feeling guilty or sorry for myself.

So picture this in your mind's eye: Ralph and I are walking hand-in-hand, talking and just enjoying our togetherness. All the while I'm looking for a white rock on the beach.

Why? Well, I've started a pile of white stones back at the house to remind me of our "get-aways." I pick up a new one each time we get out. And I'm continually eyeing that pile to make sure it grows.

I'm still the same triple-A, goal-oriented person. But now when I drive home I always look over at my pile of white rocks. It's a visual reminder of what's important in life and makes me feel good.

This weekend we *scheduled* thirty minutes to pick blackberries (and spent over an hour). Bee sting included, it was another special memory. No white rocks but I found a bunch of dried weeds that I thought would look good in a pot.

Remember ... live *La Dolce Vida!* Just be sure to define what "The Sweet Life" means for you!

Chapter 10

California, Here We Come!

We were off and running.

Remember, I came from a twenty-five-year corporate background, so I brought a lot of that triple A-type personality to the table. My reputation was for making things happen and the opportunity to do that with my winery unveiled itself. I soon learned that if we wanted to survive as a very small player in the wine industry we needed to focus on a niche market. We'd stumbled on our identity and our brand, Working Girl Wines, when our community labeled us the Olympic Women in Wine. We cemented the brand when I bought the Kathy Womack Women and Wine painting.

However, in the mass distributed wine market we couldn't compete on price. There was no way economies of scale would kick in, and like any industry, major acquisitions were taking place, making it even harder to compete. So, we played to our strength: we are women, we know what we liked so we created the Working Girl (WG) wines and self-proclaimed them the *Official Wine of Working Women*. I was always coming up with one-liners. This one turned into a poster of a lady lying in a hammock, obviously just getting off from work, one heel dangling off her toes, the other on the ground with her brief case and reading glasses while enjoying a glass of wine. Great visual and connection for selling the WG wines. Even if you didn't carry a briefcase or wear panty hose and pumps, women related to that liberating feeling of Work Day's End.

Another one-liner that identified what the Working Girls and wines stood for ... *Working Girl Wines – Created by Women, In Support of Women*. This message still speaks to the Working Girls and the wines today. Early on we designated a local non-profit as our charity of choice that supported women in need and wrote a check each month based on our sales.

What we hoped for came true in our small piece of the world. There was a real emotional connection to the wines. They were flying off the shelves and I started to get calls from regional distributors that heard the message. There was a positive buzz about the winery and just maybe the leaking septic tank was behind us.

Now, though, I was beginning to get concerned about inventory. If I started distributing wines beyond the winery, obviously we needed to produce more, which meant I needed a short-term infusion of cash.

As luck would have it, I had a serendipitous encounter with the Vierra brothers, Gary and George. Both had strong ties in the wine industry, especially California, making and selling wine. Emails went back and forth between us initially and one statement from George stood out for me. "I feel that establishing a good foundation in California is the # 1 priority and the correct strategy. New York, Texas, Illinois and the other key states will follow in 2006. I will allow that competition is very tough in California, but wines that have a story such as WGWs can create a significant niche. The wines are delicious and will be attractive to the vast population of women, regardless if they are wine consumers or not."

I flew to California and with their help started to put a plan in place to produce, distribute, and market the wines. And, who carries the risk? Yep, me.

ShoreBank Enterprise Pacific, a non-profit community development organization, opened a new office in Port Angeles dedicated to building strong rural communities by providing capital investment. In March 2005, Olympic Cellars received ShoreBank's first local loan, $104,000, due for repayment in six months.

I contracted with Hogue Winery for a *heart-pounding* production of 9,200 cases of the WG brand. Prior to that we had grown from 1500 to 3200 cases. Now we'd tripled that in a heartbeat.

In May 2005, we were about to go big time. It was exciting and scary but California here we come.

It had been a month to the day since Olympic Cellars announced their venture into the California wine market when we knew our California strategy wasn't working as planned. Ah, we were so brave, hopeful, and so naïve. We listened to the experts and put our initial focus on the California market. We were the classic David and Goliath, testing our product in the Lion's Den. Why? Because more wine is sold in California than in any other state. And, we had a fresh, unique story and packaging, good wine, and a concept that was sure to sell. But that wasn't good enough.

During the summer I marketed and promoted 24x7, which resulted in some key media and PR that saved our bacon, since the California market for WGWs crapped out. An article in *Wine Spectator* magazine about the wines for women featured a photo of Molly, Libby and me and included two paragraphs about us and our wines.

I'm not sure how they got the photo, which had been taken on a whim to use in a regional tourism promotion – Enjoy a Working Girl Road Trip on the Olympic Peninsula. It was taken on a Saturday and all three of us were working in the tasting room. A friend parked his red convertible with top down in front of the winery. We poured guests an extra big taste, grabbed sunglasses, threw boas around our necks and ran outside. Molly poised sitting on top of the back seat with a bottle of our champagne. Libby tied a scarf around her head like you had just been driving top down with a matching satchel and me, well I had sequin sunglasses, the purple feathered boa, and a purple silk hat. The photo just sang . . . "Girls Just Wanna Have Fun."

We got a phenomenal response from women-owned distributors across the nation and retail shops asking how they could get the Working Girl wines. Our story, the grass roots charitable support and, yes, even those fun labels attracted interest, especially in Texas where a woman-owned distribution company became our largest client. The wines were entered in the Houston Wine Competition and WG White and Rosie took Reserve Champion, which is even higher than a gold medal. And only in Texas, instead of medals for this prestigious award I got two fancy silver belt buckles.

But just as important, I got a call from family-owned Alaska Distributors in Seattle and was asked to meet with their VP of sales. Score – now our wines were distributed across our own state, Alaska and Oregon.

So even though we didn't corner the California market, by December we had sold 70% of the wine and paid back the loan. This enabled us to plan another bottling in January.

The Washington Wine Commission recognized Olympic Cellars for our innovation and marketing and referred us to a variety of wine writers. The media coverage continued, a lot of positive, good stories as well as some that really got under my skin.

One article, in particular, got my goat. The Winery and the Working Girls were described as "red neck," just offering up a lot of clichés like "created by women for women." The article left off the most important part of the tag line, In Support of Women. Let me tell you . . . we do what we say, are what we are, and damn proud of it.

I realized I needed thicker skin and must keep focused on the end game – growing the brand and supporting women through our donations. I also needed an outlet to vent and started writing a series of *Rants and Raves* emails to my customer list on a range of topics. Side note, if you haven't noticed, by now my emails had become a big focus of my customer outreach. The R&Rs were written as if I were speaking to a friend, reaching out, sometimes asking for advice and sometimes saying, I just need to get this off my chest. We've all done it. But, to your customers? (I've included one of my Rants and Raves – Pigeon Holed. The one that follows is an example of a get-something-off-my-chest rant.)

Email replies ran the gambit from advice to support or just an atta girl. Bottom line for me, I engaged my customers and they felt a part of our business.

Remember I told you marketing was my middle name. There was a real-life story behind the Working Girls and their wines and not just another cute label. It connected us with our customers, distributors of our wines and the media. But that would've all fizzled out unless I kept the marketing fresh and on-going, continuing down the non-traditional path of running the winery and reaching out to the most important people in our lives, our customers. And, not just for the sale.

I didn't want to communicate with my customers only when I wanted them to buy wine. That gets old fast. We're all sick of being badgered to death to buy, buy, buy. I just delete, delete, delete and then unsubscribe.

My goal was to initially generate curiosity. What are the Working Girls up to next? Then sometimes educate. But always showing the love. This last statement might have you rolling your eyes and think I'm dishing out some lame marketing voodoo.

I just knew in my heart that my customers needed to know I valued them. They had a choice of where to spend their money. And, they were part of our winery family.

WINE BITES

Tonight, I feel like a sparkling wine, bubbly and festive. Why? I finished the first section of this book. You've met our cast of characters and while there's more to the story, I'm going to pull out the perfect pairing with a bubbly - a bag of potato chips and I'm just going to enjoy.

Let me tell you about tonight's bubbly, a Brut Blanc de Blancs from Treveri Cellars, which is Washington's only sparkling wine house. Since its opening, Treveri sparkling wines have been served at White House State Department receptions and the James Beard Foundation in New York.

I think of Juergen Grieb, Head Winemaker and Owner, as sort of the winery's mentor. Early on we could only afford to buy small quantities of bulk wine to bottle as we built up our own cellar. Juergen who was then the VP and head winemaker for Coventry Vale, a custom winemaking facility, helped us out again and again. Imagine us pulling up in a U-Haul truck with a 375-gallon tank in the back and park next to tankers that transported the approximate 850,000 gallons production to other wineries.

My fondest memory was sitting with Juergen as he helped me blend the Rosé the Riveter that would be sold in distribution. Juergen even let me hire a bottling truck and his crew to bottle the Working Girl Wines at his facility. Thank you Juergen for all your help over the years.

Rant and Rave #3: Pigeon Holed - Stereotyped. Heck NO!

Some of the media coverage of the Working Girl Wines sort of got under my skin. Articles showing up categorizing the wines as Just for Women or Flash-in-the-Pan Gimmick Wines and then berating us because the wines were not vintage dated.

So, let me say this emphatically. *Working Girl Wines* are NOT just another cute label, trying to grab up new market share while trying to *Hide our Age*.

Here I sit, in my favorite pink flannel, grape stomping jammies, writing another email. But I think this one's more an exercise in helping me sort through all the feedback we're getting on the *Working Girl Wines* as they're released across the country.

Wines for Women. We've had a lot of interest and media attention regarding the release of the Working Girl Wines beyond our winery doors. There has also been a flurry of articles about "Wine for Women." Our marketing tag line for *Working Girl Wines* used to be "Created by Women, For Women, In Support of Women." I realized early on you couldn't create a wine for a gender so we dropped the 'For Women.' Everyone's tastes are too different. I like big, bold reds. In fact, I didn't personally drink the *Working Girl* wines until we came out with *Handyman Red "dedicated to Michael Smith, all the husbands, neighbors and other men in the community who we could always call on when we need strong helping hands or the 'MacGyver' touch."*

But, the situation I'm facing is . . . here we are, three women, with labels that reflect our personality, our philosophy and approach to the wine industry, our life and our business. So I'm torn. But there's little time to twiddle and anyway, the upside . . . maybe we're still on the right track: women-owned distribution companies around the country have found us and THEY want our wines! We'll keep on truckin.

I want to personally thank many of you for asking for the wines when you're eating out or shopping in a wine store. Your personal testament has generated inquiries and resulting sales. Our heartfelt thanks.

Gimmick Wines. Like any industry, gimmick products always pop up to grab attention during narrow "windows of opportunity." It's no different with wine. Cute labels are all over the place. And why not? It's the label that draws your eye and helps a wine "jump out" in a sea of choices. But a cutesy label often gets purchased once and then vanishes forever into the wine graveyard ... unless the bottle content is memorable. Otherwise, it's on to the next cute label that grabs your attention.

Our challenge is to get the *Working Girl* story out there. The "*Girls*" have been around since 2003 and their popularity has grown the old fashion way ... grass roots word of mouth! Our wines are built on a foundation of charitable and community support and it's our vision to have them continue to support local communities in which they are sold.

Ugh! No Vintage. Even though I could consider myself an *industry insider* now, I'm not fixated on vintage designations (that's the calendar year the grapes were harvested that you see listed on a bottle). I AM very serious about our wine ... and want medals just like everyone else (most of 'em are only handed out to "vintage" wines ... it's just one of the "traditions" that goes with this industry). Now, I know on average when certain types of varietals should get bottled after harvest. So when I look at a vintage on a shelf, I may be wondering, "Why is a wine this old still on the shelf?" or "How come they bottled this one so soon?" But for most wines that fall in my "norm range" of vintages, I don't care. That's because I'm not a collector (I don't lay my wines down ... I'm sure that term did not originate with us gals.) I always find an excuse to drink that really good bottle of wine I purchased, after all I worked hard today and deserve it! I try a lot of wines for taste, style and food pairing, basically because of reputation, medals, write-ups, etc. Remember, four years ago I was schlepping semi-conductors instead of wines! Market research: someone has to do it.

But what I've learned to TRULY love ... is the power of blending wines! I'm told all the great French winemakers were master blenders, including Benoit, our French winemaker.

I can't tell you how many times during our tasting and blending trials a blend wins out over the straight varietal. That's why if you don't consider vintages, whoa, things can get really fun!

The *Working Girl* wines are blends. And even though the same grape varietals go into our *Working Girl* wines, because we designate them as "non-vintage," we're not constrained to putting just one year's vintage into a bottle. We're free to make the absolute best wine we can make ... even if it's a blend of 50% from one year and 50% from another! Now, the law requires us to call these "Table Wines" instead of a nice fancy vintage name (like Merlot), but for you it means just one thing ... ENJOY ... because the wine will be good! We've staked our reputation on it.

So what's this diatribe gotten me?

I guess a confirmation at least to myself that *Working Girl Wines* are not just another cute label, trying to grab up new market share while trying to hide our age.

We believe in what these wines stand for long term ... and hope you do to. You know I always want to hear from you ... any thoughts, advice?

Update:

The Working Girl Wines finally went to California – to Hollywood!

Olympic Cellars was honored by a request from the Women's Sport Foundation to include our Working Girl *White and Go Girl Red* in the celebrity bags for their annual Billie Event.

The Billie Awards honor media excellence in the portrayal of girls and women in sports and physical activity. The Billies were held on April 15, 2008 at the Beverly Hilton Hotel in Beverly Hill, Calif. This event gathered celebrities from film, television and professional athletics, including Billie Jean King, and featured a special performance by Sir Elton John.

The Women's Sports Foundation is an educational nonprofit (501(c)(3) charity) organization founded in 1974 by tennis legend Billie Jean King so that girls following in her footsteps would not have to face the barriers she faced playing sports.

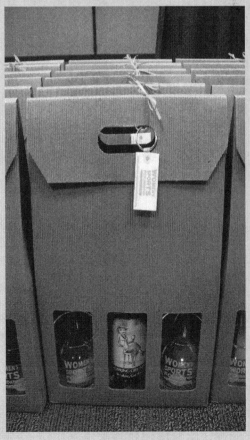

PART TWO
RUNNING YOUR OWN BUSINESS – ADVICE FROM THE FRONT LINES

CHAPTER 11
Marketing and Chardonnay

Colleagues and friends have commented that they liked my marketing skills and approach to getting the word out about the Working Girls, and they encouraged me to write about it. Initially I approached this book more as a marketing manual for a small business with lots of bulleted advice. Then I sent my first draft to some friends for some feedback. They hinted that it was very businesslike and probably very boring.

When I heard, "Kathy, tell your story first," I got it.

It became clear that the book had to be more than a marketing checklist. I had too much valuable experience to share, too many pitfalls to warn those readers who might be thinking of starting a small online or off-line business; too many wonderful stories to tell. So, I started over.

You've only read a part of our story up to now, but I think this is a perfect place to talk more the business and marketing aspects of a small, bankrupted winery in an economically challenged small town. You know, just in case somebody leaves you a bankrupt business or some such, and you're looking for some advice.

In Part Two of the book I'm going to break down some of the basic business strategies I learned from my prior life in the corporate world and how I applied them to a small business. I think they will be helpful to anyone who shares my entrepreneurial DNA.

Yes, there are many business manuals out there that can tell you about setting up your books, keeping track of inventory and the like. But that's not what helped Olympic Cellars pay the bills. How did we draw in the customers, day after day, year after year? That's what I want to share with you. So to rephrase an old saying, how do you run your own business? Ask the woman who owned one. After all, we survived and many, including me, would say we thrived. A big part of that success is because we braided our relationships with our customers, our distributors, and our community into our marketing approach, which is a bigger story than simply a business or marketing checklist.

And for those of you who think business/marketing is a dull or even scary topic, or something introverts must avoid, it might help you to know that I spell marketing "FUN."

However, that *Fun* involved a lot of OJT: On the job training. But in the beginning, just like I didn't know the wine business at first, I didn't how to market our business, either.

But as I traveled down memory lane putting together the initial outline for this book I realized that over time we had built long-lasting relationships with our customers and volunteers who had become a part of the winery family and they had helped the winery succeed. They were invested in the winery's success. And these relationships were what our marketing success was all about.

Many knew about the septic system, the bankruptcy, the struggles and then the success of the Working Girl Wines. But they also knew that our link to the community went much deeper than selling as many cases of wine as was humanly possible.

The winery supported the community and the community supported our business. The celebration of International Women's Day at the winery kicked off each year's charitable support for local non-profits that supported women and families in our community.

Like the wake of a ship, all this history is easier to see from the rear, looking back at where we've come from. In the beginning it was a different story. I've mentioned that marketing became my middle name. I knew what it was supposed to do, sell your product to a customer. But the thing I had to figure out was how do you communicate with the customer; what was the best media? Deep down I knew the communication couldn't be one way, it needed to be a two-way dialogue that focused on earning, not buying my customer's attention.

I've said it before, but I'll say it again: I just knew in my heart that my customers needed to know I valued them. I needed to reach out in a personal way and show the love.

Despite my years in the corporate world, I had absolutely zilch experience with marketing. Initially, my philosophy was throw something at the wall, if it stuck then great, if it didn't try something else. At least I was smart enough to know that just opening the doors and hoping someone would walk through and buy a case of wine was Whistling Dixie.

I had looked at a lot of wine magazines and the ads that I couldn't afford. To me though, they all blurred together and they didn't engage me as a customer or make me want to buy the product.

Working Girl and its non-traditional persona was definitely working. We were selling wine and winning awards but that's what wineries were supposed to do. I wanted to grow my business and be recognized in the industry so I threw caution to the wind, tradition be damned. My new marketing philosophy, if it's legal and "death or injury" is not a by-product of an idea, at least to my customers and team, then I charged ahead – although when skydiving out of plane into Washington Wine Country, I didn't say "death or injury" too loud. Tuck and roll, that's what I had to remember that time.

There are similarities between any business, be it brick and mortar or on-line. But one thing stands out more than anything else: the one thing we all have in common is – Customers. And what do we value above everything else? Our Customers. If we don't, we're out of business.

It all boils down to this. You want your customer to want your product enough to drive out of their way to buy it or order it from your website.

As I said, this section of my book deals with marketing and business advice learned on the front lines ... connecting with my customers, standing out in the sea of wines and having fun doing it. It's real life with a dose of laughter, a few tears and some zany antics to keep things interesting.

Wait. Stop here. I can hear my husband Ralph say, "Kathy, so get to the point."

Ah yes, why am I writing this book? I've rambled a bit, I know.

Maybe I'm a bit uncomfortable offering marketing advice since I've taken no formal classes on the subject. But I wouldn't finish this book if I didn't feel that I had something of value to offer you for your business.

There is a story to this advice, just like there was the story about how I went from a corporate career to owning a bankrupt winery. This story comes with the same twists, bumps, and an epiphany of sorts regarding my marketing.

And just like the first section of the book, I wanted to share some more wines to sip along the way. Except this time, I didn't refer to the *Wine and Mood* suggestions.

Chapter 13

What's In It For You

I've told you my story and now in the following chapters I'm going to tell you how you might apply my life lessons to your business. But, as I just started writing I realized you are now my customer and I need to get in your shoes. My message – what's in it for you?

Each one of the areas I'm going to focus on below was an integral part of moving my business forward and all were interrelated. After writing about each of these areas and coming back to this chapter, I realized that each had a fundamental goal – communications that were personalized to what's in it for our customer.

Here's what I'm going to talk about.

Chapter 14: Social Responsibility
Chapter 15: Attract more customers with events
Chapter 16: Shaking it up, a non-traditional approach
Chapter 17: Low hanging grapes
Chapter 18: Advertising and Public Relations
Chapter 19: The Team is #1
Chapter 20: Community involvement
Chapter 21: Email Marketing

When I joined the *club* of small business owners it was an eye-opening experience and a bit scary. Most of us didn't have the time to even network, but we had a pretty strong rumor mill with the *did you know* type conversations where we shared the difficulties we were facing. Businesses were in competition with each other and it seemed to me, the newbie of the bunch, that collaboration could be difficult.

But looking back, this was my first ah-hah. You have to give first, to receive. I wanted help to break in to this business community, but what was I offering in return? I joined the Chamber of Commerce, volunteered on committees, and realized that this was the most amazing and giving community. In time we built relationships, and when I had questions or needed help I could pick up the phone.

Here are a few Business 101s that jumped out at me early on:

Business acumen: I found out that I was also very fortunate to have an accounting background and that for a lot of businesses the main issue was the lack of business acumen and the understanding of the importance of cash flow. This is not an area I'm going to cover, but if you don't have that financial background then hire it. It will be the best money you ever spent.

Logic plus Creativity: What surprised me, though, was the need for both left brain logic and right brain creativity to run my business. I was fortunate to be able to think and operate out of both sides of my brain; although I found out I had a ping pong ball inside my brain sometimes screwing around with my thought processes. Again, no worries. Know yourself, build a team or build a network where you can brainstorm or work through an operations issue. You'll make yourself crazy talking through your business issues with yourself.

Put yourself at the top of your list: Whatever your business, dedicate some part of your day or week as yours and yours alone. You're going to need your own private TLC. Owning my own business brought more demands on me than I would have ever imagined. Without some time alone, by myself, for re-grouping – not to mention exercise, nutrition and sleep – (well, at least sleep) – I would never have succeeded. I would be headed down that slippery slope to the proverbial Wall. Then . . . Splat! I know because that is what happened to me at Texas Instruments.

The gift of a small business: With the winery, things were different. I had a payroll that supported people that I knew personally, not just employees on a list. I knew their spouses, their kids. We were a small core team; we became a family of sorts. This was a gift, one that is still most precious to me that I never even thought I would receive when I took over Olympic Cellars Winery.

I've learned a lot about marketing since I bought the winery and done most kinds of marketing. Print ads, PR, face to face contact with customers at conventions and tastings in grocery stores, community events—you name it. What stands out for me in these days of the importance of the Internet is email marketing.

Remember my fourth priority from chapter six; start communicating with my customers beyond the tasting room. As I mentioned above each chapter in this marketing sections focuses on a fundamental goal – communications that were personalized to what's in it for our customer. What worked for me and the big thing I have to offer you is email marketing starting with Chapter 21 through 25.

By now, you've read a few of my emails and probably noticed I go off on tangents with hands and arms moving as fast as I could type, passionately telling a story to my customers, pulling them in and making them feel a part of the winery.

That's what I really want to share with you, how we engaged our customers with emails. It wasn't a bunch of expensive marketing and ads, 'cause I sure didn't have the money in the early years. I got ideas from some of the craziest places that I just adapted to the winery. And, it's what I'm hoping to pass on to you as you read this book. Ideas that you can mold to fit your own business. Yes, I had a blog/website, but it was our regular, sometimes weekly emails to our customers that made the connection. The blog was dependent on someone finding my site and was a placeholder for my emails. Whereas an email was like a phone call, I wrote directly to the customer who had signed up to our list, via the guest book in the tasting room or some other email collection device.

My marketing style via emails was personal, usually written as an engaging story in my best Working Girl persona keeping the focus on my customer, not on my product.

But let me backtrack. Email marketing alone for the winery, or for any brick and mortar business that also has online sales, wouldn't have been enough. It also had to include building relationships through community involvement and winery events.

Finally, it may look like I have this female focus going on. I didn't write this book specifically for women business owners, but for anyone, male or female, looking for advice or encouragement as you start your business or try to jumpstart a stalled business, or an interested reader looking for a good story. But, after all, I'm a woman in business writing about my experiences. There's no way to keep the female perspective out of it, just like I can't ignore the female aspects of what happened with our winery and our wines. Women created the Working Girl Wines. Of course, our wines transcend gender, just like I hope this book will. And since I'm writing from my gut, there's no getting around the fact that it's a women's gut. No way to change that.

And no way to take 25 years in Corporate America out of this gal.

Wine Bites

If you were here, I would pour you a glass from The Expedition Chardonnay, 2015, Canoe Ridge Vineyard and Winery in Walla Walla, Washington, as I continue to taste my way through Safeway looking for my favorite Chard. The tasting notes for this wine were right down my alley - scents of butterscotch and honeysuckle mix with flavors of ripe pear and honeydew for a rich, elegant texture on the finish. And it's 50% barrel ferment, three-quarters American oak and one-quarter French oak.

Canoe Ridge Vineyard focuses primarily on Chardonnay, Merlot and Cabernet Sauvignon. The Chardonnay grapes are from the Horse Heave Hills Appellation, which is the same appellation that our Lemberger grapes are grown.

Chapter 14

Social Responsibility: The Heart of the Winery

First let me start with *The Heart* because to me it set my moral compass. I told myself, Yes, Kathy you need to make money and get us out of debt. Then I pondered, but at what cost? Is there more to this new business of mine then just making money?

I'm not sure when I read about running a business with a Triple Bottom Line (TBL) instead of just focusing on making a profit, but it felt right and got me thinking.

Definition of TBL in the accounting world; consideration is given to the company's financial, social, and environmental performance over time. Also, called "Profit, People, Planet." I still used QuickBooks with standard financial reporting, but I started thinking in the Three P framework when making decisions.

Obviously, my business goal was to operate profitably and in doing so we could also give back to the community and be sensitive to environmental concerns. I think these were the words on a poster that I wrote down: The Olympic Peninsula ... beauty abounds, from sea to towering mountains, from majestic forests to fertile fields.

You could say Profit, People, Planet had become our mission.

Every day in the mail along with the BILLS, I would get multiple donation requests from local, state and national charitable organizations. Early on I made the decision to give to local charities and civic organizations, as that was all we could afford and that's who we needed to support. We honored these requests with donations of a few bottles of wine in a gift basket.

Initially, we set an annual limit because if we weren't careful we could donate our entire production, given the number of non-profits and fund-raising events in our community.

Now, this is the accountant in me talking ... financially there is no advantage on your bottom line when you donate goods, because they are already accounted for at cost and you can't write off the retail value. But you also can't put a price on the goodwill generated from your donation. And, don't discount the opportunity of future sales from individuals who passionately

I was thinking what wine at the winery to pour. What I really wanted was our oaked Chardonnay with hints of butterscotch on the nose and a lingering buttery finish. But we had sold out.

So, like searching for the best way to write about what I can offer you on the marketing and business front, I was on the search for a good Chardonnay for this writing part of my journey.

In our small town, we don't have a wine store, so Safeway was where I headed. You might wonder why I just don't select from my own wine cellar. To tell the truth, I don't have one. I had my own cellar at the winery and if I was trying different wines to keep up with what was going on with my competitors, I normally only bought a bottle or two. And if the wine was really good I would come up with a reason that I deserved that second bottle of wine. I'm not into delayed gratification and long-term storage.

Back to Safeway. I didn't select from the top shelf because those Chards were pretty pricey, but when this section of the book is done, I've eyed a couple of wines on the top shelf that I will have deserved and then I'll shell out the dollars. But for now, I selected one shelf down, purchased six different bottles to get my 10% discount, read all the labels looking for the descriptors that defined my taste in Chardonnay and headed to the checkout line.

WINE BITES

Glass in hand, let's begin with the next chapter while sipping a 2015 Waterbrook Reserve Chardonnay from Washington State. When tasting the competition, I would often pick a Waterbrook wine. Their winemaker, John Freeman, joined the Waterbrook team in 2003. He's amassed more than eighty 90+ scores and 100 Best Buy wines. This winery is located in Walla Walla and recognized for producing wines that exemplify the outstanding vineyards in the Walla Walla Valley and the Columbia Valley.

Chapter 12

Marketing: Out of Sight, Out of Mind, Out of Business

This old saying has always said it ALL for me. If you're out of sight to your customers, you're out of their minds. So how do you connect and stay connected? And if you could look over my monitor you would see this bit of wisdom framed on the wall; one that I lived by every day at the winery.

While this section of the book deals with how I tackled growing my business in a small rural community, your business challenges I know are different and require different strategies. Yours may be total e-commerce, located in a much larger city, with no employees. But bottom line, all of us face the same challenge. How do we attract, connect with, and keep our customers?

I think regardless of your business and how you communicate with your customers there are definite overlaps between any business types. I'm writing about what I found worked for me, and while it is specific to a winery, I'm hoping it will get you thinking or give you an idea to implement especially if you're starting a new business.

My storefront is an historic barn. It attracted visitors, but accounted for a significant percentage of monthly expenses (payroll, mortgage, utilities, cleaning). An on-line business, such as a successful blog, web development, or content marketing website also has expenses but maintaining a physical store and production facility are usually not one of them. I had to learn how to take advantage of both. Visitors, the tourist season and events helped grow my email/customer list. Some joined our quarterly online wine club and others purchased from promotional wine emails.

I always tried to put myself in my customer's shoes . . . providing a great product and/or shopping experience will only get me so far . . . that is if the customer even finds my business. I needed to find a communication vehicle that made sense, and which <u>I could do regularly</u> to stay in front of my customer. Email? Social Media (Facebook, Twitter, YouTube, Pinterest, Instagram) Blog? Or a combination? Didn't want to bombard them but communicate as if I were talking to them face to face. And I learned early on at the bar pouring wine . . . that face to face contact was priceless because you can personally connect. Never short cut that opportunity to build a relationship, which I began to think could also be done via my emails.

Facebook worked for me. There just wasn't enough time in the day to learn and leverage all the social media platforms. I only dabbled in Twitter,

YouTube and Pinterest. The winery's customer demographic (Baby Boomers: born 1946-1964 and Gen X: born mid-60's to early 1980s) responded better to Facebook and my emails. I used my blog as a placeholder. I would post my emails to the blog, which I would then link to from Facebook, from my website, or in a follow-up email.

Another aspect I considered for my target customer was disposable income, which on average was higher for these two generations. Small boutique wineries such as Olympic Cellars could never match high production wineries that could sell at a much lower price. Individuals spent more if they wanted handcrafted wines, not found on every store shelf.

Always at the forefront for me was reaching those with time-starved lifestyles. Again, in my customer's shoes (and mine) it would be so much easier to buy wine at the grocery store: one-stop shopping. Why would someone want to drive out of their way or pay for shipping to get Olympic Cellars wine? Or shop at a small business when generally you will get a better price online and shipping is free.

I've already talked about quality of product, but I knew social responsibility and community involvement would also keep my business front of mind. Again, the latter two was just part of belonging and doing business in a small community, although I think social responsibility now for any business is a given.

At the risk of repeating myself, customer interaction (phone, email or in person) is paramount to success. We all know people talk about their experiences, good or bad. And each of us wants to be valued as a customer. After all, we have a choice of where to spend our money. An old saying ... People don't care about you, until they know you care about them.

So, my advice, find a way to always make it personal to the customer. Relationship equals value equals sales. Your message: <u>what's in it for the customer?</u>

A very different wine pouring experience cemented this message for me. Although it didn't jump out at me at first, that particular evening wouldn't leave my mind. If I'm having trouble coming up with *what's in it for my customer*, when I'm writing a press release, ad or email, I always think about this night and get in my customer's shoes.

The Port Angeles Chamber of Commerce sponsored "after hours" gatherings for its members at local businesses once a month. It helped promote the business and got all of us small business owners to gather for some well-deserved time away from work. The local wineries rotated and poured their wine at these events.

Believe it or not, my turn was in the most unexpected place for a wine tasting, a local funeral home. I hauled in my Working Girl Wines and asked where they wanted me to set up. I was steered into a room that held a stainless-steel casket filled with ice. Sooooo ... I iced down the White and the Rosé right next to Dead Man's beer. I guess there was some tongue and cheek humor going on.

As you can imagine, this wasn't a well-attended event and those that did come got the full tour, downstairs to the rooms normally closed to the public. One lady came up looking a bit pale and was reaching for a beer as she asked why the casket was made of metal. Very matter-of-factly, she got her answer ... it was used for badly decomposed bodies ... and she let go of the beer and walked away.

I tell you this story because of what I learned that evening. Regardless of your business purpose, when you go home each day you know you've given it your all. The owners and employees at the funeral home were sincere and had immense pride it what they did (it's emotionally demanding).

But, those that visited that night were told <u>What They Do, Not What's in It for Them</u>, i.e. the care and emotional support they provide to the families they serve.

If I hadn't been pouring wine that night, I probably wouldn't have attended this After-Hour Chamber Gathering. We don't like to think about death. Standing in a funeral home socializing with drinks in hand just didn't feel right and probably why many opted not to attend. I think instead of the basement tour, maybe a short presentation to those attending about their business finding common challenges other businesses faced. That starts conversation. And maybe weaving in some personal stories on how they supported the families at the sadist of times would have been another approach.

WINE BITES

I'm a happy woman. Tonight's sipping wine is a 2015 JaM Cellars Butter Chardonnay. And the operative word is butter – on the finish, just how I like it. JaM Cellars is all about easy-to-love, everyday wines. I loved their tag line and of course thought of WGWs – Your Go To Wine at Day's End.

John and Michele are the "J" and "M" in JaM Cellars and are second-generation Napa Valley vintners. After almost a decade crafting ultra-premium wines in the Napa Valley, they decided to make some super-approachable wines that we could enjoy anytime we wanted—whether that's a special occasion, everyday celebration, or just a day of the week with a "y" in it.

Chapter 14

Social Responsibility: The Heart of the Winery

First let me start with *The Heart* because to me it set my moral compass. I told myself, Yes, Kathy you need to make money and get us out of debt. Then I pondered, but at what cost? Is there more to this new business of mine then just making money?

I'm not sure when I read about running a business with a Triple Bottom Line (TBL) instead of just focusing on making a profit, but it felt right and got me thinking.

Definition of TBL in the accounting world; consideration is given to the company's financial, social, and environmental performance over time. Also, called "Profit, People, Planet." I still used QuickBooks with standard financial reporting, but I started thinking in the Three P framework when making decisions.

Obviously, my business goal was to operate profitably and in doing so we could also give back to the community and be sensitive to environmental concerns. I think these were the words on a poster that I wrote down: The Olympic Peninsula ... beauty abounds, from sea to towering mountains, from majestic forests to fertile fields.

You could say Profit, People, Planet had become our mission.

Every day in the mail along with the BILLS, I would get multiple donation requests from local, state and national charitable organizations. Early on I made the decision to give to local charities and civic organizations, as that was all we could afford and that's who we needed to support. We honored these requests with donations of a few bottles of wine in a gift basket.

Initially, we set an annual limit because if we weren't careful we could donate our entire production, given the number of non-profits and fund-raising events in our community.

Now, this is the accountant in me talking ... financially there is no advantage on your bottom line when you donate goods, because they are already accounted for at cost and you can't write off the retail value. But you also can't put a price on the goodwill generated from your donation. And, don't discount the opportunity of future sales from individuals who passionately you as you read this book. Ideas that you can mold to fit your own business. Yes, I had a blog/website, but it was our regular, sometimes weekly emails to our customers that made the connection. The blog was dependent on someone finding my site and was a placeholder for my emails. Whereas an email was like a phone call, I wrote directly to the customer who had signed up to our list, via the guest book in the tasting room or some other email collection device.

My marketing style via emails was personal, usually written as an engaging story in my best Working Girl persona keeping the focus on my customer, not on my product.

But let me backtrack. Email marketing alone for the winery, or for any brick and mortar business that also has online sales, wouldn't have been enough. It also had to include building relationships through community involvement and winery events.

Finally, it may look like I have this female focus going on. I didn't write this book specifically for women business owners, but for anyone, male or female, looking for advice or encouragement as you start your business or try to jumpstart a stalled business, or an interested reader looking for a good story. But, after all, I'm a woman in business writing about my experiences. There's no way to keep the female perspective out of it, just like I can't ignore the female aspects of what happened with our winery and our wines. Women created the Working Girl Wines. Of course, our wines transcend gender, just like I hope this book will. And since I'm writing from my gut, there's no getting around the fact that it's a women's gut. No way to change that.

And no way to take 25 years in Corporate America out of this gal.

Wine Bites

If you were here, I would pour you a glass from The Expedition Chardonnay, 2015, Canoe Ridge Vineyard and Winery in Walla Walla, Washington, as I continue to taste my way through Safeway looking for my favorite Chard. The tasting notes for this wine were right down my alley - scents of butterscotch and honeysuckle mix with flavors of ripe pear and honeydew for a rich, elegant texture on the finish. And it's 50% barrel ferment, three-quarters American oak and one-quarter French oak.

Canoe Ridge Vineyard focuses primarily on Chardonnay, Merlot and Cabernet Sauvignon. The Chardonnay grapes are from the Horse Heave Hills Appellation, which is the same appellation that our Lemberger grapes are grown.

financial background then hire it. It will be the best money you ever spent.

<u>Logic plus Creativity</u>: What surprised me, though, was the need for both left brain logic and right brain creativity to run my business. I was fortunate to be able to think and operate out of both sides of my brain; although I found out I had a ping pong ball inside my brain sometimes screwing around with my thought processes. Again, no worries. Know yourself, build a team or build a network where you can brainstorm or work through an operations issue. You'll make yourself crazy talking through your business issues with yourself.

<u>Put yourself at the top of your list</u>: Whatever your business, dedicate some part of your day or week as yours and yours alone. You're going to need your own private TLC. Owning my own business brought more demands on me than I would have ever imagined. Without some time alone, by myself, for re-grouping – not to mention exercise, nutrition and sleep – (well, at least sleep) – I would never have succeeded. I would be headed down that slippery slope to the proverbial Wall. Then … Splat! I know because that is what happened to me at Texas Instruments.

<u>The gift of a small business</u>: With the winery, things were different. I had a payroll that supported people that I knew personally, not just employees on a list. I knew their spouses, their kids. We were a small core team; we became a family of sorts. This was a gift, one that is still most precious to me that I never even thought I would receive when I took over Olympic Cellars Winery.

I've learned a lot about marketing since I bought the winery and done most kinds of marketing. Print ads, PR, face to face contact with customers at conventions and tastings in grocery stores, community events—you name it. What stands out for me in these days of the importance of the Internet is email marketing.

Remember my fourth priority from chapter six; start communicating with my customers beyond the tasting room. As I mentioned above each chapter in this marketing sections focuses on a fundamental goal – communications that were personalized to what's in it for our customer. What worked for me and the big thing I have to offer you is email marketing starting with Chapter 21 through 25.

By now, you've read a few of my emails and probably noticed I go off on tangents with hands and arms moving as fast as I could type, passionately telling a story to my customers, pulling them in and making them feel a part of the winery.

That's what I really want to share with you, how we engaged our customers with emails. It wasn't a bunch of expensive marketing and ads, 'cause I sure didn't have the money in the early years. I got ideas from some of the craziest places that I just adapted to the winery. And, it's what I'm hoping to pass on to

Chapter 13

What's In It For You

I've told you my story and now in the following chapters I'm going to tell you how you might apply my life lessons to your business. But, as I just started writing I realized you are now my customer and I need to get in your shoes. My message – what's in it for you?

Each one of the areas I'm going to focus on below was an integral part of moving my business forward and all were interrelated. After writing about each of these areas and coming back to this chapter, I realized that each had a fundamental goal – communications that were personalized to what's in it for our customer.

Here's what I'm going to talk about.

Chapter 14: Social Responsibility
Chapter 15: Attract more customers with events
Chapter 16: Shaking it up, a non-traditional approach
Chapter 17: Low hanging grapes
Chapter 18: Advertising and Public Relations
Chapter 19: The Team is #1
Chapter 20: Community involvement
Chapter 21: Email Marketing

When I joined the *club* of small business owners it was an eye-opening experience and a bit scary. Most of us didn't have the time to even network, but we had a pretty strong rumor mill with the *did you know* type conversations where we shared the difficulties we were facing. Businesses were in competition with each other and it seemed to me, the newbie of the bunch, that collaboration could be difficult.

But looking back, this was my first ah-hah. You have to give first, to receive. I wanted help to break in to this business community, but what was I offering in return? I joined the Chamber of Commerce, volunteered on committees, and realized that this was the most amazing and giving community. In time we built relationships, and when I had questions or needed help I could pick up the phone.

Here are a few Business 101s that jumped out at me early on:

Business acumen: I found out that I was also very fortunate to have an accounting background and that for a lot of businesses the main issue was the lack of business acumen and the understanding of the importance of cash flow. This is not an area I'm going to cover, but if you don't have that support the organization your donation supported (and who develop a taste for your product).

Okay, back to the accountant in me. I kept thinking from an impact standpoint, making a real difference, did our donation of a few bottles significantly impact their bottom line either?

I felt the winery needed to focus the money/wine we could contribute to a non-profit that would significantly help their cause, which then became our cause.

In 2004 I decided to participate in the Walk for the Cure event - my father and mother both died of cancer in their very early 60's. I ended up talking as we walked to the Executive Director of Family Planning of Clallam County. She told me about their Gynocare program, which provided free diagnostic testing and treatment for underserved women on the Olympic Peninsula. (Clallam County stretches from Cape Flattery, the westernmost point in the continental U.S. along the Strait of Juan de Fuca to just East of Sequim.) She further explained that a lot of women in our community fell through the cracks because they made too much money for government funded health care, but not enough to afford insurance. The decision they faced: put food on the table or get a pap smear. You know their decision.

We decided to designate the local Gynocare Program as our "Charity of Choice," donating two percent of monthly profits from sales of all Working Girl wines, plus $1.00 for every Working Girl branded item sold in our gift shop. Our first check to this program was $88.00. It was a start. They needed money, not wine.

Our charitable giving evolved as the winery grew. Events supported local non-profits and later we partnered with a non-profit for each of our summer concert series. By the end of 2016 Olympic Cellars had donated over $122,000. These cash donations don't include the wine that was contributed, which totals over $45,000 retail value. Many of the non-profits we donated to also had fundraising events and they would buy our wines to pour for their guests. One or more of the Working Girls would attend these events, talk about the wines, meet new folks and talk about upcoming events at the winery. We were there to support the mission of the non-profit not to push our wines. We did, though, have the opportunity to start building relationships.

Olympic Cellars was honored in 2009 and 2010 when it was named to the List of Top 78 Corporate Philanthropists in Washington State in an expanded Corporate Citizenship Program that recognized companies of all sizes for their staunch support of philanthropic causes and organizations. (2009 was the first year small businesses were recognized for their charitable giving.)

As I've mentioned before, small wineries rely on volunteers for the labor intense jobs like bottling. I found out early on that sometimes the volunteers didn't know what they had gotten themselves into, suddenly realizing what the intense 8-10 hour work day entailed (although we told everyone). Some folks had to back out right in the middle of bottling. A lack of volunteers in key positions could crater the bottling line.

Then I hit on the idea of partnering for mutual success. We called this partnership 2X Success™.

This program paired a non-profit organization's need for funding with the winery's need for dedicated volunteers. It allowed each organization to share in the other's success. For each volunteer hour provided, the non-profit organization can purchase one bottle of Olympic Cellars Working Girl wines at "our cost." The 501(c)(3) non-profit organization could then sell or auction these wines at a fundraising event.

The concept was so unique that the Washington State Liquor Control Board (WSLCB) worked with us throughout the design of the program to ensure that it met all legal requirements.

An example of an ongoing partnership is with our local United States Coast Guard. Eight to ten Coast Guard men and women volunteered for two long days each year. The wine they earn for volunteering is sold at the PX and the profit goes to helping Coast Guard families in need. Our Coast Guard crew touched over 168,000 bottles of wine that we've produced and they earned over sixty-four cases to sell.

With the growth of the winery and expanded sales of Working Girl Wines our charitable support also expanded. Our Summer Concert Series is now the cornerstone of the winery's fundraising activities. We partnered with a different local non-profit for each weekly concert. Volunteers from the non-profit help us the night of the concert and Olympic Cellars donates a portion of our ticket sales, all tips and proceeds of our now famous "Dollar Dance." And, the concerts have grown to as many as 500 attending which is our limit.

During the break a representative from the non-profit heads to the stage to talk about their mission. Then the first song in the next set is the Dollar Dance. The only way you can get on the dance floor is to drop dollar(s) into a basket, usually held by three or four really adorable kids. Who could turn a cute child down? Both the non-profit and the winery market the concert. More people, more donations.

With each concert and different non-profits, we could showcase the winery and the wines to folks who might not have ever been to the winery before, but lived on the Peninsula. Their cause became our cause. Each January non-profits applied to volunteer at a winery concert or event for the following year.

Community involvement and support along with growing a successful business became an integral part of my Working Girl way of doing business.

We were then able to focus on the third P in the Triple Bottom Line, Planet.

Guests who visited the winery generally had two questions. Where are the bathrooms? And, where are the grapes? After all, when you think of winery you think of vineyards.

We finally got smart and put up a sign for the restrooms. And then explained that wineries on the North Olympic Peninsula got their grapes from vineyards in hot, dry Eastern Washington, which had gained a reputation as some of the best wine country in the United States.

But personally, I didn't like that answer. I wanted to know if grapes could be grown here on the Peninsula so we could make a local wine.

Then I met Tom Miller, who lived a short distance from my house. Again, this is another one of those signs, another rainbow over our barn. His house and small vineyard was across the street from Dungeness Bay Cemetery where Gene Neuharth, the founder of our winery, was buried. Gene brought vines from California when he moved to Sequim in the 70s. He wanted to grow grapes but those grape varietals couldn't adapt to the Peninsula coastal environment. And, now a vineyard is right across the street.

Tom and his wife, Isabelle, bought their Sequim property in 1995 and grew kale and oats to feed their sheep. In 2000 he visited the small Bainbridge Island Winery, which was well known for their 100% estate grown grapes and wines. Located on the wet side of the Cascade Mountains, this winery had seven acres of grapes that were carefully selected for their ability to thrive in Puget Sound's cooler climate. Madeleine Angevine, Siegerree, Pinot Gris and Pinot Noir were the primary grapes.

Tom retuned home and started planting cuttings from Bainbridge Island Vineyard and christened his vineyard, Dungeness Bay Vineyard.

In 2006, Libby and I picked grapes from Tom's vineyard. It was a gorgeous, sunny fall day. And there we were snipping grape clusters and laying them gently in the bin. We loaded the grapes in Tom's truck and drove to the winery. The amount was so small I almost thought we should hand press the grapes instead of all the work to get the crusher set-up, but we set it up anyway. I was so proud. Our first harvest produced 35 cases which is 2/3 of a ton. The wine sold out fast. And that was all the grapes Tom had.

Now my question ... is there any real interest in growing grapes on the North Olympic Peninsula? Tom did it but he only had a *garden-size vineyard*. Do we have the right land with southern exposure and the right soil available for larger scale vineyards? So many unanswered questions.

Although the Dungeness Valley area is a relatively short distance from Bainbridge Island (56 miles) the Island is more sheltered then the Sequim Dungeness Valley on the Straits of Juan de Fuca. But Sequim is located under the Blue Hole, the Rain Shadow of the Olympic Mountains, which means more sunshine and less rain. The valley is already known as the mecca of organic farming, berry farms, dairies, and grass-fed cattle. The climate is moderate and the land is fertile.

When you don't know, you ask the expert and in the case of grape growing, that was Southern Oregon University Professor Greg Jones. Jones' research focused on the role of climate and the characteristics of agricultural systems. He studied how climate influences whether a crop is suitable to a given region, how climate controls crop production, quality and ultimately drives economic sustainability. Bottom line, Dr. Jones' focus on climate is the critical aspect of where to grow grapes and which varietals would be economically viable to plant.

In 2006 Olympic Cellars spearheaded a micro-climate grape study of the Olympic Peninsula conducted by Dr. Jones. The cost was $15,000. I presented the study throughout our community. The Economic Development Council, City of Port Angeles, Port Angeles Chamber of Commerce, Clallam County Extension, Shore Bank, Olympic Cellars and over twenty individuals and businesses contributed. But we were still short of the funds needed to support the study. Then three friends, Karen Rogers, Edna Petersen and Rhonda Curry, organized a last minute fundraising event called Women for Community Prosperity. This is what *Community Support* is all about. The Working Girl way of doing business.

There was a lot of press surrounding this study, but the article that stood out was written by Gene Johnson of The Associated Press and published in the Seattle Times. Title: Vintners look for right grapes to grow in rainy Puget Sound.

These two quotes from the article says it all.

"Western Washington is the great untapped vineyard resource," says Keith Love, a spokesman for the state's most prominent winery, Chateau Ste. Michelle in Woodinville. "The potential is there, but there hasn't been enough research done. We are glad somebody's able to do it."

"The interest is just getting going," says Gary Moulton, the lead

Washington State University researcher. "As people start moving from hobby winemaking to cottage industry, you're going to see a lot of boutique-type wineries. We don't have a lot of big, thousand-acre chunks of land like they do in Eastern Washington, but we're going to have a lot of smaller vineyards that can make a [tourist] destination. People want to try local wines."

Benoit planted our vineyard in March 2007, a landmark anniversary for Olympic Cellars. I keep referring to the vineyard as the *Le Petit* vineyard. It may be small but it's our first and completes 'the circle' that the founder of the winery, Gene Neuharth, started over 28 years ago.

Benoit also continued my French lessons: Vineyard is *vignoble* in French and Benoit informed me, "Kathyeee, *vignoble* is a masculine word, of course." Well I had to Google this and found out that in French all nouns have a gender, either masculine or feminine. Vin, French for the grape or wine is also masculine.

Poor Benoit. Surrounded by women, at least he was working with a *masculine* product.

And he could get the last word. "*Vignoble*" trumps Working Girls.

Benoit planted: 80 Siegerrebe one-year-old vines, 60 Madeleine Angevine cuttings, three each Pinot Gris, Sauvignon Blanc, Chardonnay and Madeleine Sylvaner (test plantings)

We officially dedicated our new vineyard that May. In the early 1900's our land and barn was Wayside Farm. It is only fitting that our vineyard should be "Wayside Vineyard" with a Working Girl or should I say Vineyard Angel watching over the vines.

Benoit told me he has really missed the vineyards. I can't even describe how I felt and how incredible it was to drive into the winery and see Benoit standing in the middle of the vineyard with the Olympic Mountains in the background. It takes my breath away.

Fast forward to 2015. The winery crushed six tons of local grapes from Dungeness Bay and Dungeness Valley Vineyards. The coastal grape varietals were Madeleine Angevine and Siegerrebe. Harbinger Winery also made wine from locally grown grapes and new vineyards are maturing. Also, local wineries took advantage of the Peninsula's abundant fruit crops and local ciders are now available.

The Triple Bottom Line mission was the right choice for me and my business. PEOPLE: Community and non-profit support with our time, dollars, and wine. PLANET: Spearheaded grape study, supported sustainable vineyards and made wine from locally grown grapes. PROFIT: Went from bankruptcy to over $1M in sales in five years.

I believe, more than ever, that social responsibility is an integral part of our/your business model in today's world. And it can take many forms.

Depending on your business, product and especially your personal passion there are lots of ways to give back. The winery chose to support smaller non-profits. Just like small businesses fighting to stay profitable, getting needed funding for a small non-profit is just as hard.

We all know that our customers have a choice where and when to spend their money. Knowing their money also supports more than a financial bottom line is an important part of their decision to purchase and remain loyal to the business.

WINE BITES

No new Chardonnay. Hey, I have three bottles still in the fridge. Tonight I enjoyed a sample of all three: Waterbrook, JaM Butter and Canoe Ridge. Dang, I liked all three but couldn't decide which was my favorite so I'm still looking. But this got me thinking. These are large wineries with stellar reputations with a vast distribution network. But in Safeway they are just another bottle next to other Chardonnays of similar price. How do you stand out in the crowd?

CHAPTER 15

Attract More Customers with Events

Whoever coined the phrase, *laughter is wine for the soul*, likely did so after attending one of our Olympic Cellars' events.

I doubt you're starting a winery, but brainstorm your product line to see if you can come up with events of your own, either online or in your brick and mortar store, as I tell you about mine.

As I've mentioned earlier, we needed to get folks to the winery and I was willing to do most anything except stand on the corner (ha ha). My marketing philosophy was throw any and all at the wall ... what stuck we used. If it didn't work we moved on to something else. My husband called it guerilla marketing, which in his marketing-eze definition is an advertising strategy to promote products or services in an unconventional way with little money. It involved high energy and imagination focused on grasping the attention of the public, making it more personal and definitely memorable.

Well we did just that. We came up with some pretty wacky and zany events in our 'throw it at the wall and see if sticks' strategy that brought folks to the winery from near and far. Fun was the operative word. You could say we stood out in the crowd.

None of these events cost that much in dollars but they did require a lot of work, team coordination, and creativity on my part to write emails, press releases, and ads. We needed to stand out. Then pray for good weather. As the event drew near you would find me standing at the door asking, will they come? Build it and they will come is a lot of poppycock. If you haven't done your upfront work you might as well close the door.

We tried to tailor each event to appeal to a different demographic so we could expand our customer base. Establishing a sense of community was also an integral part, with most events supporting a local non-profit.

We profited from these events by selling lots of wine, meeting potential new customers, asking them if they would like to be on our mailing list so as not to miss future fun events and finding opportunities to collaborate with other businesses in the community.

Now you might be thinking, well Kathy has a winery and can do all this cool stuff. What can you do? LOTS. Check out the National Days of everything. There you'll find all kinds of opportunities and angles for some guerilla marketing for your business. The National Chocolate Chip and Flip Flop Days came out of this Google search.

Below I've listed some of our events. Which ones worked and which ones didn't. Also, you can't just do the same event over and over. Keeping events fresh and new was another key learning for me. I've included a few examples of press releases, emails and ads, all written to engage, forward to friends, share on Facebook and so on.

Whatever the event, Olympic Cellars kept 'em laughing, dancing and coming back for more!

Rosie the Riveter Contest

In the summer of 2004 we released the third lady in our trio of Working Girl Wines, Rosé the Riveter. It was also the 60th anniversary of the real Rosie the Riveters and we wanted a special event to commemorate these women. The symbol of Rosie The Riveter represents women in non-traditional careers and was the reason we wanted a similar label for our wine. Sara Gagnon, our winemaker, was in a non-traditional career herself at this time, representing a very small percentage of female wine-makers in the wine industry.

None of our ideas for a Rosie event were cutting it. One evening Bob Smith, a friend of Molly's, dropped by and we all sat on the patio and continued brainstorming. If you looked east from where we sat, you could see and hear the Port Angeles Speedway where a bunch of cars were doing what they do, race around the track. One idea led to another and we had our event. A We Can Do It, Too! contest for Can-Do Women.

The contest – a three-woman team had to change/rotate the two tires on the passenger side of a race car. Sound easy? The fastest team wins. Ten diverse local businesses sponsored teams.

Port Angeles Ford provided *advanced* tire-changing training to the teams. Peg Buell, the Parts Manager used her own car for the teams' trainees. I think she began to rethink this after training Molly, Libby, and me when I kept referring to the pneumatic impact wrench as the ZZT-ZZT thing.

It was also only fitting that in *our own backyard* we found an opportunity to support the G.I.R.L.S. Summer Camp, Gifted Individuals Realizing Leadership Skills, which was a four-day non-traditional career exploration camp where twenty girls, ages 13-14 attend. All team sponsorship fees were donated by the teams and paid the tuition for six girls that summer.

Re-enacted *I Love Lucy* Chocolate Factory Scene

The actual 1952 episode was called Job Switching. Fred and Ricky took on household chores while the women went to work at the chocolate factory. In our version, Libby was Ethel to my Lucy and of course, Molly was the supervisor. Libby and her then husband Dan built a hand-cranked conveyor belt. We watched the Lucy video a gazillion times and practiced in the evenings. We performed at the first Chocolate Festival sponsored by the Sequim Chamber of Commerce and local businesses. A link to the original episode and our performance is in the appendix. Thank goodness someone took a video on their phone. How'd we do? In subsequent years "Lucy" teams signed up for a Chocolate Factory contest during the festival.

Unleashed the Christmas Elves as Personal Shoppers

This one failed miserably. The idea was to get women to come to the winery and write their Christmas letters to Santa. Then the Working Girl Elves would contact the significant other, get them to the winery, let them read the letter to Santa and help them shop. Only two women joined us on the first night and we cancelled the rest. We did look pretty cool, though, dressed up like elves. So, we re-grouped with a bottle of champagne and told lots of elf jokes.

Dressing up like elves didn't work but a lot of our events did. If you're afraid to try, you get nothing. You know what I mean.

Conducted the Most Romantic Man contest on Valentine's Day

And, this one was a doozy. You never know where your inspiration or idea is going to come from, but when it shows up, jump on it. This event was so popular that the Peninsula Daily News offered to sponsor it a few years later with a special insert that promoted the contest and also got them ad income from local businesses. Below is the full-page letter to readers that was printed in the pre-Valentine Holiday insert. I left in the 'how it works' details in case you want to hold your own Most Romantic Man contest. We learned some important lessons that first year. Like, let the winner and runner-up know they should come to the winery for the big announcement. The winery was packed, but the most romantic couples were MIA.

Peninsula's Most Romantic... Meets *Sleepless in Seattle*

A few weeks ago, I watched the movie Sleepless in Seattle again for what seems like the 99th time, fast-forwarding to all my favorite parts. I got all excited watching it and thinking about our third annual Olympic Cellars' *Most Romantic Man Contest.*

I kept getting ideas, seeing connections, similarities and began planning for this contest. I looked up the movie on the Internet and found out there is a tagline: *What if someone you never met, someone you never saw, someone you never knew was the only someone for you?*

So, I wrote a tagline for us:

> What if someone you see every day,
> someone you've known for what seems like a lifetime,
> doesn't really know why's he's the only one for you?

And, I know you remember the scene where Rosie O'Donnell and Meg Ryan are watching an Affair to Remember and Meg Ryan is writing THE LETTER. All it takes to nominate your man is a 250-word letter.

And, if you want to do it in the tradition of the movie . . . grab a box of tissues, make some popcorn, rent the video, invite your girlfriend(s) over and write your letter answering the all-important question: Why Should Your Man Be Voted the Peninsula's "Most Romantic?"

This year I'm really thrilled because we have two great prizes, the winning letter continues the movie theme and both are very romantic!

<u>First Prize</u>: Weekend in Seattle, overnight accommodations at the Hotel Vintage Park in the Olympic Cellars room #802, dinner at Tulios, theater tickets and an Olympic Cellars wine basket.

<u>Second Prize</u>: Two-Nights at Chito Beach Resort on Clallam Bay, a gourmet picnic basket and an Olympic Cellars wine basket.

Ladies, this is how it works.

1. Send your letter by January 18 to the Most Romantic Man Contest, P.O. Box 1330, Port Angeles, WA 98362.

2. Drop your letter off at any Peninsula Daily News office in Port Angeles (305 W First St), Sequim (510 W. Washington St., St. A) or Port Townsend (1939 E. Sims Way).

3. Drop off your letter at Olympic Cellars Winery: 255410 Highway 101 or email to <u>kathy@olympiccellars.com.</u>

4. Our panel of judges using our Swoon-o-meter will pick the top 14 letters. The top 14 letters will be published in a special section on January 29 in the Peninsula Daily News. News readers will be asked to vote on which letter they think should be chosen by the winery.

And don't forget the best part, <u>The Evening of Romance</u>, on Friday February 10 at 5:30. Make this evening a tradition and share the excitement and a very special time with that person you love. Enjoy music by Carlos Xavier and the Flutets. The highlight, his solo of An Affair to Remember. Wine is sold by the glass. Light snacks and chocolates will be served.

Then the announcement! When you leave you might even hear Tom Hank's words whispered,

It Was Like . . . Magic!

Celebrated National Flip Flop Day

Dear Friends of Olympic Cellars,

Well, I thought I was brilliant ... have been espousing for the last week or so around the winery that I was going to declare Saturday, June 21 "National Flip Flop Day." It's also the first day of summer. So just to make sure (you know you can Google everything), on my first search I found someone had already taken this honor. The 2nd Annual National Flip Flop Day is being celebrated at the Tropical Smoothie Café in Destin, FL.

Dang ... they're serving smoothies but I'm serving wine!

I know many of you have already experienced hot summer days, but for those of us on the North Olympic Peninsula we're not sure summer will ever arrive. We just want to feel the heat and the sun on our face!

Also, just wearing fun, colorful flip flops has good karma and lifts your spirits. Just imagine thousands of people *flip flopping away* on Saturday (or maybe just Olympic Cellar's customer list) but it still makes you smile.

On a more serious note, we all know that there is a lot of bad stuff happening that we have no control over. We all help where we can but there is that uncertainty which may still leave you anxious thinking about the future. Wearing flip flops for one day is not going to solve the issues facing our country and I'm not trying to make light of them. But, we all can make a difference by impacting our own sphere of influence that surrounds us.

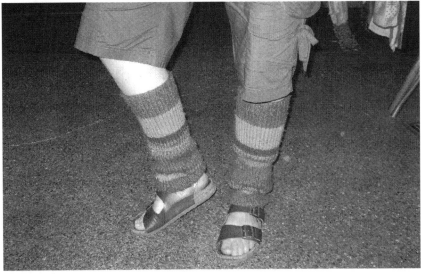

And, for one day you can. Reach out to those dearest to you and celebrate life and National Flip Flop Day! As we like to say at the winery...

Savor the moment and cherish the memories, Kathy

PS. If you live close to the winery, wine tasting is on us Saturday if you walk through our doors wearing your favorite flip flops!

PPS. In the Pacific Northwest some might view our "sandal" foot attire as not being at the height of fashion when you have to add SOCKS to keep warm!

Dedicated a holiday to us – "NO" Labor Day

Labor Day Weekend we had music, skydiving, and wine tasting. Since we are the WORKING Girls and Labor is synonymous with Working, this was supposed to be our holiday too, get it ... NO Labor Day. It just worked for us.

Started the Working Girl "First Jump Club"

I was invited to tandem skydive into *Wine Country* in Eastern Washington as part of a Washington State Tourism Promotion. You have to do it at least once. An experience you will never forget. I also knew I had a way better view plummeting to earth on the Peninsula. Hence, the First Jump Club. Guess what gave me the idea for the name, yep I was watching an oldie but goodie; The First Wives Club.

Join the Working Girl First Jump Club. New Members Welcome. Anyone who would like to experience the thrill of dropping in at the winery from 13,500 feet is invited. For the second year, our "No Labor" Day event kicks off with tandem skydiving (the easiest way to make your first jump) into the BIG field behind Olympic Cellars Winery. Imagine getting a bird's eye view of the pristine lakes and majestic Olympic Mountains. It's a once in a lifetime experience.

Dreamed up the Working Girl Road Trip

The media continued their focus on women's buying habits, age demographics and disposable income. The focus moved from women and wine to girlfriend travel, the hottest trend in the travel industry.

Our Peninsula joint marketing organizations and tourism-based businesses started brainstorming. It resulted in a year-long promotion of girlfriend travel to the scenic beauty of the Olympic Peninsula. And Olympic Cellars and the Working Girls were right in the middle of it. I did my research and presented it around town. I printed the following paragraph from my presentation and thumbtacked it to the wall by my desk. It may have been written nine or so years ago but it's not out of date.

Baby Boomers (those aged 41-60) make up, at almost 80 million, the largest generational demographic today. And, among Boomers, women not only outnumber men but also influence as much as 80% of household purchase decisions. In the next decade, women will control two-thirds of the consumer wealth in the U.S. <u>These women are not a niche market – they are the market</u> for companies savvy enough to understand their needs and perceptions, their life transitions, and their deep-seated hopes and fears. By cultivating brands that resonate and connect with these women your company wins their trust, loyalty and their incredible purchasing power.

We launched a Working Girl Road Trip and added a section to our website with sample itineraries, shopping destinations, event schedules, crazy pictures, restaurants, lodging, you name it. We encouraged women to put themselves at the top of their list (you know we don't tend to do that) and schedule a getaway with girlfriends that included but not limited to . . . laughter, good heart-to-heart conversations, chocolate, and good wine. Molly, Libby and I took *working* road trips to check out the competition. But we had massages, great food, went to plays (the best for us was *The Vagina Monologues*).

We came up with the Working Girl Goodie Bag and sent it out to a select group of travel writers and received immediate interest because it was a new angle. We got free ink for about six months. Also, the Goody

Bag, full of surprises, were given out to Road Trippers who stopped by the winery and showed us their overnight reservation or camping confirmation. Then we took a picture, the ladies signed and dated it and pinned it to the Road Trip Wall of Fame. More photo ops.

Remember the picture in the red convertible. That became the inspiration for the Working Girl Road Trip graphic and also used for our annual event card which was handed out at the winery. All the events for the summer season were listed on the back.

Held contest for the Best Chocolate Chip Cookie

The contest was done in conjunction and promotion of a new business.

Dear Chocolate Chip Cookie and Wine Lovers,

This is really tough duty, but we need your help in tasting and picking the best Chocolate Chip Cookie. Then, if that is not hard enough, we need to also pick the best wine to pair with the cookies.

This contest started with the recognition of National Chocolate Chip Cookie Day on May 15. We decided to hold our own Working Girl contest and received over fifteen recipes. We narrowed it down to five.

You're invited to <u>The Showcase, 833 E. Front Street, in Port Angeles</u> on Wednesday, June 17 at 5:30 p.m. to taste, vote and have fun.

Molly and I will prepare and bake one of the recipes in the Showcase's beautiful demonstration kitchen to get you in the mood . . . aaah the smell of warm cookies.

Then your real work begins . . .

The five trays of cookies (identified by numbers 1 to 5) that made the finals will be unveiled

You will receive a ballot for voting and begin your tasting

Once the cookie tasting and your scoring is complete, we will start tabulating the results

New ballot will be handed out for wine tasting and pairing from a selection of three Olympic Cellars Wines

Announcement, Awards, Cheers!!!!!

This is an open invitation to chocolate chip cookie lovers . . . The Working Girls

Finally, my favorite... the Grape Stomping Harvest Party

They All Stared in Disbelief at My Big Feet, But When I Started to Stomp ...

I Felt the THRILL of Victory and then the AGONY of de-FEET

7:30 a.m. Tuesday, September 6

My coffee is steaming on my desk and I find myself daydreaming. Seven years ago I was on a flight from Tokyo to Dallas watching one of Lucille Ball's classic episodes ... The Grape Stomp. (More accurately it was the 150th episode, Lucy's Italian Movie, that aired on April 16, 1956). I remember thinking, I should do this at the winery someday. Now I'm planning our 5th Annual Grape Stomping on September 15.

Who would have thunk that a 25-year corporate veteran would retire, move to about the farthest Northwest corner of the country and try her hands at rebuilding one of the oldest wineries in the state of Washington? Believe me, semi-conductors to grapes is not the most natural career path.

Wine does have the ability to "sucker and seduce" you into doing things totally out of your comfort zone . . . so when researching how to do a grape stomp and buying prizes, I got myself some rather "not so sexy but warm" grape stomping flannel pajamas. I've got them on right now . . . got to be in the right mood to plan out the gazillion details that go into this event.

Oh, we learned so much the first year . . . I ordered two tons of grapes. That's a lot. Michael built the huge grape stomp tank (barrel staves encircling a 6-foot aluminum tank) to look just like the one in the Lucy Show. I

pitchforked about 500 pounds into the tub, then tried it out and fell flat on my butt. The tank was slick as "snot" loaded with grapes. So, then out came the grapes (now it's a total of 1000 pounds shoveled) and in went a piece of old carpet, Voila!! Again, I shoveled the grapes back in ... now 1500 pounds. I'm more than sweaty and not so perky any more in my "most classic harvest costume" and a red wig that now looks more like road kill.

After six years, this is still my favorite of all the winery events (even the skydiving). You can get a real sense of the "grape" even if it is squishing up through your toes cold, sticky and wet. And yes, your

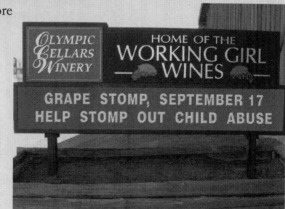

stomp partners might have a bit of those grapes adorning their head since you're really stomping to win your "competition heat" so you advance to the finals, "The Grand Stomp Off." The Thrill of Victory or The Agony of de-FEET. It's still one of those life's experiences that will not be forgotten.

Imagine yourself now, the competition is over. You have a celebratory wine glass in hand. The band is doing a sound check and you're just about to listen to LeRoy Bell. This is going to be a magical performance. He's written for Elton John and opened for artists as diverse as B.B. King, Al Green, Taj Mahal and Lee Ann Rimes. And, you have A FRONT ROW seat on the winery patio. It doesn't get any better than this.

On a more serious note, Olympic Cellars is donating ticket proceeds from the Grape Stomp and Concert to Healthy Families of Clallam County to help Stomp Out Child Abuse. We want to pack the winery grounds!

WINE BITES

Back to Safeway scanning the Chardonnays for my next bottle. Nothing jumped out. In fact, as I perused the wines for a second time, I noticed none of the labels jumped out. Most labels focused on the winery's name. The brand was the winery. Then I noticed *The Jack, 2015 Saviah Cellars*, which featured the graphic of a playing card. What flashed through my mind was playing cards with my sister and brother on our last visit. Well, that stopped me and I picked up the bottle but saw no description on the back. I took a chance anyhow. The wine was good, just not my style.

The point being: there was an emotional connection that got me to buy. We're talking a wine label here but look at your product and service and get in your customer's shoes, what's in it for them and how do you stay emotionally connected.

Then I got home and looked up the winery. Saviah Cellars was founded in 2000 in the Walla Walla Valley. Their first vintage was just 300 cases. By 2009 was named One of the Top 100 Wineries by Wine & Spirits Magazine, in 2010 Saviah Cellars was called One of the Rising Stars in Washington by Wine Spectator and in 2013 The Jack brand was named one of the Top Value Brands of the Year by Wine & Spirits Magazine. Another heritage winery of Washington State.

CHAPTER 16

Shake It Up, A Non-Traditional Approach

I'll tell you a little wine story. It has to do with the wines I chose to inspire me as I work on this book. There I was in Safeway again, looking at the Chardonnays. One bottle surprised the hell out of me. Robert Mondavi's Private Selection <u>Bourbon</u> Barrel-Aged Chardonnay. Of course, I bought it, Googled it and said, "Damn." They notched up the traditional barrel aging to a whole new level. Beer is aged in bourbon barrels sometimes but who would have thunk, a white wine?

And, it was the perfect wine for this chapter. Sometimes you got to shake things up. Don't get complacent. Stand out in the crowd. Consider a different path, not the predictable one. Be flexible.

During my 25-year career at Texas Instruments I learned that you had to change with the company, keep your skills <u>current</u> and not get mired in "<u>the way things used to be</u>." Downsizing, reengineering, layoffs, doing more with less, turning on a dime when something is not working, focusing on the top 10% employees were the new norms. And, I was a survivor.

While the Working Girl Wines helped save Olympic Cellars, it also led us down a very non-traditional winery path.

Good or bad, I didn't have any experience in the wine industry. Tradition and success were steeped in the fame and accolades anointing a winery, its wines, and the winemaker who produced the best Washington wines. Top wine ratings by *Wine Spectator*, Robert Parker and even Gary Vaynerchuk's wine blog could sell out a vintage and put you on stage with the likes of Washington's renowned Leonetti Cellars.

And here I was, by day, this wacky, 50++ year old broad espousing the Official Wines for Working Women. By night, focused on paying down the bills, rebuilding our cellar, and making payroll every two weeks.

So to me I needed to *change lanes* because I couldn't run this business like a normal winery or I would *get run over* because I couldn't go head to head with Merlot or Cabernet Sauvignon against established wineries. I needed a different angle even though the business was a winery. I asked myself, "What do our customers want?"

With the help of the Working Girl Wines and three new wines with the marketing behind them, our product line-up embodied this non-traditional, non-intimidating approach to rebuilding our business and enabled us to go from bankruptcy to $1M in sales in five years.

I've already told you about our Sweet Syrah, an easy drinking soft Syrah that was slightly sweet. It was blended with 20% sweet Late Harvest Riesling. We knew our customers would like it and it became our cash cow.

We listened to our customers again and took advantage of what was popular when we made the next two wines.

Benoit, our French winemaker, WAS very traditional as you would expect and wanted to make red wines similar to the wines he made in France. When we finally had enough cash flow I told him we could notch up our grape budget and make the wine he wanted. "Go for the best," I said. That meant the best grapes from well-known vineyards. The cost of premium varietal grapes could be double, even triple the price we were used to paying, if we could even get an allocation from the vineyard. So instead of $1500 a ton, it could be $3500 a ton. One of the vineyards wouldn't sell grapes to Benoit until they met him and tasted wine he had made.

We had built his cellar back – new oak barrels each year, a new crusher/press, tanks and even a new fork lift to replace *Big Bertha* that had to be jump-started every day.

What I didn't mention is how I intended to bring in additional sales and pay for the grapes from the top vineyards in Washington.

I've already mentioned that we were the first to make a local wine from Madeleine Angevine grapes grown in the Dungeness Valley.

We got a heavy influx of tourists in the summer, especially during the Lavender Festival. Sequim, Washington, is known as the Lavender Capital of North America. Mid-July is the Lavender Festival and over twenty-five to thirty thousand tourists pour into town during the season. Remember when I said that our tourists asked for a local wine? Well, it wasn't long till I heard this question frequently, "Do you have a lavender wine?" What can I say? At the time, I would say, "No," but the wheels were turning. I knew we had an opportunity.

We were always looking for opportunities, but we had to decide if it was financially worth our time and investment. I bounced all my ideas off Molly and Libby, and later Lisa, because we were all really connected to our customers, and Benoit if it involved wine. Molly was great with her feedback. Often she would say, "Kathy, great idea but we can't do it now, so park it."

I knew a lavender wine wouldn't go over well with Benoit, and I wasn't wrong. I pulled up my big girl panties again and asked Benoit how we could make a Lavender Wine and he just blew another gasket. "Kathyeee, lavender smells like my grandmother," he said and stormed back into the cellar again.

There was no talking about it. I waited a few days hoping he would come around, like with the Sweet Syrah, but the subject was closed.

That didn't stop us though. Molly and I got to talking and we enlisted advice from Angels Lavender Farm. Their suggestion was to infuse organic lavender into the wine. It wouldn't alter the taste much, but give it a slight lavender aroma. And, we had Madeleine Angevine wine in the cellar awaiting bottling.

And that's what we did. We had a cheese cloth bag filled with dried organic lavender and suspended it in the Madeleine Angevine wine tank about a week before bottling. We would check the wine frequently pulling the bag out at night and putting back during the day.

But this vintage of grapes didn't ripen as much as Benoit would have liked and we had to pick it before the fall rains commenced. The wine needed a bit more alcohol and sweetness to balance it, or so the non-winemakers, Molly and me, thought. By this time Benoit said all he would do was bottle the damn wine.

So I went to Safeway and bought 24 bottles of cheap, $5.99, Late Harvest Riesling. It tasted just plain sweet and had 12.5% alcohol. As I pushed my cart up to the checkout lane I ran into folks who knew me. Of course, they asked about the wine in my cart maybe thinking this was my secret stash? Please no. I looked them straight in the eye, lied and told them it was for my mother-in-law's bridge tournament that weekend. Well, it worked.

I drove back to the winery and walked into the cellar with four six-pack totes. Dang it if I didn't get caught by Benoit. He looked at me, looked at the wine then looked at me again and said, "You must be out of your mind." I thought I came up with a pretty good retort. "Well, the late harvest Riesling made the Sweet Syrah so special, so it couldn't hurt this wine. It needs a pick me up." He had nothing more to say.

Our lavender-infused wine became very popular and sold out during the summer months at a premium price. For a few years we had the market cornered until others capitalized on the opportunity. But we were first, had the advantage at the right time and then moved on.

Okay, now for the third wine. Do you remember the Twilight phenomenon?

Frankly, I didn't know much or have reason to care about Twilight until the summer of 2008. We had a mother and daughter visit the winery from Scotland on their way back to Seattle after spending two days in Forks, a logging community and, I soon learned, the setting for the Twilight book series. Forks is about sixty miles west of the winery.

This international visit got my attention and I started asking questions and occasionally searched the Internet for stories, but was still under the impression that Twilight was a teen book on vampires and werewolves. Lisa Martin had started working at the winery and promptly brought in the first three books for me to read. Twilight visitors continued to grow, and while Moms tasted wine, their daughters would sit on our coaches reading or re-reading the books. Amazing to me was that the first book was released in 2005 and it was now 2008 and I'm just tuning in.

I started getting requests for a Twilight wine but didn't seriously pursue it because I didn't see a connection. First, I thought it was a teen book. And, there were vampire-labeled wines already on the market. There was no connection to the heritage of Olympic Cellars or the Working Girls.

Then that fall we partnered with a local B&B on a Twilight package before the movie release. We gave the B&B wine glasses and complimentary wine tasting for their guests. By that time I noticed that our visitor demographic had changed and groups of women were on a Twilight journey. Was this another incarnation of the Working Girl Road Trip?

I did my research, Googling everything I could find about tourism and Twilight. And, I finally read the first two books and watched the movie. I highlighted all the passages in the books that I connected to either personally or from a "wine" perspective.

Two major insights:

First, disregarding the vampire and werewolf characters, to me Twilight is a beautiful love story describing the purest form of love.

Second and most important, I felt so proud reading Stephanie Meyer's descriptions of the Olympic Peninsula, our mountains, forests, the beaches and the rain. This is our home and we love it. After re-reading my highlighted passages, I could almost visualize the wine label and knew I wanted to do a sparkling wine. The label needed to capture the essence of the Olympic Mountains at Twilight and offer a heartfelt thank you to all that visit the Peninsula.

I knew exactly where to go to capture my vision for the label. When I drive back from Seattle, about twenty miles outside of Sequim you drive around a big curve and there towering above the road is the quintessential Olympic Mountains cascading into the far away distance, each mountain a different hue of gray to pink to a deep purple depending on the time of day.

On June 13, 2009, we released our sparkling Syrah. The back label words:

> A sparkling wine that bubbles with enthusiasm
> in celebration of your day's journey and adventures.

> Sipped at Twilight as the Olympic Mountains take on the dazzling hues of the coming night, tiny bubbles mirror the Sparkling sky.

> Enjoy the berry fruit character of this lively and refreshing Syrah. Off-dry, ruby in color, with fresh flavors of raspberries, cherries and red fruit.

We heard from visitors every day how much they loved the Peninsula and on their next visit would schedule more time to just ENJOY the beauty, serenity, earth's bounty and the abundance of mountain and water activities.

Four years after the first movie release and on the brink of the last movie to be released, Breaking Dawn II in 2012, Forks had greeted over 200,000 visitors on their Twilight journey. And those that planned their itinerary and Googled Anything Twilight found our small winery and the Sparkling Twilight wine on the road to Forks.

WINE BITES

I started this chapter with my selection - Robert Mondavi's Private Selection 2015 Bourbon Barrel-Aged Chardonnay. It's the first ever Chardonnay to be aged in bourbon barrels. Described as a surprising twist on a classic wine it is a match made in toasty oak heaven. Oh, yeah.

Since first tasting this wine, I've told a number of friends about it but when I went back to Safeway for some more the wine was sold out. (I put in a special order).

I didn't start out thinking that by ending a chapter with my latest *sipping advice* would actually connect to my marketing messages. This Chardonnay bucked tradition and by telling my friends how great the wine was it created a word of mouth marketing experience, one that is valued by consumers above all else. It was a personal connection.

CHAPTER 17

The Business - Some Basic Marketing Strategies

Or, for me it was the Low Hanging Grapes. I know the phrase is properly called Low Hanging Fruit, but a grape is fruit and I like the comparison. The official definition of the phrase refers to goals that are easily achievable and do not require a lot of effort. And, a course of action that can be undertaken quickly and easily as part of a wider range of changes or solutions to a problem.

Not sure about the 'effort' or the 'undertaken quickly' parts of the definition, but when cash flow is limited you definitely need to go after the *low hanging Grapes*, so to speak, in the short term. For me it was some of the basics of marketing and just good business you forget in the heat of battle.

Stand Out Business Cards

This may be old school but people still use business cards. I remember looking at the business cards that I was handed after an event trying to remember who or why they gave them to me. I ended up throwing most of them out. Then it hit me, if I can't remember, I'm sure there are others in the same boat as me.

Looking at my business card more closely the problem hit me between the eyes. It was all text. At that time I didn't have a recognizable logo. And, logos may mean something to you but not to me. I wanted something more personal, something that would make people remember Working Girls. And I knew a logo wouldn't cut it. So, I arranged for a camera shoot with a local photographer, struck a jaunty pose held up my wine glass as if I were toasting someone (I was, my customers) and smiled right into the camera. I had this photo printed on the front in gloss with the winery name and Home of the Working Girls, with the rest of the contact info on the back in non-glossy stock, so folks could actually write on it. Molly, Libby, then Lisa and I all had photo-style business cards linking our persona to the three Working Girl wines. Guests at the winery would take all three. Our business cards were such a hit, we designed post cards around the idea and sold them. I guarantee you, the personal touch in marketing will sell more product than following the herd.

Thank You Notes

Spend the money on classic, high quality note cards folded (cream or white) with your business name on front. Envelopes lined in a metallic paper are stunning.

Then use them! Hand written notes are almost a lost art. And receiving one in the mail is very special. Yes, it's quicker to send an email but not as personal. Send thank you, congratulatory or just-because notes whenever you think about sending the same in an email.

I have to type out my message first then hand-write it. Whatever it takes. You know it meant something special to the individual who received it when you see the response. It was rare when I didn't get a call or an email thanking me for the card.

Remember Names

"A person's *name* is to him or her the sweetest and most *important* sound in any language," wrote Dale Carnegie in his classic book, *How to Win Friends and Influence People*. When you use someone's *name*, it shows you see that person as an individual.

At the winery, when it was busy the names would just go in one ear and out the other. That's not good. Often, I had to ask the customer more than once after they had introduced themselves. As embarrassing as it was, I knew the importance of this personal touch, so would rather apologize, blame it on my senior moment and log it in my brain rather than not have greeted my customer by name at all. I tried all the memory tricks. Repeat their name three times in a conversation and the four steps: Commit, Concentrate, Repeat and Associate.

My biggest challenge was remembering names, especially if I met the individual again away from the winery. I could remember their face but not the name. When my husband was with me and we were at some event with a lot of familiar faces I told him to start the conversation by first saying, "Hi, I'm Ralph, Kathy's husband." The other people would introduce themselves and all was well.

Winery's Voicemail . . . easy, no cost marketing!

WAIT! But I'd hold on . . . that's what I remember years and years ago when I would call Southwest Airlines for a reservation back in my Texas days and they were still a pretty small airline. Their voicemail would start off with the expected message and then, wham you'd hear, *WAIT! But I'd hold on* . . . then some funny but informative spiel continued.

Southwest Airline's voicemail was my inspiration; entertaining and informative while on hold and marketing at no cost. So, I created a basic template, with a Working Girl persona and updated it regularly depending on winery events, the seasons, sales or the introduction of a new wine.

So consider your voice mail as another easy, no cost, marketing tool for any business. Make it personal, fun and, when appropriate, find a 'soft' sales angle to get customers through the door or ordering online. And update it regularly.

Believe it or not, the voicemails had a following. Customers listened all the way through and then sent me emails with their input, thumbs up or down *before Facebook*. And when I was pouring at an event or just chatting with a customer or a business colleague my *voicemails* frequently came up in the conversation. So, I guess I was doing something right.

The Walla Walla Enology and Viticulture Institute, founded in 2000, also used my voicemails as examples of good marketing. Their program was hands-on learning, from planting a vineyard to the finished bottle teaching their students all aspects of wine making and the business of wine.

Updating the voicemail was usually the last thing I would do in the evening. Probably not the best time because I was tired but I would pour a glass of wine, close the door to my office, write my script and try to say it within my time limit without mistakes. Easier said than done. I don't know what my record was for re-recording the voicemail to get it right but it was a lot . . . maybe that second glass of wine had something to do with it.

My basic template: In the example below the *italic verbiage* changed with the message and **bolded** verbiage were words I emphasized when I recorded the message.

Opening of voicemail:

Welcome to Olympic Cellars. If you got this message, **the Working Girls** are with customers *or out in the cellar.*

If you want to skip this message, press the # key now **but I'd hold on** because *you don't want to miss my spring line-up (or, what's happening in July, my Fall update, my holiday message, and so on.)*

The middle portion of voicemail - Promotion:

Are you ready for this? It's time to Free Your Feet! That's what I said. ***It's time to free your feet.*** *Flip flops and a winery? Maybe not the most natural connection, but to the Working Girls it signifies something pretty special - summer, warmth and sunshine! We've been shouting,* **Down with fleece***.*

========

Neither snow nor rain nor gloom of night stays us Working Girls from the swift completion of our appointed rounds. *We're so linked with UPS and the postal service during this time of year, this motto is pretty much our "modus operandi" during the holidays - EXCEPT that snow and cold can get in the way of our appointed rounds, such as* ***packing and shipping!*** *It's mid November and the weather is still looking good! We all know this can change rapidly and we'd hate not to be able to ship your Thanksgiving or Holiday wines.*

========

It was a glorious harvest with over 51 tons, that's 102 thousand pounds of grapes. That means we shoveled about 291 bins at 650 pounds each. Did we earn our title of Working Girls of Olympic Cellars? ***You betcha****. And bottling is November 10.*

Our holiday wine, Cranberry Jubilee, will be available November 11. Place your order. 100 cases are gone by Christmas.

========

Voicemail wrap-up:

Now back to our pre-recorded announcement. We are located in a huge, historic barn on Highway 101, 9 miles west of Sequim. Going west, there is a turn-around at O'Brian Road just past the barn. Easy access including ample parking for your RVs.

Leave a message, Molly, Lisa, or Kathy (**that's me**) will call you back **and remember, Stop, Enjoy the moment and Live La Dolce Vida**

Start and Never Stop Building Your Customer Contact List

If you have a storefront or an on-line business how will *you* stay in touch with your customers? Decide right away and be consistent. Early on we didn't have a customer database. The customer had to write their name and email in a notebook by the door. We lost a lot of names. As soon as we could afford it we installed a point-of-sale database and got rid our cash register. We entered all the emails and could track sales and wine club members.

Before we asked for a customer's email, we tried to establish a rapport and personalize their experience during our time discussing wines over the bar. Then at the end we would ask for their email. Back when I got into this business asking for an email was a BIG ask. Now it's a pretty common question but I still don't take it lightly. Customers are giving us a valuable and personal piece of their private information. We promised not to bombard them and shared that we hated that type of marketing too. And at any time, they could unsubscribe.

A large majority of our customers were tourists visiting the Olympic Peninsula and then went home to their lives. Buying a bottle or two on vacation, we've all done it. Did we order again? Maybe, but more often not. That's why our initial connection to the customer was so important. Getting their email gave me more opportunities to connect and retain them as a customer.

At the end of the day, we look at dollars sold but just as important is the number of new contacts added to our list that will/could be future sales if we did our job right.

The Girlfriend's Corner – Gift Shop

I don't know if you would call having gifts for sale to go along with wine sales as low hanging grapes. Well, I guess you could if you just order from one of the merchandise catalogs that regularly appeared in our mailbox. The winery sold the usual suspects when it came to winery gadgets, but if you weren't really into wine or already had multiple corkscrews and bottle stoppers these products wouldn't generate a lot of income.

But if you wanted a steady income stream that made a difference on your bottom line, then it takes effort and time. The winery is also a tourist attraction. The huge, 100+ year old barn towers off the side of Highway 101, the only road in and out of the Peninsula. And our sign says, Olympic Cellars – Home of the Working Girl Wines. It does tend to draw curious tourists. We realized that not every customer is going to buy or even like wine, and we didn't want them to leave empty handed. That

created a new mission.

We went to our first Gift Show in Seattle and walked the aisles. We expanded our vision on what we purchased choosing gifts we liked personally as women.

And when we discovered the right gifts sold, wow. Now it didn't matter who the customer was, whether they liked wine, didn't like wine. Thanks to our savvy shopping we were appealing to both.

Some of my favorites included the wine purses, which I think got used more as a regular purse because they were dang cute. The wine sippy cup – picture your kid's sippy cup. Nothing spills. Now visualize a clear plastic glass with a plastic wine glass inside. You fill the wine glass, attach the non-spill lid and sip away. A real mother's little helper.

And my personal favorites, a morning coffee cup and evening wine glass that I use routinely. The cup has three silent directives written on it. It's morning and you've poured your first cup, sniffed the aroma and haven't hardly taken a sip. You point to it and tap the top line "Shhh" if you're not ready to be interrupted. Still need more coffee? The next line gives you a bit more time before you start your day in full force. Point to "Almost."

Sighing as you finish your coffee and now ready, your family gathered and waiting for you to point to "Now you may speak." Works every time.

And the glass is a stemless wine glass also with three lines denoting fill levels. Good Day, Bad Day, Don't Ask. I bet you can figure out which one requires a full glass.

Buying the perfect products took work, really. Molly, Libby, then Lisa and I traveled to January gift shows (NY, Dallas, Atlanta, Las Vegas or Seattle) once a year. We would walk endless aisles looking for that one new something and usually found it in what was called the "Temporaries." Every gift show had one and it was for new businesses trying to launch their product. We met many creative entrepreneurs and often ended up sharing stories about our businesses. And as you would guess, we purchased a lot of these gifts from new businesses owned by women with a story we could share with our customers.

I was the wimp of the group. Somewhere about mid-afternoon my eyes would glaze over. Just too much stuff closing in around me. Molly would look at me and say, "Do you need your alone time?" I'd nod and go find a quiet place to just chill.

But early on we learned that all three of us had to vote "yes" before we committed to a purchase order. Before we placed our orders and flew back home, we'd have our Working Girl discussions over drinks and a good dinner (our reward) each night voting on our product choices.

We displayed the gifts aimed at women together in what became known as the Girlfriend Corner. Again, Pam taught us about merchandising to catch the eye. And when women gathered, laughed and squealed, "Remember when we did . . . or this would be perfect for my sister," we knew we had nailed it.

"Tasting Room Magazine" named Olympic Cellars Gift Shop to the Top 10 Winery Gift Shops in 2016.

Here are a few emails inspired by the gift shop. One is just fun for our customers to read, no sales pitch. The other has a soft sales pitch. Both kept our customers up on the goings on with the Working Girls.

WINE BITES

I've tried to pick Chardonnays that are distributed widely and might be sold where you live. You can always order directly from the winery but I'm not good at delayed gratification.

Tonight's wine, a 2015 Chard from Chateau Ste. Michelle is made with grapes from their Indian Wells vineyard. I like this Chardonnay's ripe pineapple and butterscotch flavors and rich, creamy texture.

Chateau Ste. Michelle is the founding winery in Washington State located in Woodinville. 2017 celebrates their 50th anniversary. When we visited Seattle on vacation, this is the first winery we visited. The tasting room is housed in a beautiful French style chateau and the summer months are packed with events and concerts.

Nerd Approved

I was working through a pile at my desk yesterday and came across sales material for a *Wine Whisk* that I had picked up at the San Francisco Gift Market about a year ago. Remember thinking then ... what will they invent next to sell to wine lovers or folks looking for the next gadget to buy for wine loving friends?

The Wine Whisk booth at the gift market was packed. Molly, Lisa, and I inched our way to the front and were totally speechless. There were all these glasses of wine being "whisked" like scrambled eggs. We backed out of the crowd and burst into laughter.

All I could think was Benoit will kill us if we bought this gadget for the winery. Whisking is not in his top three ways to aerate his beautiful wines.

But, in our time-starved lives, maybe just maybe, this whisk might be a good thing. So I bought one and never told Molly or Lisa. I knew they would make fun of me.

Also, I should have done a little research on-line before my test of this product. I opened a really good bottle of wine and poured it into one of my crystal glasses. I got a little too energetic "trying to beat my wine into a frothy goodness." (Whisks are naturally meant for beating not for stirring and it didn't come with a warning.) It didn't take long. I broke my glass and spent the next twenty minutes cleaning up Syrah. *The force of the words that passed my lips was aeration enough.*

Since then I found the **NerdApproved.com** website, the source for preposterous products. Their write-up on the whisk warns the user from being too zealous! And furthermore, the website also recommended **a coordinated look** . . . a link to purchase "whisk earrings".

Now my wine loving friends, you can have it all. Perfect holiday gifts or NOT.

A Wine Glass That Is 'One' With You

While I know that the better the wine glass -- the right lead content, the right shape and the correct rim – the better your tasting experience, I also have my favorite glass which does not meet any of these standards.

This glass is "just me." It was given to me by my best friend who knows my most favorite flower in the world is the sunflower. The glass is literally drenched in bright yellow flowers and green leaves making it impossible to see the wine, the legs of the wine on the glass, or even the color of the wine.

But I don't care because the nuances I miss drinking wine from this glass is more than made up for by the warmth of memories. I will hand wash this glass each evening just so it is ready for the next day.

Molly, Lisa, and I all shop together for the gifts at the winery. We all have to agree before we buy anything. And if you know any of us, we all have strong opinions.

Our space at the winery is limited, so what we buy has to "speak to us," i.e. we need to immediately relate and can think of someone in our lives who would just love it. If it meets that test and even better yet is made by a small or fair-trade business, then it's a done deal.

For the holidays we have a large selection of what I describe as 'hostess, co-worker, girlfriend gifts' in an affordable price range that I can guarantee won't hit the "re-gifting" shelf because they will be treasured. When you pick out a gift it will remind you of the person you're buying it for and that makes it special ... for you and for them.

And if you want to buy wine you're at the right place. We've always specialized in a wider variety of wines because we know that individual tastes vary. The wines are award winning ... white, red, dry, sweet, and sparkling. Your choice.

Happy Holidays, The Working Girls

CHAPTER 18

Advertising vs. Public Relations

When do you start spending money on marketing?

The short answer, when you have the money.

A better answer, when you've got a plan.

When it's time to decide where to allocate a marketing budget, you need to ask yourself some questions.

For me it was where will I get the most bang for my bucks? Should I try social media, newspaper, magazine or even mailing snail mail?

I looked at local advertising first, given I live in a small community and people still read newspapers. I sell locally and with print I could better track the success of my advertising.

Our newspapers weren't all that big and depending on my ad, it had a higher probability of being seen and read then compared to say the Seattle Times, where ads would get lost. Even if you live in a larger city there may be community type publications that are available.

As I looked through my ads, they were primarily event-focused and placed in local and regional newspapers or wine magazines that had a longer shelf life. Here are my words of wisdom that I wish someone had written down and pasted on my forehead. It would have save me time and money when I started advertising.

- First set an annual and/or event budget.

- Plan out your year.

- Sit down with the local papers for a couple of weeks and just flip through them. What catches your eye (good or bad)? Where is the placement of the ad? How big is it? What day does it run? Are there days with more ads?

- Save the pages with the ads you like. Would you have bought from that ad?

- Get to know your advertising representative.

- Meet with your representative at your business and give him/her a tour. Ask lots of questions. Get their input on ad copy, graphics, and other aspects of print ads. Keep in touch. You also want your rep to feel a part of your business success that comes from their ads. So, let them know how well or poorly the ad performed.

- Share your plan and the ads that most interested you with your rep but not necessarily your budget.

- Ask for an annual cost for your whole plan, or by event. If you want to keep your business in front of the public on a regular basis, factor that in as well.

- Also, ask about any 'advertising specials' during a large community event such as our Lavender and Crab & Seafood Festivals, when there are special event pullout sections that tourists read. These pullout sections often get inserted in regional newspapers at no cost to you.

- For events, I placed ads in the Friday Weekend events issue and requested the right page, right side because research showed the eye travels from left to right, from the top of the page to the bottom. Many publications charge extra for a page on the right-hand side, but it's often easy to negotiate this placement at no extra charge. And I kept the ad size large enough for a good headline, graphics, and decent amount of words at a readable font size.

- Many times I got a second ad on Thurs for next to nothing when I did a Sunday ad. These ads were more "stay in front of your customer," but also could promote Summer Season or whatever high-volume business season, such as a holiday.

- If you can, provide print ready PDF copy. While most publications will design your ad, I always wanted total control. If you can afford one color it helps the ad pop from all the B&W ads.

- I guess I use this phrase often . . . what goes around comes around! When you run ads on a consistent basis based on your budget your press releases usually get printed. And, depending on your event there's a high probability that it will get a special mention or even an article.

- I've gotten some good deals at fundraising community auctions when I bid and won on an advertising package donated by our local newspaper.

- One last thought, research whether sponsorships will give you a return on your investment. Events need sponsors to cover the out-of-pocket costs. Generally, the sponsor is named on the event website, on a banner in a prominent space, and in press releases. But what does the sponsorship buy you? Do you see an up tic in sales during the event because they saw your name as a sponsor? I learned to ask what will I get in return for my sponsorship money.

Now on-line media advertising is another whole can of worms. It has changed dramatically as we all know over the years. My husband is responsible for the marketing in the self-defense business he and his partner own. A large majority of his media advertising goes to display and Facebook ads, which are managed by a consultant.

The ad advertises an introductory digital training product that is affordable and a great value. It's important to understand front end and back end marketing. The first purchase by your customer is your front end. After this initial sale the customer is added into a list and receives additional pitches for product. Called back-end marketing, Ralph's email sequence is a mixture of content only, video training tips and a soft sale pitch. On a regular basis they will promote a more expensive product. In this way the business builds their *list*. This valuable commodity, the names and emails of all actual and prospective customers, can be a veritable goldmine if you are a digital marketer.

Have you heard the phrase, "The money is in the list?" It's because your list is a valuable asset and you need to treat it right. This is why collecting emails is so important. You may collect an email with one sale; but if you use that email to stay in touch with the customer over time you build a relationship and that one sale can blossom into many sales, and that one customer becomes a loyal friend to your business. Put a pin in this, because I'm going to have a lot more to say about email lists and email marketing.

While the winery has a Facebook page, we haven't advertised on Facebook because of age restrictions and targeted location laws for alcohol ads. Just haven't wanted to crack that nut. We do boost a post if it's getting lots of likes and shares. You can set a budget on your post boost and expand your audience. That I understand.

I am not an expert on media advertising and it changes along with the technology way faster than my wine vintages. There are a lot of resources available on line if that is the direction you're heading.

If you're a business that tourists frequent, don't forget rack cards, which are often distributed in your local city's visitors center. An eye-catching card still gets picked up. And just like "the above the fold" in a newspaper, the top half of the card is most visible, so focus on that first. I visited our local visitor's bureau and stood in front of the rack cards display. Then I gave myself thirty seconds to pick out the ones that caught my eye. I continued to study them to pick out the ones I wouldn't have normally seen. This helped a lot when I sat down to rough out my thoughts for a rack card.

Public Relations, Publicity

There is a tradeoff in publicity versus advertising. When seeking publicity, you cannot control the message. There's a risk that what you want to say may not appear as you intended in print – it's the journalist's prerogative to write the story he or she wants or needs to tell to suit the publication. With advertising you can say exactly what you want, when and where you want to say it – for a price.

When we were launching Working Girl Wines in the market place there was a lot of media coverage on the buying power of women. Women head up 72% of US households and make or influence 85% of all purchasing decisions. And 64% of wine consumers are women.

These types of stats generated a flurry of 'women in wine' articles and what influences a woman's buying decision. One example: women are less influenced by wine ratings, as they tend to judge the entire product. And while the wine quality is important to women, so are the label design, the bottle shape, and the philosophy of the winery.

The Working Girl Wine brand was included in this media flurry, and I knew that we needed to take advantage of it somehow. I also didn't know much about PR, media relations or how to get our story out to the wine writers and wine buying - selling community.

Then I met Deborah Black (AnastasiBlack.com). She was coming off a corporate career (we had that in common) and starting her own public relations business. She concentrated on tourism and Washington State with a focus on the Olympic Peninsula.

We worked very closely together, talking frequently. Our writing styles were similar and it wasn't long before we were writing as if in the same voice. In the beginning I would do a rough draft and Deborah would re-write my piece in a press release format for distribution. Eventually, I could just call her and give her the details and she would do the draft for my fact editing without changing the style of writing.

Deborah brought a communication plan to the table that included objectives and messaging strategy. She researched media outlets to pitch our story to and built a strong contact list that was tailored to our plan.

The beauty of publicity, beyond being free ink, is in the credibility it brings. Most people are more likely to believe a story they read in the newspaper or on-line than a paid advertisement. There's power in publicity. And, as we've recently discussed, the media feeds upon itself. Once the ball gets rolling, you may end-up with many unsolicited stories and mentions in various media. You won't end up with another ad unless you pay for it. And that can add up!

Beyond press releases, Deborah pitched story ideas to key media (electronically or verbally), which built relationships. But our message had to be NEWSWORTHY. If it appears too self-serving, it won't interest a writer or editor, and they'll probably refer you to the advertising department.

But once the media got to know us, sometimes they came knocking on our door when they were doing a particular story or were in need of specific expertise. Our story got out beyond Washington State, because we also worked in partnership with other tourism organizations and direct competitors, working together to raise the profile of the Peninsula. Everyone Wins.

NEWSWORTHY is the key. I wouldn't spend the money on public relations unless you are growing a brand and have a real story. You can write business news briefs or press releases for accolades or awards your business receives and get free ink locally. And, of course, don't forget to let your email list know about any items that appear in print. It's important to note that what is new, exciting and newsworthy to you (the publicity seeker) may not be viewed in the same light by a media contact. Print media, in particular, serve a specific geographic audience (and with budget costs forcing reductions in staff, it's rare that they will cover news/events that take place outside their coverage area). If your "news" is not local to them, it's tough to get ink. In this case, your best bet is to look for news trends or a story that took place within the medium's coverage area that you can "piggy-back" on. Your story must have a link to the medium's coverage area.

Always ask yourself the question, "Why would this media contact care?" and craft your pitch in a way that answers that question. It was hard to pick as I headed down memory lane clicking through about 100+ press releases I sent. Here are a just a few headlines crafted to get attention.

Wine, Chocolate & Shoes
Olympic Cellars and Girlfriend Factor Bring Heart and Sole to El Paseo Fashion Week

Olympic Cellars Showcases "Only Rooster in the Hen House" At Spring Barrel Tasting
Public invited to meet French winemaker Benoit Murat

Olympic Cellars Introduces the *Working Girl*® Road Trip
New web page drives popular girlfriend travel trend to the Olympic Peninsula

Olympic Cellars Helps *Stomp Out Child Abuse* at 3rd Annual Harvest Party
"Grape Stomping Boogie" supports Healthy Families of Clallam County

Olympic Cellars' 2006 Cabernet Franc Makes Seattle Magazine's Top 5 Picks
Recent recognition includes private tasting for Wine Advocate Reviewer Jay Miller

Here's a sample of the various media outlets that ran stories that featured the winery, wines or the Working Girls.

- Puget Sound Business Journal's 2009/2010 List of Top Corporate Philanthropists

- Wine magazines: Wines and Vines; *"Working Girls" is Catalyst for Olympic Cellars Turnaround*, Wine Press Northwest, Wine Adventure Magazine for Women, Wine Spectator, *From Cosmetics to Chardonnay. Taking their cues from other fields, wineries are tailoring products to women*

- International: London Financial Times; *California wines need to be more like* Rosé *the Riveter*, The Independent (London, UK): Domaine Dames, A-News – Victoria, B.C.

- Out of State: New York Times; *Changing Directions and Finding Yourself*, San Francisco Chronicle, Time Magazine, Boston Spirit Magazine, Miami Herald, Business Week Online, Girlfriend Factor, Travel Girl Magazine.

- Taste of Washington Annual Wine Expo: Speaker

- WA State: Puget Sound Business Journal; *Vital Changes – Charlton restores winery with upgrades, marketing and hard work*, Seattle Woman Magazine; *Wine, Women And . . . Business,* Northwest Woman; *Olympic Cellars – How Sweet It Is*, Seattle Homes and Lifestyles, Seattle

Metropolitan Magazine, Seattle Magazine; *YOU GO, GIRLS Olympic Cellars celebrates women and aids local charities with its line of Working Girl Wines*, Olympic Business Journal, Washington CEO, Advancing Philanthropy, Northwest Prime Time, Seattle Post, King 5 TV NBC, Channel 13 Fox News, KUOW FM Radio (NPR affiliate), KPLU FM, KMPS FM

My most treasured honor was receiving the Women for WineSense Rising Star Award at the National Women's Wine Competition for innovative marketing, inspiring women in the wine business and the development of a tier of philanthropic programs focused on helping women and families. This was their first award recognizing Women in Wine outside of California. Margrit Mondavi gave me the award and was later inducted into the Women for WineSense Hall of Fame.

Wine Bites

Bella Italia is a great Italian restaurant in Port Angeles with an extensive wine selection. On Tuesday evenings during the off-season the restaurant features a wine tasting from some of the premier Washington wineries. Recently Woodward Canyon wines were served. The email about the wine tasting talked extensively about the 2014 Chardonnay. While I couldn't attend, I called and purchased 3 bottles and I wasn't disappointed. After I picked up the wine I checked Safeway and it wasn't there but if so it would have been on the pricey shelf.

The Wine Advocate: 91 Points

An incredibly impressive white, Woodward Canyon's 2014 Chardonnay was barrel fermented and aged in 20% new French oak, with partial malolactic fermentation. It has a beautifully classy, medium-bodied, refreshing, yet also textured style to go with lots of ripe apple, citrus blossom, brioche and vanilla aromas and flavors. It's rock solid and I suspect will age gracefully for 4-5 years.

Bella Italia is also known as the restaurant where Edward took Bella (Twilight series) on their first date. Bella ordered the mushroom ravioli and you can too. It is scrumptious. Of course it was paired with our Sparkling Twilight.

Chapter 19

The Team is No. 1

A friend who is an author and was reading this book chapter by chapter giving me needed critical feedback asked me this question, *"One thing that stood out to me was the exceptional staff you managed to hire, but I found myself wanting to know, how did you find these people? And, did you know exactly the types of people and specific skillsets you were looking for, or did you just luck out, so to speak?*

That's about three questions rolled into one. In earlier chapters (Priorities and French Influence) I talked about hiring Sara, Molly, Benoit, and Libby. And yes, they were exceptional people. I knew the skillsets I needed, there was an element of luck, and the rainbow was bright over the barn.

And, I had been a supervisor/manager my entire 25-year career at TI. That means hiring, training, working side-by-side with people, providing feedback and sometimes firing employees. TI provided lots of training and I read lots of books. Though *on the job training* taught me the most.

One lesson has stuck with me to this day. I was an accounting supervisor early on in my career. All the ladies that reported to me had their desks in four to six-person cubicles. Each day I would walk in head down looking at my list and relaying to each person what they needed to do that day. Then I walked out of one cubicle and go to the next cubicle again head down, relaying the list I had made for them. Then one day, a young lady interrupted me and said, "Kathy, at least you could say good morning."

I mumbled, "I'm sorry," and left quickly, embarrassed. I was so focused on the job that I forgot the people. Thank goodness it was early on in my career and that young lady taught me a valuable lesson. Later that day I pulled all the ladies together, apologized and then we had a long two-way conversation about what it meant to work as a team. I learned the most that day.

As I sit with my fingers on the keyboard two words won't leave my head – Trust and Respect. These made up the integral glue that cemented our team. And both had to be earned by all of us, especially me. A strong, cohesive team can achieve anything.

Guess I can't get rid of communicating in bulleted lists, so bear with me. As a leader, I offer you a list of basic guidelines for building trust and gaining the respect of your team. Your team is an extension of you, so the relationship you have with your team extends to the relationship with your customers.

Build Trust:

- Don't Place Blame: We learn from our mistakes and we don't make them twice. When one of us made a mistake I always said, "We can fix anything but death." Then we figured it out.

- Lead by example

- Communicate openly

- Know each other personally

- Show Respect: Treat others with respect and dignity

- Work as hard (harder) as everyone else in your team

- Start each morning with a cheerful greeting, check in with each team member

- Ask for opinion and input

- Treat your staff as you wish to be treated

- Support your staff in times of need

- Build a sense of community spirit by doing things together

- Give compliments often, recognize achievements where ever possible

- And never forget to say Thank You. Give credit where credit is due

How and when should we say thank you to the people that work for us? Well, at least once a day.

In a small team no one and nothing can be taken for granted. Each has a role that is important to the overall success of the business. There is no 'I' in team – it is 'We.'

If you're not at your brick and mortar business during every open hour, you are trusting that business and customer interactions are handled the way you want. Really it doesn't matter – brick and mortar or e-commerce – your team (your employees, virtual assistants or contracted editors, designers, consultants) are your voice as the owner.

Your responsibility is to train, give feedback and acknowledge a job well done, EVERY DAY. And, if you don't give the feedback, if something is off, then it all rolls back to you. It is your responsibility.

This is not the book for employee training, feedback, and performance reviews. There are lots of books, experts, and training out there.

My input: Even if everyone is doing a great job and you don't acknowledge it because you're just too busy, then team attitudes and comments can disintegrate without you knowing it and then it's too late. You've all heard these types of comments or said them yourself in previous jobs: "She doesn't even notice. We worked this project hard and does she even say, Thank You?"

Depending on your business there are all kinds of special, meaningful ways to show your appreciation for a job well done.

When I was an employee I think having my boss look me in the eye and say I did a good job for whatever was on my plate was just as meaningful sometimes as an annual raise, which, based on business performance, didn't always happen. So you need other ways to show and acknowledge your appreciation of a job well done.

When you own your own business, you have a bit more flexibility than in a corporate environment. And you're way closer to the individuals that work with you.

In the first few years we ran a lean staff in the Tasting Room. Usually, only one of us was in the Tasting Room at a time. I was always on call and could be at the winery in ten minutes if I wasn't watching my speed. I would be home working the books, writing emails, updating websites, and so forth.

Staffing on the weekends was particularly difficult because you could have gaps of time with no customers and then WHAM, a couple of groups would walk through the door.

Even when the customer flow was a steady, manageable and I didn't get a call, there might not be time for a lunch break or even a bathroom break. So when I didn't get a call I generally came in sometime in the afternoon depending how things were going. (I was always calling in throughout the day.)

There is a point to this whole discussion of the staffing dilemma. One way

I could say thank you is to send Molly or Libby home early (no loss in hours) and close down the winery myself.

Another, and I know only a winery can do this, give them the tasting bottles that still had wine in them to take home, instead of gassing the bottles for the next day. But maybe you have products you can share with your staff to show your appreciation.

We were open seven days a week and only closed on major holidays; Easter, Thanksgiving, Christmas, and New Year's. If you're counting, that's just four days. For Moms (we all were) having the day before a holiday off is almost as important because the to-do list at home is long. The best Thank You I could give is work those days myself and pay them also. Or, at least we'd divide and conquer, allowing them to come in late or go home early.

How you do it is up to you and your business. Just put yourself in their shoes.

Each year during the holiday season I would take us out to dinner and usually wrote up something that went with their gift. Here's one from *December 28, 2006, for example.*

Libby and Molly,

I'm not sure what to think of 2006. Frankly, it went by very fast, just like the airplanes I spent too much time in.

I know it was another great year for the Working Girls from sales to media to a fabulous-looking tasting room and to stretching our wings!

Divide and Conquer was our mantra. The Tasting Room and all of its facets was your business to run. Thank you. I focused on distribution and learning that side of the industry. And together we made that "stretch goal" I threw out in January 2004 when we all about choked: $1M by the end of 2006!

Our accomplishments were many and our disappointments few. The business is changing along with our environment and we will evolve and reinvent ourselves and stay three steps ahead as we've always done. I look forward to our day of vision, goal setting, and just plain spending the whole day with each of you.

My biggest goal this year is to have more time at home and at the winery. The heart and soul of what we do and who we are is exemplified in our tasting room. And, when we're all together the energy and laughter just fills the room and the creativity just bubbles out of each of us.

Ralph and I talked about our respective businesses and goals for the year. I told him at the end of 2007 I wanted us all to FEEL three things:

- *That we're Satisfied with Our Accomplishments (I set big goals)*
- *That we're Energized*
- *And, that we've had Fun*

I also think for us it is the Year of the Woman, getting back to our roots (not sure I can fully express what I mean yet) but it is still best said on our t-shirt: I Am Woman, Hear Me Pour.

So, I've added to our bracelets two new symbols of who we are and where we're going – literally.

Surprise, Kathy

The charm was an airplane and I had planned a Working Girls trip to Cabo. I gave them a copy of the airline and hotel reservations. (I started gold charm bracelets the previous year where each charm symbolized our accomplishments and goals.)

One last input – transitioning from a job with a company to owning a small business requires a MAJOR shift in mindset on how you approach 'work.'

Think about what you say in the morning: "I'm off to work." But that statement has a whole lot of inner meanings, like there is a start time and stop time for work. There is a regular paycheck. Paid holidays and vacation. A regular work schedule with weekends off. <u>All that changes.</u>

Banish "work" from your vocabulary. Now, you're off to your business – the business you've birthed and are raising like your own child. It's a part of you and requires a LOT of time and energy, way more than the corporate job. Regardless of how you communicate with your team or customers you always need to be "ON." You're the Leader.

So when you get a bit of downtime, take it, even if it's just a 24-hour getaway. Pat yourself on the back and come back recharged.

Below are another series of emails that I dubbed Notes to Self - Business Advice. I didn't have a disclaimer or a list of emails topics for folks who signed up for winery emails. Most would think they would get emails regarding the winery, wine promotions and events. I'm sure they never thought I would send veiled emails with business advice or my lessons learned. But, as my relationship grew with my customer list, so did my subject matter. Expanding beyond the winery but not the Working Girl.

As you read the two email stories I picked for you, think about your team that should never be taken for granted, your responsibility not to let anything fall between the cracks and the importance of down time.

WINE BITES

I'm ready to switch wine varietals. About time you might be thinking. Enough Chardonnay for a while. Writing my marketing chapters got me thinking how I promoted the wines at Olympic Cellars. When we bottled a new vintage or a new varietal the first thing we had to do was write the tasting notes. This required some very hard work by the team. We had to taste and taste and taste . . . then write down what we smelled, tasted, what foods would pair well and just overall impressions. I'd gather all input and write the tasting notes for our website and our tasting room.

The wines I am highlighting in the next few chapters are current releases at Olympic Cellars.

Tonight's wine is a 2016 Madeleine Angevine from Dungeness Valley Vineyard, Sequim, Washington. The cool weather grape grows well in our climate and we're very proud of our local wine. The nose has layers of honey, tropical fruit and grapefruit. The mouth has a delicious combination of quince, light green apple and a nice minerality. We enjoy this light, crisp wine on a sunny day with Dungeness crab salad.

I Am So 'Not Cool' Anymore!

My husband, Ralph, and I were shopping at a natural foods Co-Op up on Seattle's Capitol Hill a while ago. I'd left my glasses in the car so I was letting Ralph pick the produce while I'm off wandering the aisles.

As I passed a display of bottled water I noticed a brand I hadn't seen before and picked up a bottle. I could just read the words "Send a Message in a Bottle."

Well, that captured my attention, you know, the marketing person inside me. So I put it in our basket.

On the way home I drank the water and tossed the empty bottle in my basket to take to the winery to show Molly and Libby (we each lug around these great African baskets that we use to haul all our stuff that goes to and from home, winery, and events).

So, this story continues a few days later when I get to the winery for a Working Girl meeting.

I pull out this water bottle, again not really looking at it closely, and hand it to Molly while blabbering on about, "Wouldn't it be cool to do a promotional mailing to our customers in a plastic wine bottle?"

I can barely get the words out because Molly is laughing so hard she's tearing up as she hands the bottle to Libby.

"Kathy," Molly says, "Don't you know what this is?"

Again, I touch the bottle and say something like, "Well, it has a plant on the front and it say's 'Legalize It.'"

Still NOT GETTING IT, Libby rolls her eyes and informs me the plant in the picture is marijuana, and the label asks folks to send a message "in the bottle" addressed to the Chief Justice of the Supreme Court asking for marijuana to be legalized.

Well. Details.

You know, if it was something techie I didn't get I could understand, but for goodness sakes, I even grew up in the 60's and 70's.

I guess I DO get going a bit too fast sometimes (well, maybe a lot of the time, according to the others).

I know the course we're headed and the goals, but sometimes I'm just not the one to fill in all the details (that's probably why I got such poor scores in school for not coloring within the lines!).

Like when I was proofing an ad for one of our last winery events. I knew something wasn't right but I just couldn't put my finger on it. Until it hit me. I'd forgotten the "date, time and place." Minor details. Guess I was hoping "women's intuition" would get most folks here at the right time.

What's the old saying? "The devil is in the details?"

My take-away from these embarrassing "brain farts?"

Two Points:

9. <u>You need to work with a team who has complimentary skills.</u> For the Working Girls here at the Winery, that means not all of us better be going through "menopause therapy" at the same time!

10. <u>To stay competitive, you've got to be cool!</u> Well, maybe not on the ragged edge of "cool," but since your customers span multiple generations, your business sure as heck better reflect that, too. Between Benoit, Kathy Kidwell who works in the winery office, Libby, Molly and me, we cover three (and really close to four) decades. Good enough.

Ah well, at least when my grandkids call me "Grandma Wine Chick," I still feel cool!

My Secret T

It's been quite a while (eight months) since I've written a "rant and rave" but I still can get all riled up sometimes, wave my arms and get tongue tied and say "I'm waanting and waving".

Next week I'm going to be interviewed by Seattle TV Station Q13 Fox News for a story on the Washington wine industry. The gist of my segment is what's it like to be a woman in the wine industry and that I'm considered to be somewhat of a pioneer. This is quite an honor, especially the "pioneer" label, as I've only owned Olympic Cellars five years. I think Olympic Cellars is on the radar more because we've approached the business from a non-traditional, no prior experience road. Marketing is our mantra.

But as I sat down to try to write answers to the list of questions I was given, my mind kept going back and remembering my last thirty years in business (twenty-five years in corporate America). Then I looked down and remembered that I was wearing My Secret T-Shirt, which sums up some key lessons I've learned that have absolutely nothing to do with my gender and business acumen. Frankly, I'm a bit tired of the subject of "women in any business." Sure there are more glass ceilings to shatter, but our world has many more issues needing the attention and talent of our collective society. But, I'm not going there now.

Molly just called from the winery and I told her I was writing a rant and rave. She laughed and exclaimed, "What now?"

So back to My Secret T-Shirt and the lessons I've learned in business. Boring but they're dead-on. I'll try to be brief.

1. People Don't Always Meet Their Commitments
2. Never Assume
3. Following Up is My Responsibility

Now this doesn't sound very positive and I don't like how those three statements reflect on me personally. It sounds like I don't trust people to do what they say. But I do, I just know how over-committed people are these days. You've read it, lived it, know all the clichés about our bombarding electronic world, 24x7 lives as employees, parents, friends, care givers, everyone having to maintain home and hearth. Dare I go on?

This morning I missed a massage that I had scheduled for two weeks. I was really looking forward to it, but I thought it was at noon but it was at nine a.m. But I won't miss my teeth cleaning at four p.m. because I got my "reminder" call. I can't even keep up with my calendar. I'm a perfect example of my own lessons.

And, owning the winery has me even more in-tune to my lessons learned above. With a tasting room open seven days a week, add in events, bottling, grape harvest, making wine, trucking, marketing, government regulations, monthly reports, and watering/weeding the flower beds, I can get sort of grumpy sometimes. I'm not proud of it but it happens. You know how it feels. In my case it is usually open mouth and insert very large foot. Benoit, Libby, and Molly would be fast to agree.

I'm also fond of saying "Does Anyone Ever Do What They Say?" I'm an information junkie. Just give me updates and I'm okay. If there is a lack of feedback then guess what? "I Follow-up." I've got to know that when something is supposed to get done, or shipped or cleaned, you name it, I Need to Know That What I Want, What I Need, Happens on Schedule.

I also learned early on in my life "never assume." In fact, at one point I did a needlepoint picture and had it framed for my office that said, "NEVER ASSUME ANYTHING." I don't know where it finally ended up but I hope it helped someone along the way.

So I've become a fanatic "Follow-Upperer." You won't find this word in the dictionary but obviously it means to "follow-up" on everything. I warn everyone in the beginning – the team, vendors, family, friends, wine label printers and truckers – that I call on a regular basis to check on the status. I can drive people crazy. I explain in the beginning when I first make contact, place an order or start a project that I need regular feedback, status updates or I will be calling. In today's busy world, I think everyone over commits even though all of our customer service training said, "Under Commit and Over Deliver."

So what is my Secret T-Shirt?

Molly and Libby asked me what I wanted for my birthday this year and I said, "All I want is a t-shirt that says, "I'm Tired of Being the Bitch." Sometimes you just feel that way. You get tired. I love this t-shirt. It is nothing I'm going to wear out in public, but as I sit at my desk dealing with "whatever" and I have to follow-up or push, go up the chain or get mad, it just makes me feel that there are others out there that would understand.

OK, I feel better, Kathy

CHAPTER 20

One with Your Community

Remember when I said you need to work 'on' your business and not 'in' your business. Well getting involved in your community is part of the "on," but if you don't watch it, you'll find yourself overextended, losing the laser focus you need for your business with no time, and I mean *no* time for you and your family. Benoit took me aside once and told me I was doing too much outside the winery. Big, BIG wake-up call.

But involvement in your community, its priorities, business-related organizations, and non-profits keeps you linked in and you can take advantage and/or promote your business when opportunities arise.

It can also be very personally fulfilling depending on your passions and interests.

I got involved in a wide variety of organizations and events over the years. Like your business, your community focuses on different priorities depending on outside influences, economy, and even politics.

Molly called me during Christmas week 2008. "Kathy," she said, "I want to have a party. Well, maybe a dance. I guess what I really want to do is hold an Inaugural Ball to celebrate Barack Obama's presidency!" My response after I could speak again (I think when my jaw dropped it unhinged), "OoooKaaay, let's try it but January 20th is not far off."

A little over a week and many phone calls later we sent out a press release and business leaders in the community helped with seed funding to get it off the ground. We also had wine glasses engraved with President Obama's campaign logo and the words, Together We Can. And to this day, people call us and say they broke their glass and do we have any more.

Tickets sold out fast. I know we exceeded the fire marshal's occupancy limit, especially, after we stopped taking tickets and folks could just walk in, but It was an amazing night. No politics, hope for the future and a Community Gathering. And, no one wanted to go home even it if the next day was a work day. I kept begging our local band, Fat Chance, to play just one more, just one more song, PLEASE.

We held the Olympic Peninsula Community Inaugural Ball on Tuesday, January 20, 2009. With much support from our local community the winery invited the public to celebrate an historic inauguration

Looking back, Molly stepped out of her comfort zone along with thousands of other Americans the year before, to campaign door-to-door for Barack Obama. Molly exemplified the type of informed, involved, active citizen we needed to help drive change at the community level. We both believed that together we must act *locally* and think *globally* to help renew America's promise. The Community Inaugural Ball was an opportunity to unite our community in sharing a passion for that kind of change.

As you already know, Molly and I are both fond of acknowledging 'signs' when they appear to us. The sign that Port Angeles should host a West Coast Inaugural Ball hit us both between the eyes – and it came in the form of a history lesson.

Port Angeles was established in 1862 via an executive order issued by President Abraham Lincoln. The town site came to be known as the "Second National City" following the federal government's establishment of Washington D.C. Tributes to Lincoln's influence are found in the naming of Lincoln Street in the heart of the town, Lincoln School, and Lincoln Park.

In 2009, the United States commemorated the 200th anniversary of Lincoln's birth. President-elect Obama had approved *A New Birth of Freedom* as his 2009 inaugural theme, a phrase taken from a lesser-known part of Lincoln's Gettysburg address.

It was a sure sign. Thousands will be gathering in the First National City on this historic day. It's time for the 'Second National City' in the 'Other Washington' to join our nation's capital in celebrating a new day.

Our Community at Work – Painting Downtown Project

The Port Angeles community came together to paint over forty-five buildings the summer of 2009 when the Hood Canal Floating Bridge was closed for construction during tourist season and critical to the local economy. This bridge is the major route between Washington's northern Olympic Peninsula and the rest of the state. While the bridge was closed only six weeks, our community project just kept growing. When the tourists returned, a fresh, cleaned up and very proud community awaited them.

A side project was filling an empty storefront with local art so when tourists strolled the town an empty building was a place of interest and full of information about Port Angeles.

Each of the eight local wineries donated a used wine barrel no longer in production. Ralph and I delivered the barrels to local artists who committed to painting them at no cost for a future auction event to support the Port Angeles Art Council. One of my favorites is in my tasting room.

Seattle media covered this project; print, radio and TV. It was great exposure for the community and its business.

Memorial Day 2011. My best friend's son, Captain Joseph Schultz, was killed in Afghanistan.

Betsy Schultz and I moved to the Peninsula at the same time. She walked into the winery in August 2001 and exclaimed, "I just bought a B&B. Can I have a glass of wine?" I responded in kind, "I just bought this winery. I'll pour us both a glass of wine."

We are the same age; actually, Betsy is one day older. We worked our businesses side by side over the years. Not always seeing each other as much as we wanted, but connecting at some of the community events. I thought I got involved – but Betsy did it all.

We closed the winery and held the memorial for her son, Joseph, at the winery in June. And it wasn't long after that she founded the Captain Joseph House Foundation (CJHF) and donated the Tudor Inn, her award winning, historic B&B to the Foundation. The House serves as the only Family to Family respite for Gold Star Veteran Families of our military's Fallen Heroes. There is currently no federally mandated support for Gold Star Families.

I've served on the Board of Directors since CJHF was founded.

On September 28, 2011, just four months after Joseph's death, the winery hosted the American Veterans Traveling Tribute, an 80 percent scale replica of the Vietnam Veterans Memorial Wall in Washington, D.C. We've always thought of the winery as a community gathering place and were honored when we were asked if the Wall could be set up on our grounds. And, if we could leave the grounds open 24 hours a day.

Volunteers were available at night for veterans who didn't want to visit by the light of day and needed their time alone. The volunteers would offer a flashlight and guide the veterans to the names on the wall they came to visit.

The purpose of this traveling tribute is to Honor, Respect and Remember all who served, are serving and have sacrificed their lives for our Country's freedom: Military, Police and Firefighters.

Annual Fundraising Auction for Friends of the Field and the North Olympic Land Trust

I've supported and worked a number of fundraisers in my community, but I had never been asked to speak and ask for donations, which scared me to death. I'd learned at the winery to ask for the 'sale' but never 'please just give us money.' I worked on the words below for days and as I walked up to the podium I had an idea. But, I had only seconds to tell the organizer and didn't wait for his response. Figured if it worked, good. If it didn't, well, I would ask for forgiveness and wouldn't be asked back.

Here's my speech. The success of this auction for these two organizations was important to me and our community. I tried to relay that with passion and a sense of humor. I put emphasis on the bolded words throughout to set up the need for donations, our connection to this community, and the land we wanted to preserve. I started off by asking all the farmers and their families to stand up and be recognized. I caught my husband's eye and took a deep breath and launched in to my speech.

> *I am one of your most devoted admirers . . . owning a small business is one thing, having Mother Nature as your partner is another . . .* **Thank you for Growing Our Food.**
>
> *For those of you that don't know me, I moved to Sequim in 2001 from Dallas. Olympic Cellars Winery is my business. I'm your* **classic city gal.** *Small fenced yards, lots of hot concrete, skyscrapers and traffic jams were my every day landscape.*
>
> *Food to me was restaurants and limpy salad bars. I'm not much of cook. To me, food grew in grocery stores. Yes, that's what I said. While I knew that there were farms someplace, I never gave them much thought. Whole Foods became THE place to shop . . . but now that I know what real,* **fresh, straight from the ground, farmers market produce taste like**, *I think maybe that's why we covered everything with salsa.*
>
> *I know many of you can relate if you moved here like we did. Ralph and I arrived in August from 110 degrees, smog-filled days to 55 degrees, star-filled nights. One of my first morning walks before opening the tasting room took me past Farmer Brown's flower and vegetable stand with an unlocked cash box and a chalkboard with prices. Looking around I realized that all I had to do is drop in my money, make the correct change and take my produce. I'll never forget that day because in Dallas I didn't know my neighbors and we all had security systems. So very early on I learned* **Trust and Neighbors** *were part of this new* **community** *I joined. Sadly, Farmer Brown passed away on Sept 1.*

*We rented a house that backed up to Jack and Max Wayne. There was a white picket fence dividing the yards. Jack had a huge garden. He fished, crabbed, canned and rarely needed food from the grocery stores. He was very much self-sustaining. Jack also liked his wine and when he found out I was the "winery lady" we traded. Each day fresh vegetables hung in a plastic sack on my side of the fence. I would hang one of that day's tasting bottles in a sack on his side of the fence. I pulled up my first vegetables from his garden. And he lectured me about waste and why I needed a compost pile. When I think of Jack I add **Self-sustaining** to the attributes of my new community.*

*One other thing you need to know about me, I married into a **pioneer farm family** in Ellensburg Washington. I was pretty much "**that city gal**" again. I listened to the stories of stacking hay or milking before school. Feeding the cattle in sub-zero weather. The huge garden and the goat that butted Ralph's Mom right off her feet. But it really wasn't inside me. I didn't truly understand until the **land, their legacy, was "threatened"** and Ralph's father became ill. We fought the courts for two years to save his family's pioneer farm and land. The family didn't want it broken into lots, they wanted it kept whole for generations to follow.*

*Neuharth Winery, now Olympic Cellars, was the first winery on the Peninsula. Gene Neuharth's vision was to have a vineyard, which we've pioneered. Local vineyards and wines are now a reality. The winery's home is a 100-year-old barn/dairy farm once owned by the Chambers family. Many people shared their stories about growing up here, working in and on the barn and playing in the loft. The land and barn now have become **my heritage** to preserve.*

One last community experience. Remember I said I couldn't cook? That's how I met Molly Rivard, in her cooking class. I may have not learned to cook but I met my best friend who also taught me a great deal about living life. And through her I met her family, Josh, Elisa and their girls, Hannah and Lily, a young farm family and their extended community.

*Young families are **again** choosing the farm life. But they're going to need help to find and afford the land. **They're our future. They're our legacy.***

*All these experiences began adding up. You might say a **seed** started growing inside me nine years ago. Safeguarding farm land, growing real food in a sustainable system, preserving a way of life that is **now my** community ... it is why I support Friends of the Field and the North Olympic Land Trust and why I stand before you tonight.*

*I've talked about community, neighbors, trust, heritage, legacy. One community attribute that stands out now more than ever is **sustainability**. A strong, healthy community is self-sustaining, taking care of its own. We **can't depend** on the continued flow of outside money to save our farmland. The economic future is uncertain. Literally, the safeguard of farmland is in our hands.*

But we **can depend** *on a steady stream of semi-trucks bringing in packaged food that is no longer living, that takes money out of our community and erodes a community lifestyle that I know you treasure because you're here tonight. This is* **your community.**

The Friends of the Field has a nest egg of $225K they have worked tirelessly over four years and sold lots of strawberry short cakes to build. It needs to grow to be a viable match or funding base to help save the next farm. And I need your help tonight.

In prior years there were **matching money grants** *to work towards; not this year. So we need to help* **Seed** *this fund ourselves. There are folks around the room with pledge sheets.*

So I'm going to ask in my best Julie Gratton style for $20K "then you can go home." Hmmm, **I'll have to ask for forgiveness later ... what about a $20,000 donation in return for vegetables for life?** *(BTW, we got a donation for $20,000. I was so excited I jumped down off the stage and shook their hands. Wasn't very professional of me but Holy Toledo.)*

OK, $5,000 and five years of seasonal vegetable boxes. It only takes four and we're at our goal. (Got a few here, too. But then there was some fun dealing going back and forth like ... "I don't like beets, you can have mine if I can have your carrots.")

Last ... I think I need a 'carrot' to get this going... $2500 donors ... Nash's carrot for two years. Nash's organic farm is FAMOUS for its carrots. **(It was a good night!)**

WINE BITES

Another wine or in this case dessert wine, 2016 Sailing Moon Rose' Dessert Wine, is made from local Regent grapes. Regent is a cool-weather red wine grape. This grape does best in a cool, dry area with a long growing season. If we have a rainy season, this grape might not make it.

This Port-Styled wine fortified with brandy distilled from our Madeleine Angevine wine. The vivid Rose' color hints at the fresh, delightful flavors of strawberry, rhubarb and pie cherry. Enjoy lightly chilled.

Chapter 21

Marketing with Emails

Before I knew it was a marketing strategy I used emails as my primary method of staying in touch with my customers outside of the tasting room. Why? I think by now you could guess. There was no cost.

Previously I mentioned we purchased a point-of-sale system. It wasn't until 2005 and the timing was critical given the expansion of the Working Girl brand. We updated it with all the customer emails gathered over the first four years and started collecting sales data. It was a beautiful site.

Periodically I would do a bit of research as I had time. I Googled a lot of iterations of *Marketing on a Budget*. Most articles I read suggested Email Marketing as an option and often said it was one of the best returns on investment of your time.

TIME: that I understood because I never had enough of it. In addition, these articles stressed sharing useful information on a periodic basis while trying to make the sale. And the clincher for me – an overarching principal that governs your writing – write compelling copy, always thinking more about the customer. So the way I looked at it – if I was the customer, would I want to read the email that showed up from Olympic Cellars in my inbox?

We obtained the majority of the non-local emails when the customers personally visited the winery while on vacation or on weekend get-aways. That's when we made our first connection with them, be it at the tasting bar or when they attended an event. The customer met one of us Working Girls and maybe even Benoit. Many had perused our website prior to visiting, when planning their trip. There was a personal interaction and it was strengthened with a good dose of storytelling and laughter as we poured wines for tasting.

When I read more about the strategy of using mini stories in email marketing I knew this was up my alley. I focused on continuing the customer's initial winery experience via my emails. Written personally from me in my voice on what's happening at the winery. You know, like when you get on the phone with an old friend and the first thing you say, "whatcha been doing?" And yes, I also sold wine but not in every email. And, of course, if I used the proper marketing-ese strategy words, then these emails were written to build loyalty, trust, and brand awareness.

It didn't take me long to realize I needed additional software for sending out emails. We integrated our Point of Sale with MailChimp. Finally, I could segment my customers by location, interests, wine club(s). Also, it was much easier to track the success of an email given all the stats this email system provided. Again, feeling tech savvy.

As I put myself in my customer's shoes, my gut said email marketing is where I needed to focus. Why? Because people check their email all the time and there isn't much in our mailboxes anymore.

Again Googling – stats said greater than 90% of people go online to check their email, the #1 activity on the Internet, and spend 2.6 hours a day checking, reading, and sending email. And 66% of online customers have purchased as a result of an email. And the average purchase that comes from an email is more than three times higher than that of social media. And you don't pay for social media advertising when you email your list.

Google became my writing partner and sometimes my inspiration. It was easy to crank out an email about the What, Where and When of an event. The hard part was writing compelling copy that engaged the customer.

When I was promoting the Working Girl Wines and I had to travel all the time to visit distributors across the US, I did a lot of my emails in the hotel restaurant or bar. I could sip a glass of wine or a martini forever and just get into a zone. As I think about this, it was the energy of the room, the laughter, conversations all swirling around helping me find my words.

Also, my marketing husband would say you have to write regularly to keep your rhythm, focus and voice. He was right. My creative spark would sort of die if I didn't regularly communicate with my customers.

While I have a logical-financial left brain, my right brain can ping from thought to thought and idea to idea. Which is good because I knew that to keep customers opening my emails, I always needed to look to the future, not get stale or cranking out emails just on events or to promote and sell wines.

For me, writing ideas came from cosmic sources, i.e. who knows. Something would just get stuck in my brain and the internal ping pong ball started bouncing around trying to find an angle to the winery, our wines or just something interesting to engage customers. Sometimes it took days to write an email that had a compelling story. As an example, I read a wine review that described a wine as a *Bony Ass Wine*. These three words generated an idea for an email that bounced around for days till I found my words. I've included it in this chapter as an example.

Unless I was on a deadline, I didn't try to force my writing, especially if it was a story angle that I connected to the winery. If I tried to push through it, I would spend more time deleting because the words weren't flowing. I gave it time, let it percolate. Also, I found that I wrote better once my to-dos were ticked off my list and my brain could just flow – and yes while sipping a glass of wine.

I've never been one to beat my email list to death. Three to four emails each month was my goal. Each had a specific purpose. And, the subject line was just as important as the content. If it was a wimpy subject line customers often wouldn't click thru to read the email.

A Working Girl Welcome from Olympic Cellars was the first email a new customer would receive. Every couple of weeks I would send out the Welcome email to new emails on our list. This email was updated throughout the year to be current with the season. It wasn't long but just told our new customer what to expect from me and gave them links to some of the more popular emails I had written.

Welcome Email

Subject: A Working Girl Welcome from Olympic Cellars

Hello, I'm Kathy Charlton, one of the Working Girls, and I just wanted to reach out and thank you for stopping by the winery recently and sharing your email with us.

I hope you enjoyed your wine tasting and visiting our 110+year-old-barn. It is the oldest standing barn on the Peninsula and we are honored to call it our winery home.

One or all of the Working Girls, Molly, Libby or me, are usually behind the bar or working in the cellar alongside our winemaker, Benoit, most every day. We are headed in to fall and grapes are ripening fast in Eastern Washington. We had a hot summer so we expect that we will start crushing two weeks early, late September. Libby and I, now called cellar rats, pull on our fleece and start shoveling tons of grapes.

I will keep you updated on the happenings at the winery and promise not to bombard you with emails. Generally, you will receive three or four emails a month giving you an update on the goings on at the winery, the Working Girls, new wine releases and specials. Sometimes, well, I also get on a roll writing, no subject is sacred. But the email usually has something to do about wine. It could be informative or put a smile on your face.

Here's links to a few: Pinot Envy, Serve Your Cellars Best Before Dinner and My Most Embarrassing Wine Moment. Enjoy.

Kind regards,
The Working Girls and Benoit

Then on a regular basis these are the list of emails for each month.

1. <u>Content</u> that had something to do with wines. It had to be interesting and non-traditional. No sale. These emails I researched looking for something unique and interesting about wines then added my own touch.

2. <u>Soft sale</u> had a story with a connection to one of our wines and a link to the website.

3. <u>Direct sale</u> was a promotion with a time limit. Get it now, at this great price, etc.

4. <u>My Choice</u> - This fourth and optional email was dependent on seasons, events or whatever rant or rave that got my creative juices flowing.

I've also broken out separately a few categories of emails (holidays, pets, laughing at yourself and showing the love) that fall into this fourth list but have a strong marketing purpose and included them in their own chapters. All of these emails relate to your life and life's experiences letting your customer feel that they know you.

Also, I didn't want the fourth email to ever become routine. I would go on jags like writing a TGIF email. But I got busy one Friday and ended up writing *It's TGIF on Monday*. That email got way more opens then the series of TGIF emails that were becoming routine to my customers. So, I had fun with the variations of TGIF and then moved on to the Rants and Raves I've already mentioned.

As I'm writing I realized I never wanted to have my customer get used to any regular anything from me. If everyone got use to a TGIF or another regular category email, they might skip it. And when I wrote about taking a stand it was to rock the boat a bit.

For me, one of the main reasons for sending non-sales emails was a responsibility to my customers. I couldn't let the only time I communicated with them be to ask for their hard-earned dollars. So, I tried to create a sense of curiosity, humor and personal caring with my customer communication. Then when there was a wine promotion I hoped that they would take the time to read and consider the email.

I would usually post my content, events, rants and raves emails to my Working Girl Blog and promote them by including the link on the Olympic Cellars Facebook page. I didn't put any sales, soft or direct, on the blog posts because of alcohol regulations. But all the emails were sent to my winery customer list.

The Working Girl Blog got hits from Facebook links but people rarely signed up for the blog. I didn't promote it.

A detailed email calendar helped me stay on track for each quarter and an overall high-level annual calendar was kept for year-to-year planning. Then researched and planned in advance so I didn't find myself under pressure saying, *I gotta get an email out before I go to bed*. I always carried a notebook with me or recorded thoughts on my phone for later, because when I'd get an idea and then forget I'd want to kick myself.

Sitting in close proximity to my husband in our home office I would hear him talking about marketing strategies with colleagues. I'd hear them say every business has their own persona and USP. I asked him what USP meant. Bottom line it is your unique selling proposition, i.e. what makes your product different from your competition, makes it stand out in the crowd and tells your customers what is special about you. Then you need to focus on your ideal customer, tailoring your story to what's in it for them. Then let them get to know you, how/why you got into business, a family connection or history to the business. What your brand stands for.

The Working Girl Wines appealed to women. It wasn't just the wines. Women related to the brand name, Working Girl. That's who we are. As Working Women ourselves we understood the challenge of work and family. As Working Women we encouraged women to put themselves at the top of their list if even for 24 hours. We valued Working Women and supported them and their families through our charitable giving.

From the beginning I developed the persona of Working Girl (me), the winery and how our wines evolved. I tried to stick to that persona and used these descriptors, phases and tag lines wherever they made sense.

Me: The Working Girl. Wore hats a lot because didn't have a good hair day. Couldn't cook. Believed in signs and the rainbow over the winery. Spoke my mind. Gracefully Aging. Loved Lucille Ball. Grandma Wine Chick. Savor the Moment, Cherish the Memories. I Am Woman, Hear Me Pour.

Winery: Heritage Washington Winery. Historic Barn, Oldest on Peninsula. Olympic Cellars, Home of the Working Girl Wines. Hot August Nights – Music Venue. A Gathering Place. Supported the community and local non-profits.

Wines: Award winning. Wide variety. Wines for you no matter where you are on your wine journey. Working Girl Wines, the Heart of Our Charitable Giving Program. Working Girl, Your Go-To Wine At Day's End. Dungeness Wines – Our Heritage. La Dolce Vida – The Sweet Life.

I've shared an example or two of each category of email I wrote just to give you an idea how you can start off with an obscure but interesting angle and draw your customers into the content. Also, I spent time Googling images that I could include in the email. If it was an email-blog that got promoted via Facebook, a picture helped it stand out in the newsfeed as you well know.

Think about your business especially when you read the content emails. What about your business can you share that your customers would find interesting, learn something in the process, and maybe talk about with friends while, of course, mentioning where he or she got that special little tidbit of knowledge?

Two Examples of Content Emails

A Bony Ass Wine

This had my jaw dropping. I've read a lot of wine reviews and tasting notes but had to admit this was a first.

I've even gotten over the disgusting use of how cat-pee aromas in wine are good, yet horse manure is bad. Wet slate is in, wet dog is out? Sweat is positive, but dirty gym socks are not?

But, A Bony Ass Wine? Now where did that come from? Of course, I Googled it but no references to bony ass wine anywhere.

So it got me thinking. What does that phrase conjure up? A few words immediately popped into my head (all non-gender specific). Thin, flabby, flat, sharp, okay . . . and sort of bony.

Then I thought of wine in those terms and I got it. Wow, I thought, this may become my favorite expression to describe a red wine I don't like.

I went back to Google and the eParker.com glossary of wine terms.

And, eureka. I found the words that perfectly sum up this very descriptive and a bit outrageous wine term, A Bony Ass Wine. Maybe Robert Parker will add it to his list!

Angular: Angular wines are wines that lack roundness, generosity, and depth. Wine from poor vintages or wines that are too acidic are often described as angular.

Flabby: A wine without enough structure, particularly too much acid or tannin. It feels flat and without intensity and can even seem syrupy.

Sharp: An undesirable trait. Sharp wines are bitter and unpleasant with hard, pointed edges.

Now, what is the opposite of A Bony Ass Wine? Hmm, I'm not going there. But I can describe what makes a good red wine for me. Good structure, full-bodied, not overly fat but with good fleshy notes, round, mature, big, with depth.

That is so much poppycock wine-speak. What I should have said is I like my red wine Big, Bold and Bodacious.

Follow These Steps to Wine Loving

I happened on the *8 Step Program to Enjoying Wines*. It got me to wondering, are there other multiple step wine programs out there that might teach me a thing or three.

Well, with just a few quick Google searches I bring to you the ultimate in *Follow These Steps to True Wine Loving Consumption*.

    4 Steps to Wine Tasting
    6 Steps to Loving Red Wines
    8 Steps to Enjoying Wines
    10 Steps to Ordering Wines in a Romantic Restaurant

In the first two I just provided the links. The 8 Steps is summarized.

The 10 Steps was just so much fun to read, I kept trying to summarize it. Frankly I would just click on the link and read the original, unadulterated version!

Now obviously, you might be thinking, I bet Kathy didn't stop at 10 Steps.

Of course, not! I continued my Google search for the 12 Steps to Wine. And, you know what I got; The 12 Step Program but not to wine enjoyment.

So, if your wine drinking dramatically increases after following all of these programs, the 12 Step Program might be an option and is only a click away.

Four Steps to Wine Tasting
http://www.askmen.com/money/body_and_mind_150/186_better_living.html

Six Easy Steps to Loving Red Wines
http://www.doityourself.com/stry/loveredwine

Eight Step Program to Enjoying Wine
http://www.winecurmudgeon.com/my_weblog/the-eightstep-program-to-.html

1. The best wine is wine that you like. If you don't like it, don't drink it.

2. Don't be afraid to try something different.

3. Price is not always an indication of quality. Inexpensive wine can be well-made, just like expensive wine.

4. Wine is supposed to be fun.

5. Wine snobs are not fun.

6. Wine speak is for wine snobs.

7. Wine is not rocket science. Anyone can learn about wine, as long as they're willing to drink it.

8. Wine and food pairings, no matter how good, they're just suggestions. The wine police will not come and arrest you if you drink white wine with beef or red wine with chicken.

10 Steps to Ordering Wine in a Romantic Restaurant
http://www.hawaiidiner.com/articles/article.php?article=147

So, gentlemen: for once, you've had the presence of mind to make dinner reservations ahead of time for Valentine's night – the second busiest day of the year (after Mother's Day) for restaurants.

What are you going to do if you know she prefers wine, but you know absolutely nothing about it? Tell her, "Why don't we just go for two pints of Guinness?" Wrong! If your dining partner is truly important to you, it is to your advantage to whisper the three magic words: "Let's have wine." And this I can say after 25-plus years in the restaurant business: women prefer wine! Here's my guide to help you out.

1. Bone up. It doesn't take more than a few minutes to prepare by absorbing the introduction of a book on wine. So now that you've done some homework, here's what you do once you've made it to the restaurant, and you've just been seated.

2. First, a waiter will approach to ask if you would like to start with a cocktail or glass of wine. Rule #1: remember that you are there to please your date, not a server. So without breaking the gaze between your eyes and hers, the thing to do is to simply ask, "Would you care to join me with a glass of Champagne?"

3. Plan to order a full bottle of wine. Why? Bottles are so much more romantic than glasses! Don't worry about quantity. If you say something like, "Let's not worry about finishing it, since the best wines always come in full bottles," how do you think she'll feel? Do words like dashing and debonair mean anything to you?

4. Do take a good look at the wine list, whether you know what you're looking at or not. The important thing is to look good doing it this is romance, after all, not a driver's test. You might consider practicing beforehand furrowing your brows, raising one side or the other or glancing up with a smile as you turn the pages.

5. Now it's time to order the wine. If you've already forgotten what little you've learned, don't panic. Just follow this full-proof method: select one of the two most food-flexible wines in the world, one of which is a white, and the other a red. So you ask her, "Would you prefer a white or a red?" If she says white, look for a Riesling (pronounced "REEZ-ling").

6. If she says she prefers a red, look for a Pinot Noir ("PEE-no NWAH")

from either California or Oregon. Like Rieslings, Pinot Noirs tend to be light yet zesty enough to go with everything from fish to red meats.

7. Say you are hopeless and can't navigate through a wine list no matter what. Then it doesn't hurt to ask for help! I believe most women are impressed by that anyhow like asking for directions on the road. Again, the idea is to look good doing it. Call over your waiter or in the finest places, the sommelier ("so-mo-YAY"), also known as a wine steward and ask for a recommendation for a good, medium range German Riesling or American style Pinot Noir. Practice this letting the names roll off your tongue like a native language. If you must, invite the sommelier to look over your shoulder and point out his suggestions on the list. Make it look like a conspiracy like the two of you are cooking up something truly special for your date.

8. Now I need to prepare you for two possible curves; because as in all things in life, not everything goes as planned. First, if your date happens to say she likes a very DRY white wine as opposed to a slightly sweet Riesling then the coolest, most food-versatile dry white you can possibly order is a Pinot Gris (PEE-no GREE) from Oregon or California, also known as Pinot Grigio (GREE-gee-o) when it comes from Italy. Secondly, if you happen to be in an Italian restaurant, the best possible red wine to order is a Chianti Classico (kee-AHN-tee CLASS-see-ko).

9. The waiter or sommelier will then wish to perform the serving ritual, which is when he shows you the bottle, opens it, and asks you to taste and approve it. There are few ordeals (like circumcision) worse than this, and so the least made of the entire rigmarole the better. When he brings over the bottle, look him straight in the eye and ask, "Is this the wine we ordered?" This will make him read the label himself and tell you yes or no, and all you need to do is nod knowingly. Then you ask him to do this simple favor: "Please open the bottle and leave it on the table" (or in the ice bucket, if it's a white). Once he has departed, you can go ahead and do the honors for her and for you the proper amount to pour, by the way, is no more than half-way at a time before raising your glasses with an appropriate, or even rakishly clever, toast.

10. Finally, the finishing touch: how many women don't like chocolate, or sweets in general? Not many at all. So if you really want to make a mark, do not automatically order coffee with your chocolate desserts but a small glass of Tawny Port from Portugal.

Two Examples of Soft Sale Email

Aim Pop Fire ... You Took Out a Vampire
SPARKLING TWILIGHT

I can't think of a more perfect wine for Halloween.

At a party? Deep dark wine bubbles to the top of your glass as you sip and stir your bubbling caldron with your witch's broom.

Handing out candy? One Hershey for Batman and two for you ... sip sip.

Watching one of the top ten Halloween Movies ... A Nightmare on Elm Street? Drink champagne ... no nightmares! I'm not making this up :)

Or, maybe the night is Dark, the fog is rolling in, the trees are dripping creepy with rain and the wind is howling ... or is it the werewolves???

Pop a bottle of Sparkling Twilight ... Aim, Pop, Fire ... **Bulls Eye**! You took out a vampire!

Saturday only ... Sparkling Twilight wants to fly out of the winery and protect you on Halloween. Mention my email and I will take $10 off.

I really have to do this ... *need to provide you with extra protection* ... especially on the Olympic Peninsula!

Serve Your Cellars' Best Before Dinner

Last year I bought a five-foot long, red metal sign that simply just spelled out the word, *Gather*.

Displayed on our long farm table in our appropriately named "Gathering Room" it just speaks to me. I can almost smell my mother's dressing, see my father carving the turkey, and my son sneaking treats to our Scottish terrier under the table.

As the holidays approach, we get a lot more questions on food and wine pairings. And after doing a little more research and reading the overwhelming amount of advice, I found some notes that banished all the complexity and stress. Even for me who's in the wine business, this was a relief, and it *pairs* nicely with my innate desire to *Gather*. After all, much of the appeal of Thanksgiving dinner is found in the kitchen with wonderful aromas enveloping all the cooks!

So here's a fresh look at what you might offer.

First, for big holiday meals don't overcomplicate the wine selection. It can be as easy as simply opening a few different types of wine and letting people choose their favorites.

It's the perfect time to serve your wines 'family style,' the way you serve your meal. Just open your selections and put them out on the table.

And of course, if you have that special bottle of prized wine in your cellar, bring it up for the holidays.

But here's where most people make a mistake.

Typically, they like to make their special wine the showcase, serving some less expensive variety beforehand.

I recommend the opposite.

Before dinner, open that prized bottle and let people enjoy all its delicate flavors – without food affecting the taste. And while all are savoring the bouquet, you might actually get a word in and offer that special toast to those most special in your life.

After this, the food takes center stage. Serve several bottles of food-friendly, not so expensive, wines that blend well with the wide variety of dishes on your table.

Then, sit back and enjoy your *gathering*.

Best Wishes, Kathy

Ps. Wine suggestions and a Holiday "Gathering" Wine Package Below. (Included in original email)

Two Examples of Promotion, Direct Sale Emails

Bubba Gump – Riesling Special

Last week I was in California visiting my son and his family. We spent one day in San Francisco and walked around all the shops and restaurants around Pier 39. When we passed the Bubba Gump Shrimp Company, I thought of Riesling. Why I don't know, but after my last email on Riesling, this wine has been rumbling in the back of my mind.

As we walked, I made a mental note to research Riesling Wine Pairings with Shrimp because I couldn't get the scenes from the movie, Forest

Gump, out of my mind. You know, when Private Benjamin Buford 'Bubba' Blue recited all the ways his mama and her mama cooked shrimp.

So, with a few key strokes on Riesling and Shrimp pairing, here's my list of shrimp dishes in true Bubba style. And if you're a bit nostalgic today, at the bottom is the YouTube video of Bubba's famous rendition of shrimp dishes.

Shrimp Risotto – Fried Shrimp, Shrimp & Papaya Salad – Mu Shu Shrimp – Peel & Eat Shrimp with BBQ Spices – Shrimp Sushi – Shrimp with Curry/Coconut Milk – Shrimp Tacos – Shrimp Salad with Sweet Chili Dressing – Simple Grilled Shrimp – And so on . . .

April's Featured Wine: Olympic Cellars Dungeness White Riesling: Regular $12.99, this month $9.75, a 25% savings.

Overall, Rieslings are delicious, versatile wines that are terrific with food, playing lively apple, peach or citrus flavors against a zing of acidity. The best Rieslings have an intense brightness — one sip should wake the most jaded palate. This description is our 2008 Dungeness White in the bottle!

You would be hard-pressed to find a wine that is more versatile with foods from bland to spicy, salty to exotic; Riesling wines can just about cover them all. The key is their acidity and depth of fruit flavors.

Tax Free Wine

Dear Olympic Cellars Customers,

I don't have my taxes done; are you surprised! You know from previous emails that I'm sometimes a *bit* behind on my deadlines. Every year I tell Ralph we are going to do our taxes in March, but I guess I just need to face facts: we are Tax-Crastinators!

So, I had an idea while I was adding up all the *gazillion* little receipts we saved this year to track our sales tax.

Why not offer TAX FREE wine for the next week to our customers while others like me struggle to make the April 15 deadline and to congratulate those of you who have filed, and better yet, already got a refund.

Here's the deal. If you order wine or stop by the winery between now and Monday, April 17, you get your purchases tax free. That includes our gift shop. That's an automatic 8.3% discount.

Remember, My Sweet Syrah is already on sale for $16 (20% discount). Now it would be discounted 28.3% but only for the next 7 days.

Remember, if you EVER deserved a glass of wine it is this week and I just remembered . . . we have to pay our property taxes at the end of the month. Ahh, I need a nice glass of Syrah!

Best Wishes, The Working Girls

Two Examples of My Choice Emails

Why Don't We Use Our Good Wine Glasses?

OK, ladies, are you old enough to remember that game show, The $64,000 Question?

Last night I go to pour myself a glass of wine.

I open the cabinet with all my glasses and cups (and yes, my collection of mismatched, dishwasher-banged-up, ratty-looking wine glasses).

I grab a wine glass (it's a give-away from a wine event pouring), pour my wine and then . . . stare across the kitchen.

There, neatly arranged behind soft back-lit glass cabinet doors, stand a sparkling array of beautiful wine glasses.

Some handed down to me from my mother. Of course, there's my good wedding crystal. And others I've picked up along the way because I just had to have them.

There they sat (probably needing dusting) because I never used them this Thanksgiving – you know the one time of year we're sure to pull out the "good stuff" and set a beautiful table. But not this year because we went out for that holiday dinner.

So what is it, some generational thing? My mom only used the "good china" for special occasions and so did her mom.

Am I just too lazy to hand-wash the glasses?

Or are wine glasses just like shoes? We buy them even if we don't need them.

Do I not think a hard day (or any day, for that matter) doesn't deserve that moment of pleasure when we sip from the proverbial glass slipper?

Well, whatever the reason, it all came crashing down at that moment.

Literally.

I wish you could have heard the sound of breaking glass. My husband sure did.

He comes running up the stairs thinking a small Pacific Northwest earthquake has just hit.

There I stood with this sheepish look on my face.

I had just pitched every one of my mismatched misfits into the trash, the last one with a tad bit too much "oomph." Watching the glass break, I just couldn't help yelling out, Mazel Tov as I threw my arm in the air.

Poor Ralph. He just shook his head, no questions asked. I'm sure he thought it was, you know, one of those hormonal things, and went back downstairs.

Do you want to join me in this New Year's Resolution: Every time we pour a glass of wine, let's all resolve to use a different glass. One of the *good* ones.

The scary thing: how many days will it take 'til you start back through yours a second time?

Happy Holidays, Kathy

What next - A Vibrating Wine Glass?

The day of the Olympic Peninsula Community Inaugural Ball sponsored by Olympic Cellars and I realized I was out of mascara.

What does this have to do with a vibrating wine glass you ask? Read on!

So, I ran out of the Elks' ballroom where we were decorating and across the street to Gottschalks, a small department store in Port Angeles. Made a bee line straight for the cosmetic counter, asked for black mascara that washed off with soap and didn't smudge.

The lady at the counter said, "Well, I have one more of the *vibrating* mascara wands. We've gotten great feedback (no clumping, nice separation of lashes, yadda-yadda)."

I was in a hurry and said I'd take it but gulped when I went to sign my credit card receipt. Yikes, $35. My only excuse for not asking for a cheaper brand? I was in a hurry and well, I wanted to look good for the Ball.

OK, so I've been using the mascara for six weeks now. I've had some good laughs talking about the vibrating wand but feel foolish every time I use it. Frankly, I still use the pointed end of a large safety pin to separate out the lashes or remove clumps (just like my mom). My lashes may be *stimulated* but they still clump.

Last week I was getting ready for an event, so my mind was on wine when I pulled out my trusty mascara. As I unscrewed the cap and it started vibrating I got to thinking about wine glasses.

What if a wine glass was battery operated, played your favorite song and vibrated to music, of course releasing the bouquet of the wine to the beat of the song.

I walked into the kitchen and looked at my wine glasses – different sizes and shapes for different wines – and I got to musing about the perfect song for a wine glass (white, sparkling and red wines).

Here are my top picks.

White Wine Glass: "It's Five O' Clock Somewhere" (If you need an excuse)

Champagne Flute: "*Afternoon Delight*" (well just because)

Red Wine Glass: "*Amarillo by Morning*" (Reminiscent of my Most Embarrassing Wine Moment)

Water Tumbler: "*Slip Sliding Away*" (It must have been one of those days)

Don't worry; I'm not inventing another gimmicky wine product. But you've got to admit, you might think about your wine glass a little differently, especially while applying "vibrating" mascara.

TGIF, Kathy

WINE BITES

Well after reading all the examples of emails sent to our winery family, I picked out the Olympic Cellars team's favorite for you tonight. You deserve it. Drum roll . . . the 2014 Mt. Olympus Red is a delicious blend of Zinfandel, Syrah, Cabernet Sauvignon and *Carménère*. Swirling the wine in the glass, it pulls you in with its lovely garnet color and loganberry nose. The oak is well balanced against brilliant berry and subtle spice. Red berry and current flavors cascade into a long fruit forward finish.

I wasn't familiar with the *Carménère grape grown in Walla Walla region of Washington. The largest area planted with this variety is in Chile and is known for its brilliant crimson color, red fruit flavors along with an unmistakable pepper note.*

Chapter 22

Holidays – It's Not All About Sales

During any Holiday season, Valentines to New Year's Day, we are all bombarded with emails trying to sell us something. For me it was important for the winery not to be lumped in with all the *Buy Now and Save 60% or Doors Open at 4 a.m.* kind of emails. And face it, who would come to a winery at the hour of the day. It seemed each year the spirit of the holidays, those special days when families gather, were buried ever deeper under an increasing avalanche of retail sales advertising.

Yeah, I know that 20-30% of retail sales occur during the winter holidays, November and December. And yes, I did promote wine specials, but I also reached out with emails because the holidays were special for me, too. The holiday emails, from Valentines to New Years, included personal memories, a funny story and even a poem.

I firmly believe if you've built up a relationship with your customer list, this is the time you can really connect on a lasting level and know that the sales will come. I got more feedback in the form of personal emails to me from the holiday examples below then any of my other content emails. I related personal stories and customers would take the time to share something from their lives, too.

It's like when you write a heart-felt letter to someone special in your life, it just feels good inside.

I've been writing this book for a few months now, reliving fifteen years of memories. I think this chapter and the email stories is one of my favorites. I've found myself re-reading the emails multiple times and just smiling. Enjoy.

Romantic Get-Away *Do's* and *Don'ts*
As many of you know, my husband and I used to live in Dallas before moving to Washington to take over winery operations. Shortly after getting married we flew to Seattle to meet his family!

One afternoon Ralph announced that he was going to take me sightseeing in downtown Seattle. We were in the car looking at a map when his sister, Jan, came running toward the car with a large black garbage bag.

She handed it to Ralph who put it in the back seat mumbling that he needed to drop it off at blah-blah-blah. I didn't really listen and didn't ask questions. I was busy looking through "Seattle Magazine" picking out a restaurant for dinner.

Our first stop was supposed to be the Space Needle but as we turned a corner, Ralph pointed out the rounded towers of the Westin Hotel. He had mentioned long ago that he always wanted to stay at that hotel someday and see the view of the city by night, but that wasn't even registering in my mind.

All of sudden he pulled into the hotel lobby driveway, turned to me and said, "Surprise, we're staying here. I love you!"

Well, I'm in a *romantic glow* as the bellman opens my door and welcomes us to The Westin. Next question was to Ralph, "Sir, can I get your luggage?"

I watch Ralph's face turn a bright shade of red, and he stuttered with a reply about a *surprise* and handed the bellman The Black Plastic Garbage Bag!

Well, maybe I did feel a little embarrassed checking in like a Bag Lady, but I got over that really fast. Just think about the movie "Sleepless in Seattle." I know it's a chick flick, but I get the same warm and fuzzy feelings watching that movie as I do thinking about my "*Romantic Get-Away in a Bag.*"

So by all means ... plan your get-away soon and maybe pack a suitcase first, 'cause clothes get sort of wrinkled stuffed in a bag. Last piece of advice ... if it's a special *decade*-type birthday celebration don't give your sweetie a set of knives like Ralph gave me on my 40th ... keep it a bit more romantic.

Red Wine, Chocolate and "Your Heart" are all we need.

Valentine Day Cheers, Kathy

Mom-isms!

Ralph and I were heading out the door and as usual my husband picked up his wallet and put two quarters in his pocket.

I don't know why today I decided to ask.

"Honey, why do you always put two quarters in your pocket?" He just stood there for a minute with a puzzled look on his face, then replied "My mom always told me to in case I was in trouble and needed to call home."

Laughing, we realized we didn't even know how much it cost to use a pay phone and if we needed one could we find one in a hurry?

We both paused, each in our own world with a distant look and a smile on our face, thinking about our moms offering wisdom in the days before cellphones.

Of course, Ralph couldn't resist, "What did your mom always say?"

At first, all I could think about was my grandmother who told me always to put on clean underwear in case I was in an accident. Even as a kid I found that pretty silly.

Well that started it, back and forth, 'til we were almost crying with laughter.

Some of our favorite Mom-isms!

- Do you want me to call your dad?
- Turn off the lights, do you think we live in a barn?
- Don't make me stop this car!
- If everyone else jumped off a cliff, would you?
- Eat your vegetables, there are starving kids in China.
- Put that down, you don't know where it's been!
- Kathleen Ann, if I've told you once, I've told you a thousand times . . .

I'm going to finish this last Mom-ism.

Kathleen Ann, if I've told you once, I've told you a thousand times *how much I Love You.*

That's what I remember most.
Happy Mother's Day, Kathy

Father-isms and special memories...

Ralph and I are headed to Ellensburg today. His father passed away in February and all the family is gathering for a "Celebration of Life" on Father's Day – up in the hills at their Charlton hunting cabin where the memories are documented in a series of spiral notebooks going back for years. Whenever you visit the cabin you are supposed to write a note in the book and date it. This was a whole new side of his family that I began to love on my first trip.

When I visited the cabin after Ralph and I got married I wrote, "We will move to Washington in four years." It actually took six and we started a new chapter in our life.

As you might remember, I wrote a blog on Mother's Day titled Mom-isms. Thought it would be a real easy follow-up to do Father-isms for my weekly TGIF email. Not So!

In thinking back through my childhood and talking to Ralph we both said, "Our fathers didn't talk as much as our mothers."

I have a lot of favorite memories but few Father-isms quotes. Ralph and I agreed on two.

If we asked our Dad if we could do something, the usual response was,

"What Did Your Mother Say?"

And the Best of All, I can close my eyes and see my dad mouthing these words

Go Ask Your Mother!

Memories . . . there are many. Close your eyes with me and remember yours.

- Dancing with my father while standing on his feet.
- Dad coming home from work at 5:15 p.m. every day. Both my parents would have a "little toddy" before dinner and we would all gather (maybe that is why we have the Gathering Room at the winery).
- Dad cooking every Sunday after church. BIG PRODUCTION. As I grew older, all I wanted to do was eat fast and go out with my friends. Now I remember the BBQs, the Caesar salad made from scratch, and cleaning the shrimp together over the sink.

Father's Day - Enjoy, Remember, Share, Connect . . .

Cheers, Kathy

PS. Some other Father-isms I found on the Internet . . .

- You can't have a champagne budget with a beer income.
- As long as your feet are under my supper table, you'll follow my rules.
- If you drive up to our house, park in the driveway, and honk the horn, you better be delivering a pizza because you won't be taking my daughter out.

- Good girls don't call boys.
- If you expect to be treated like a lady, you should always act as one.
- (Notice a trend of very opinionated, protective and traditional fathers?)
- Do you think I'm a millionaire?
- Do you think money grows on trees?

And, we all know the last father-ism…

No matter what happens, you can always come home!

Ode to Summer (Solstice) on the North Olympic Peninsula
by Kathy Charlton

Oh beautiful warm summer
Please don't go!
You've been so consistent
That we're so resistant
To Fall's cold and the rain that could come in an instant

The seasons must change for all to be well
And we know we need the rain for rivers to swell

So let the rain be by night and sun be by day
So we can continue to frolic and play

So please Mother Nature grant us this wish
Your magnanimous gesture would make you a good looking "dish"

And, an extended and glorious Indian summer
Would ensure a grape harvest that would be quite a "hummer"

The Working Girl's Twelve Days of Christmas

The *Twelve Days of Christmas* is part of everyone's holiday tradition. I used to drive my dad crazy singing it over and over.

I heard it on the radio today and started humming "On the first day of Christmas my true love gave to me … a bottle of Working Girl Wine." You can now just imagine – the challenge was on. So this year I created a Working Girl version of this classic.

Now if you used the original poem as inspiration for gifts you might have trouble finding that partridge in a pear tree or eight geese a laying …

But in my version, it's simple. It's all about wine and I know us Working Girls can help.

Read on and enjoy. I've left a copy for my husband and circled some critical stanzas.

Cheers & Best Holiday Wishes, Kathy

"A Working Girl's Twelve Days of Christmas"

On the first day of Christmas
My true love gave to me
<u>A bottle of Merlot</u>
And told me to go play in the snow

On the second day of Christmas
My true love gave to me
<u>Two bottles of Cabernet</u>
And said have a great day

On the third day of Christmas
My true love gave to me
<u>Three bottles of Syrah</u>
And told me to have a massage at the spa

On the fourth day of Christmas
My true love gave to me
<u>Four bottles of Lemberger</u>
And fixed me my favorite Vege-burger

On the fifth day of Christmas
My true love gave to me
<u>Five bottles of Cranberry Jubilee</u>
And told me it was time to decorate the tree

On the sixth day of Christmas
My true love gave to me
<u>Six bottles of Chardonnay</u>
And took me for a ride in a sleigh

On the seventh day of Christmas
My true love gave to me
<u>Seven bottles of Petit Verdot</u>
And told me my nose was a-glow

On the eighth day of Christmas
My true love gave to me
<u>Eight bottles of Rosé</u>
And took me to the ballet

On the ninth day of Christmas
My true love gave to me
<u>Nine bottles of Riesling</u>
And asked me to stop all that singing

On the tenth day of Christmas
My true love gave to me
<u>Ten bottles of Go Girl Red</u>
And said I probably needed to go to bed

On the eleventh day of Christmas
My true love gave to me
<u>Eleven bottles of La Galopine</u>
And told me they were fit for a Queen

On the twelfth day of Christmas
My true love gave to me
<u>Twelve bottles of Sparkling Syrah</u>
And yelled Hurrah ... Merry Christmas!

WINE BITES

Tonight's wine is Cranberry Jubilee, a blend of our 80% chardonnay and 20% cranberry wine from Pasek Cellars in Mount Vernon, WA. This blend is thanks to my husband Ralph who read something, somewhere and gave me the idea back in 2005. You never know where the next idea for a product may come from and this one has stood the test of time.

We made this as a holiday wine released each year in November. It was sold out before Christmas. Now it has transcended the holidays and is sold year-round.

My holiday tasting notes: Cranberry Jubilee has the best qualities of both wines and very food friendly. Crisp, tart and just a tiny bit sweet the wine is perfect for your holiday table. Also, it is just decadent at day's end with turkey dinner leftovers (comfort food), a good movie and a warm fire.

Chapter 23

Your Pet Is Part of the Marketing Team

Hello. I'm Kathy, Harley's Mom.

Can't believe that's how I introduce myself. But I do. My little white Maltipoo goes with me everywhere. My only saving grace; I don't dress her up in frilly dog clothes or carry her around in a purse.

Empty nest syndrome . . . do you think I'm suffering from that? Well, counting backwards, the nest has been empty for twenty-five-plus years and Harley came into our lives in 2010. I'm even embarrassed to say I don't like leaving her much even to go out to dinner. One day I Googled service dog licenses. Did you know you could get one with a doctor's order if you have emotional problems? Thank goodness I'm too embarrassed to even think about that.

So how did Harley come into our lives? Just like learning to cook, I kept saying I wanted a dog. Neither happened. Just too dang busy.

Until one day, visiting my son in California. One of his friends had told him that their neighbor had a dog that needed a home and my son said the magic words, "Mom, you should take her home."

And, I did just that. Didn't give it another thought. All I had to do was look in those black seal-like eyes.

I bought a dog carrier so I could take her on the plane. I flew to Seattle with this very scared little dog, shaking uncontrollably the whole way. Then drove two hours home with her on my lap.

As I drove into Sequim I stopped at Petco and bought a dog crate. While in the store, I put Harley down and she crawled under the shelves and crouched in the far corner. Crawling on the floor myself I had to coax and finally pull her out from under the shelf. All I could think was poor baby, I just need to get her home.

You might ask why I bought a crate. I was told she had spent a lot of her day in a crate and figured that was her safe place and she'd had enough upheaval in the past eight hours.

There's one thing I forgot. Telling Ralph I was bringing home a dog. Whoops!

I pulled into the garage, let Harley out of the car and Ralph comes through the door to greet me.

Then this little white dog rounds the car and looks at Ralph.

He did a double take and blurted out, "So that's why you've been so nice on the phone." Then he went back in and plunked down at his desk, none too happy. I guess the decision to bring home a dog should have been a joint decision. Well, I'll ask for forgiveness later, I thought.

Later than evening, Ralph knelt by me as I'm loving on Harley trying to calm her down. "I'll be nice to her," he said softly and petted Harley. Ralph is such a softie, I think he fell in love immediately.

We didn't make it 24 hours and I realized something was wrong with Harley's ears. Off to the vet we went. She had a raging ear infection and I was told she was underweight for her size. Well this is where Ralph jumped in. He researched dog nutrition, raw food diets, supplements, you name it. Harley survived our newbie parenting skills and we all settled in as a family.

Back to the crate. Well by the third night Harley had claimed her spot on our bed. No more crate for her. Picture the letter "H." Then think about two people in a bed with a dog. No longer could Ralph and I snuggle without moving Harley. She wanted to be close.

As I mentioned, Harley goes everywhere with me. Meetings, winery, errands. When working in the tasting room, she would always keep me in sight. Early on she huddled behind the bar in the far corner where the back bar doesn't quite touch the wall. As she got a little braver she would sit behind the bar while I served wine.

When our guests could see her at my feet, of course our conversation would switch to pets. I would introduce Harley as the "Winery Dog in Training." Although she never got brave enough to greet guests with a wagging tail, everyone recognized she was super sensitive and would take extra care to greet her gently.

Harley inspired "Yappy Hour" at the winery supporting our local Olympic Peninsula Humane Society (OPHS). We advertised it as a *Barking Good Time* and you didn't need a *Pet Date* to attend. We had animal-themed music, dog bone-shaped cheese crackers that paired with wine, healthy dog kibble and of course, complimentary water bowls.

There was a $10 donation at the door. OPHS brought a few dogs and cats for adoption. I know one special little dog, Skye – a Cairn Terrier, who went to her forever home with my friend Hope who is the owner of Best Friend Nutrition. She worked with her suppliers and rounded up a car full of donated cat and dog food. It was a fun happy-yappy hour with our pets and winery friends that night. Harley made an appearance at the end of the evening. All those people and noise were still too much for our sensitive little girl.

Harley has brought a precious joy and laughter into our lives. This little dog needed Ralph and me and thanks to her we stopped the 24x7 workaholic schedule.

We had pets when I was raising my kids, and I know I took care of our Scottish terrier, Pepper. However, I don't remember this overwhelming love that cradles my heart for Harley. Maybe it is the empty nest syndrome and she makes me feel I'm needed again. The little fluffy dog has complete trust that we will care for her and she loves us unconditionally.

Whatever the psychological connection, I don't care. My husband and I now refer to the three of us as the Pack Three.

There's another side benefit to having a pet if you own a business. Our pets are the loves of our lives, sharing them with our customers is a must.

Our pets engage our emotions, they're our best friends, they evoke trust and there's a kinship ... that's what you want for your business and marketing. Do a little Googling on marketing and your pets. You'll find those cute, cuddly canines are springing up everywhere – most people find dogs endearing and just plain irresistible.

In my husband's self-defense business, we were doing a promotion on 25-year shelf-life, freeze-dried survival food. The subject line of the email was, "Is Your Dog Better Prepared Than You?" The email displayed a picture of my little 'Harley' surrounded by bags of freeze-dried raw dog food that I pulled out of the drawer. This email had the highest click thru rate and dollars sold of the whole campaign.

I wrote this shortly after Harley joined our family as a promotional email for our Northwest Wine and Cheese event.

Ode to Our Slug

Harley and I visit the outdoors one last time each night

Spring is upon us and our slug is back

Each night slowly crossing the driveway toward the flowerbed

Harley's favorite sniff of the night

I stand there with flashlight in hand looking at the slug

Listening to the waves on the spit, loud but still quiet

Stars some nights, rain others but our slug moves slowly ever diligent

Toward her goal and back before the morning light

Before Harley, I never heard the night or met our slug

Missing the beauty, breathing slower... through the eyes of our slug.

Savor the Flavors. Let your senses take over ... yes, it's hard to slow down to a slug's pace. But try. Block out the world. Test it. Just for the sheer pleasure. Close your eyes, take a bit of cheese, melt it in your mouth and sip some wine. Now isn't this better?

WINE BITES

There is a reference to tonight's wine but not what you might expect. As I was writing this chapter I remembered giving my husband a hard time about his survival food promotion. At the time, I got curious and Googled survival and prepping. One thing led to another and I must have had 2 glasses of wine because I ended up writing the *7 not so logical and somewhat absurd excuses* for NOT storing long shelf life food. Obviously, Ralph didn't see the humor in it or use it in his next email.

1. My neighbors have a one year supply! (And they're going to share?)
2. I'm moving in with my children/parents! (Really?)
3. The boat and the 4 wheelers are taking up all my storage space! (Priorities?)
4. If anything DOES happen, the government will be here within hours! (Insert laughter)
5. I can't afford scrap booking AND food storage. (Did I mention priorities?)
6. I'm waiting for the Papa John's dehydrated pizza! (Served with the works!)

And My All Time Favorite Excuse!

7. I'm waiting till they perfect a robust, fruit forward 'dehydrated' Merlot.
(OK, I have no response)

Have to admit that occasionally I Google dehydrated wines for any break thru in technology.

Chapter 24

Humor and Marketing

Laugh at Yourself – Let Customers Get to Know You.

We've all told a friend about an embarrassing moment and their retort was, "I did the same thing." You both laugh and tell your stories. There is a connection, you're both human and all is good. Same thing here with marketing. You take your business seriously but not yourself.

I didn't know there was a marketing strategy about using humor in content marketing until my husband mentioned I had done a good job telling a funny story about myself and linking it to the winery. I just wrote about my most embarrassing wine moment.

But Ralph's comment did get me to research the use of humor when communicating with customers, over the bar, in an email, or on Facebook. For us, fun was the operative word, wanting our customers to come back for more. And in fun there is humor. So, I kept it in mind when I wrote my no sale, optional email each month. Again, I noted ideas in my notebook or something that happened at the winery I might be able to use in an email later.

My brand voice and persona was light and humor worked. If my brand or my message was serious, such as an email I wrote for New Year's Eve, Alcohol – Know Your Limit, then I was very careful about how I wrote. Or if I was on rant and writing in an email, the worst possible outcome would be to offend someone.

In my Google research, I found out that laughter releases endorphins (which gave me a chuckle), relaxes consumers, and makes them feel a part of a community, while also significantly increasing the likelihood that content will be shared socially (so does wine). I understood that. And, there was a lot of emphasis on the importance of humor in marketing because it's fundamental to forming positive relationships. Understood that, too.

Then my Google research came across a lot of blogs on marketing to the different generations: Baby Boomers, Gen X, or Millennials. And, obviously we didn't ask the age of our customers at the bar while putting in their email when we rang up their wine. But I wish now I had a small survey form where I asked some key questions like, How Did You Hear About Olympic Cellars and age range boxes to check. I knew we related to women but I never thought about age differences. How do I design my emails to these three entirely different generations? I started a very unscientific survey of my customers that came to the winery, i.e., I tried to silently guess their age and tried out different stories about the winery as they went through their tastings.

What I found out is that when we shared a good laugh over the bar, regardless of age, there was a connection and the conversation became two-way. So that was my guide when writing emails. I didn't worry about age so much, just the connection through humor.

Below are a few of those emails. I was usually the brunt of the stories, which mostly related to wine in some way, but there is one just for us women.

Last but not least, we added an element of fun while taking pictures at the winery. While I knew that our guests took pictures of the barn and vineyard, we added a few other tongue-in-cheek photo ops. Ringing the old farm's cowboy black triangle wrought iron dinner bell on the patio was popular with the kids. Sitting in the Working Girl Chair that was placed every day in front of our door. Then, of course, posing with the Vineyard Angel that kept a watchful eye on the grape vines. But by far, the second incarnation of the Vineyard Angel became the most popular.

My Most Embarrassing Wine Moment

Every time I visit my daughter and grandchildren in Amarillo, Texas, I am reminded of one of my not-so-finer moments in the world of wine.

A few years ago my daughter and her family moved from the cotton fields of Lubbock to the cattle ranches and feed lots of Amarillo. During my first visit I was introduced to Amarillo's unique "pungent" bouquet when the wind blows out of the west. The first whiff and I knew I was in cattle country.

During that same visit I flew to Dallas for winery business. The colleague I was to meet had scored tickets to a wine tasting at a historic and elegant 5-star restaurant. The tasting was kept to an intimate twenty-five people, dress was *cocktail casual* and the wines had been handpicked by the head sommelier. I could hardly wait!

In tux attire, the sommelier greeted most of his guests by name. I was introduced as the owner of Olympic Cellars in Washington State. That started a bit of conversation among the guests who favored French wines and California Cabernets but who had heard good things about Washington wines.

Now normally, I taste and spit at these types of events. I'm a bit of a lightweight and know my limits, especially when it comes to keeping my "mouth" in check.

Ahhh, but these wines were heaven in a bottle. As each wine was poured, my will power lessoned and I began to savor each velvety sip. The evening's *pièce de résistance* was a famous, old French Bordeaux (even I recognized the name). As this wine was poured, the atmosphere of the room changed. Hushed voices that were almost reverent replaced the boisterous conversations of before.

Anticipating nirvana, I swirled the wine and gently lowered my nose to the glass. Inhaling deeply, my senses suddenly were sent careening and I spoke before my brain engaged; "This wine smells like AMARILLO," I said none too quietly.

The room got quiet – real quiet – as the sommelier slowly walked to our table and stood right in front of me. "Madame, that is nose of a fine old Bordeaux with just a hint of the barnyard," he said with stern dignity, putting me in my place.

If only I had stopped there.

"Well frankly I think the barnyard has a little too much horse manure!" I retorted.

Whoops! I really stepped in "it" this time. Should have spit and kept my mouth shut.

But really, the wine by any other name or price tag WOULD have been poured down the drain.

But what do I know? Almost all the guests ranked the wine #1.

Pinot Envy

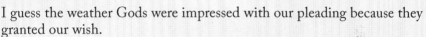

As you read in my last email, we celebrated National Flip Flop Day Saturday and ushered in the 1st day of summer.

I guess the weather Gods were impressed with our pleading because they granted our wish.

Since the email went out Thursday evening we've had nothing but glorious sunshine and warm weather. We actually crossed 70 degrees. It was an Olympic Peninsula heat wave!

At the winery, the doors kept opening to the sound of flip-flop, flipity-flop, flop-flop as our guests made their way to the bar. Remember, complimentary wine tasting was in order if you dressed appropriately.

The winery was festive with everyone showing off their feet! Molly, our tasting room goddess, really got into it and started saying goodbye with a new twist. "Thanks for flopping in," she sang out as she poured another round.

At the end of the day, Molly was getting a bit slap-happy (or by then, flap happy). Anyhow, she was serving a group of five – a mother and her four daughters. They were tasting through our wines to pick the ones they would serve in honor of their mother's 80th birthday and the mother's 60th wedding anniversary!

Molly was serving them our Dungeness Red Lemberger. Now, understand, not many have heard of this grape and usually say something like, "Is that like the cheese?" No, we say, "The grape is spelled differently and smells a whole lot better." Lately we've even taken to describing the wine as similar to Pinot Noir.

Well, Molly was on a roll, got to laughing and finally just spit out, "The wine, well, it sort of has *Pinot Envy.*"

Well of course, everyone at the bar collapsed in hysterics, Molly turned red to her hairline and the discussion quickly turned to the movie Sideways.

Seriously though, the name may stink for a grape but it's all about what's in the bottle.

Lemberger is part of Washington's heritage and should not be overlooked. These wines truly are very similar to Pinot in style, with a medium body and lots of bright fruit and soft tannins. It's a very food-friendly wine and pairs beautifully with salmon, halibut and other food right off the grill.

Oh yeah. Back to the weather. By Sunday we're headed back down to 60 degrees.

Heck, if we can skydive into the Winery, maybe next year I'll truck in a few loads of sand and we'll have a beach volleyball tournament and usher in Summer with a bang. Stay tuned.

Savor the moment, Cherish the Memories ... Kathy

My Wine Journey – Wine – Doing It Your Way

I've told the story before about how I came about owning a winery but never talked much about my wine experience or knowledge prior to getting into the business.

So, I guess you can call this, "true confession time."

Truth be known, when I started drinking wine in the 70's, I liked my reds served cold. I was even known to use an ice cube or two to get the wine to the *proper* temperature.

As I think about it now, the wait staff at the restaurants back then never even flinched or rolled their eyes when I asked for a 'cold' Merlot (or I didn't notice). I was never made to feel dumb about wine.

The only problem was, by the time they got my wine cold, it usually ended up being served with my dessert!

Then I went through a phase where I dipped bread into my red wine throughout the meal (you could always tell where I sat at the table – drips and crumbs).

Not sure how that phase came about (maybe I watched too many Italian movies) but thank goodness I got over it fairly fast.

On to REAL Wines . . .

Guess you could say my first real *wine breakthrough* came in the late 80's when I started buying 750 ml bottles instead of 1.5 liter 'jug' bottles.

I was living in Dallas back then. I remember I'd had a particularly tough day at work and decided to stop by the liquor store for some wine. There was a new display of wine *stuff* that featured a t-shirt with the all too familiar saying, "Life Is Too Short to Buy Cheap Wine."

Whatever, I ended up switching aisles – from jug wines to racks of wine with lots of *shelf talkers* (you know those 2x3 cards that describe why you should pick that wine).

I was soon overwhelmed with wine descriptions that were way over my head and in some cases sounded almost like passages from a romance novel (voluptuous, full mouth feel, lay this one down for a few years). Yeah, right!

But the shelf talkers worked, because it seemed I only bought wines with flapping tags and catchy phrases.

Business dinners, travel and a few more dollars added to my wine budget helped expand my wine education further.

At this point in my journey, I was not overly curious or particularly knowledgeable. I found a wine I liked and basically stuck to it unless something was on sale and I got adventurous.

This is about when I knew enough to 'think' I knew something about wine. Got snobbish about corks vs. screw caps, swirled and sniffed before I tasted and started spouting *wine speak* (those shelf talkers gave me enough information to talk intelligently – for about 10 seconds).

To this day I can still remember the first Napa Valley Cabernet Sauvignon I ever tasted. I was at a business dinner and our host ordered Silver Oak Cellars Cabernet. I think this is when I first really "tasted a wine," concentrating on the flavors, the aroma, the experience.

Off to Wine Country . . .

I didn't stop there. Shortly, I was off to my first wine tasting vacation in Napa. I came home with a very expensive case of – you guessed it – Silver Oak Cellars Cabernet.

I proudly displayed that wine in my new wine rack, both placed in my Dallas kitchen just under the west wall window (aka, the hottest spot in the house).

It wasn't long before I noticed wine seeping around the metal capsule that covers the cork and mouth of the bottles. Of course, I had cooked the wine and most of it went bad; an expensive way to learn about the proper storage of wine.

Years passed and I continued tasting and enjoying wines from around the world. It was during this time, while still at Texas Instruments, that my husband and I bought Olympic Cellars in 1999.

I was traveling extensively with TI then and remember coming back from India once. I dragged myself onto the plane, tired and not looking forward to the 36-hour trip. All I wanted was a good glass of wine. I was in business class (none of those little bottles for me) and kept rejecting the wines the flight attendant served. Unfortunately, I was seated by my boss who by now was embarrassed and told me to "just pick one!"

Had I become a wine snob?

Nope, I just knew the style of wine I liked – BB&B (Big, Bold and Beautiful)!

Obviously, my wine journey hadn't prepared me for running a winery.

But it did mold my thinking and later my decisions on the wines we would eventually make here at Olympic Cellars.

My wine journey had been just that, a journey.

I could have stopped it at, "Merlot over ice," and that would have been okay because that was the style of wine I enjoyed.

Remember, it's all about "Wine – Doing It YOUR Way!"

This Working Girl Can Buy More Shoes

A few years ago I came up with a new resolution, which was pretty radical: Nothing new can come into my home until something leaves via re-gifting, donation, or passing down to my kids. This I communicated to my husband who was quite impressed. My rationalization: this would stop my impulse buys.

Now, of course, this resolution did NOT involve the major three purchases in my life: clothes, jewelry and shoes. I've listed these in alphabetical order because for me priority depends on the mood of the day that sends me on the search for instant gratification.

Since clothes were not part of my resolution, I needed a solution for limited closet space. About a year ago I donated clothes to an auction to make more room and then totally regretted the decision. While I hadn't worn them in years I didn't realize I had 'attachment syndrome.' Now, I've gone as far as to buy those suck-um-up bags to store some favorites and open up a bit of space in my closet.

My rationalization for "plastic storage" was my new fashionista sense of style: Closet vintage with a hippie, hobo-lux look. Bottom line – I just can't seem to part with clothes or shoes that have special memories or cost too much or I might wear someday and for sure the style will be in fashion again!

I'm getting to the shoe part.

We all know the fashion industry has played with our heads on the whole sizing game for years. Yes, I can wear a smaller size then I did in high school but everyone knows the clothes are now made bigger.

I thought shoes on the other hand, were just the opposite. I had to buy larger sizes because the cost of making shoes had gone up so the same size shoe just kept getting smaller. This statement doesn't even make sense.

Obviously, I had no real logic for my rationalization but it worked in my head until I uncovered this really cute pair of sandals in my closet. They had the perfect heel height for a pair of jeans that had shrunk in length.

So depressing, I couldn't even slip all five toes into the sandal. Then I decided maybe my feet were sweaty, so I put some knee-high hose on. That didn't work. Then I thought, ahhh, I ate Mexican food last night and my feet are swollen from all that salt. Wrong. The next day, I still couldn't get my dang feet in those sandals.

I lamented my fate during another Working Girl meeting. I blurted out this whole story as if it was the major crisis of the day. Molly just looked at me, as only Molly can do, and said point blank, "Kathy, your feet spread with age."

Feet, too! Is nothing sacred on my body? Back to rationalization. I have a few better excuses. I'm blaming it on the winery and moving to the

Northwest. My feet just got used to work shoes, cement and socks with sandals – that's why I have feet-spread, it's not from age. I haven't had the opportunity or the time to train my feet back into cute shoes that are in my closet!

So what does a girl gotta do? I hauled out all my size 8 shoes and gave them away.

I now have a goal. I have shoe holes to fill in my closet and I can do it without a guilty conscience. It's also my birthday month.

I really do need to stop rationalizing. Shop, enjoy, and finish the day with a glass of Go Girl Red!

Cheers and TGIF, Kathy

Wine Bites

One of my favorite Chardonnays is from California. I was introduced to it at a business dinner in my corporate days. The wine choices made by our host were excellent and expensive. Rombauer Vineyards Chardonnay was the white wine and the Silver Oaks Cabernet I mentioned above was the red. No embarrassing wine moments that night but I did fall in love with the Rombauer.

So almost at the end of his marketing section I'm starting to celebrate with a 2015 Rombauer Vineyards Carneros Chardonnay. Described as perfection when the four core components are done right and all in balance: ripe fruit, creamy mid-pallet, vanilla oak and butter/acidity. No one component stands out. A seamless flow across the pallet.

Tonight, we deserve it. Cheers.

Chapter 25

Show the Love for Your Customers

Owning a winery and having fun events where people drink comes with a deep personal responsibility.

Yes, as an establishment that serves alcoholic beverages we can be held liable for selling or serving alcohol to individuals who later after leaving the winery caused injuries or death as a result of intoxication.

And, we took this very seriously to the point of being obsessive sometimes, depending on the event. During an event or concert, I rarely sat down. I constantly walked the crowd, greeting everyone, stopping to chat and watching for signs of over drinking. If I expected it, then I would get straight to the point and ask who was driving. Rarely did the conversation get contentious because they knew we cared.

During our summer concert series, we were staffed with volunteers from the non-profit organization we supported that night. All the volunteers had to come early for training, which included how to recognize someone who had too much to drink. What to watch for besides the obvious signs of intoxication; were customers buying by the bottle or by the glass? If by the bottle we checked out if it was for a table of folks, a couple or just one guest. Did they buy two or more bottles?

When the band was playing, we were also dancing, moving around through the crowd. And, if I suspected (that's all it took) that someone had too much to drink we took away their car keys.

We always closed the bar early and gave our *You Know We Love You* speech. We'd stop the band (they knew beforehand that I would pop up on the stage) and remind everyone that Olympic Cellars has the distinct honor to be located directly across Highway 101 (4 lanes) from the Highway Patrol. This always got chuckles from the crowd. Then I went through the spiel about any open bottles of wines that would be taken home had to be put in the trunk; if anyone needed a ride we would call a taxi; and that when leaving the winery one can only turn right; and that there was a turnaround about 100 yards down the road. Then we got the band playing again with as many encores as I could plead for so all would dance for 30-45 minutes more before getting in their cars.

The following email went out each holiday season prior to New Year's Eve because I felt it was my responsibility to educate and not just repeat an overused phrase such as Don't Drink and Drive. The info was sobering (no pun intended) and a lot of customers replied that they really appreciated this email and have shared it.

Because We Care...

I was listening to the radio while working today and, addition to great Christmas music, there were regular public service announcements... Drink Responsibly, Don't Drink and Drive, Alcohol – Know your Limit

The last slogan, Alcohol – Know Your Limit, had me Googling...

So here are some basic facts...

- Your body processes alcohol at a constant rate of .5 oz. per hour, regardless of how many ounces you consume
- Blood Alcohol Level (BAL) is the amount of alcohol present in your blood as you drink
- In all 50 states, the legal limit for drunk driving is a BAL level of .08 or higher
- Eating protein and fatty foods supposedly can slow down alcohol absorption but I couldn't find any detailed, statistical supporting facts
- A 120-pound woman can reach a .08 BAC level after only two drinks and a 180-pound man can be at .08 after only four drinks

What got my attention! One drink is defined as having one-half ounce of pure ethyl alcohol; each of the following is considered "one drink."

- 10 oz. to 12 oz. of beer at 4% to 5% alcohol, or
- 8 oz. to 12 oz. of wine cooler at 4% to 6% alcohol, or
- 4 oz. to 5 oz. of table wine at 9% to 12% alcohol, or
- 2.5 oz. of fortified wine at 20% alcohol, or
- 1.25 oz. of 80 proof distilled spirits at 40% alcohol

As I type this blog, I'm drinking one of my favorite beers – a 12-ounce stout at 9% alcohol. (This would be two drinks)

Wines today, especially reds, weigh in on the average of 13-14% alcohol, and our average glass pour is not 4-5 ounces.

One martini is equal to two drinks, one margarita equal to 1.5 drinks

The message is still Drink Responsibly, Don't Drink and Drive, Alcohol – Know your Limit

<u>Know Your Limit</u>, though, has a much broader message. It's way more than "don't drink and drive." We all know that when we drink, we're a bit *looser*.

So, my female friends . . . take heed of this message.

Because we care,

The Working Girls of Olympic Cellars

Writing for me was like talking through the emotions with a good friend. And, as the years went by I wrote more personally from Kathy Charlton to my customer list, not just the Working Girl. I don't know why I wrote more during the holidays, but it was a time emotions were high for various reasons. And, if I was feeling it, so were the ladies on my list.

My daughter would call all stressed out because there was just too much to do. Sound familiar. Folks that came to the winery were stressed; they had no time to chat, they had to keep going. They bought wine in a hurry, maybe with a few quick questions on pairing with food and then out the door.

But when the house is quiet and we're still up, then like me, your thoughts may wander to your heart where memories of loved ones no longer with you are cherished.

This email was written during one of those alone times, late at night.

Just Reach Out...

I went to a December Holiday Art Show in Port Angeles featuring one of my favorite artists, Melissa Klein. I've been drawn to her work because of her eccentric humor at poking fun at social convention.

The first painting I purchased was the "Curse of the Good Girl" that inspired one of my favorite email stories. Some days when my genetically inbred "Guilt-O-Meter" gets into the red zone, I think of the picture's chant . . . There's no place like home, there's no place like work and try to rid myself of the curse!

This art show, though, was different.

As usual I started to circle the room but was stopped short by one painting that immediately drew me in. I wasn't sure why, but all I could do was focus on the girl straining forward with one arm outstretched.

The painting was multi-media and there was a gossamer fabric overlaying part of the painting lightly covering the picture underneath.

Finally, I dragged my eyes away and read the card by the painting.

"Passing Through" by Melissa Klein

Melissa then walked over and stood by me. We didn't say anything for a few minutes, both lost in our thoughts. Then she quietly told me the story.

"My cousin wrote to me when I lost my friend who died very young. She said, *'The veil between life and death is very thin. Find comfort in the realization that you are not so far from those who have departed.'*"

Melissa continued quietly, "I've always felt strongly that this was a very personal piece. That it was a healing process to create and one that I almost wouldn't show. When I was preparing for my art show, here was this painting staring at me and I knew my friend would want me to show it . . . even to the point of kicking my butt to do it."

<u>So why that night and why that show?</u>

I told my husband at the last minute, I'm going. Don't know why the strong pull. But, I put a hat on my head and was out the door.

I bought the painting and Melissa emailed me to say, "I'm glad that someone I know and trust will be her new caretaker, and that the healing passes on to you."

As I walk around my house decorated for the holidays, there are so many memories of children growing up, of parents who have passed. My family gatherings also have dwindled over time because we live so far apart. And, this year dear friends have lost so much it is hard to comprehend.

This is the season when all of our feelings and emotions seem to tumble down upon us . . . sometimes more like a babbling brook with laughter floating ever so gently, then an unexpected waterfall hits that threatens to pull us under.

I'm looking at the painting and these words keep rumbling in my heart.

Just reach out, Reach Through . . . you and yours will be united within.

Thank you, Melissa, for entrusting me with such a precious gift.

WINE BITES

You might wonder from all the Chardonnays I've written about, which one is my favorite. It's hard to pick a favorite wine since we often choose a wine for different reasons. Moods, food pairing, style, celebrations, price, research (I like this excuse) or just because. No two vintages are the same. And what I might like, you might not. And that is sooo OK.

If I have to choose other than an Olympic Cellars wine, I will confess that my Go-To Chardonnay (I've tried multiple vintages) while writing the marketing section is The Expedition Chardonnay, 2015, from Canoe Ridge Vineyard and Winery. Walla Walla, Washington.

It never disappoints, I know what to expect, the price is right and I can find it in my small town. But then you haven't tried Olympic Cellars. It was just bottled in May and will be released in a couple of months. Finally!

Part Three
The Rest of the Story

Chapter 26

Meanwhile Life Happens

You could say this is the "rest of the story."

Except it's really not because thankfully it's not an obituary.

(Jeez what a sobering thought.)

But there were some unique events sprinkled throughout the day-to-day life of running my business that helped set, and sometimes dramatically alter, the course.

None fit nicely elsewhere in the book, yet it would leave some big gaps in this Working Girl's story.

Like my battle with the US Olympic Committee, becoming a mother again at age 60, and surviving the perfect storm.

I had mentioned earlier that I felt I grew up while working at Texas Instruments. Now, these last 15 years at the winery I grew up inside, no longer the same person.

Still driven, yes. But, now what I did impacted other's lives; my team, our donor organizations, my volunteer work (if I flaked out someone else was left holding the bag) and I got a sense that what I wrote mattered.

Maybe it was that sense of community I never felt part of before and in a way now felt responsible.

While there are three Working Girls and I was the character for the white wine, I fell in love with Rosie's spirit from WWII.

We're all familiar with the iconic Rosie the Riveter Poster, We Can Do It, but there was another slogan not so well known - The More Women at Work the Sooner We Win.

For now, I'll drink her wine…. And consider the possibilities.

Enjoy the rest of my story.

CHAPTER 27

Sometimes You Just Have to Take a Stand

It's all about doing what you think is right. Wherever that might be - your job, your business, your community. Taking the lead, harnessing your leadership skills is subjective, influenced by your personal feelings, challenges, or opinions.

Speak out because you know if you don't you're not being true to yourself. It just nags at you until you finally take action, step forward. There were times I felt that way. As a member of my community it was my responsibility to speak my mind even when it didn't directly concern my business. Perhaps you can see yourself in my shoes.

Taking a stand on any subject, business or social, that is important to you is a simple act but probably the most powerful thing a person can do to really effect change. It's not easy because you could be criticized, even ridiculed and both come with a level of fear. Thick skin becomes a priority. And, I hate to say this but you find out who your friends really are.

There's another consideration; do you stand <u>against</u> something or do you stand <u>for</u> something? Standing for something can be more effective in fixing it. Positive, moving forward, impacting change beats negative dialogue any day. My experience is that folks who complain about everything don't come up with ideas and suggestions to fix whatever. They just want to bitch. I believe in staying positive.

We've already discussed getting involved in your community and organizations that ignite your passions. Don't hesitate to speak out if you want to effect change and have something to say regarding issues in your community, events impacting your business or even politics. One piece of advice: write it, let it sit for a day, read it again, edit if needed and then get feedback from individuals that you respect. Once it's out there, you can't take it back. I've written letters to the editor, emailed my list, submitted articles for our local newspaper, and spoke at City Council meetings.

If your message is important to you, don't let your medium hold you down. Emails or blogs can't always do the job. Take it upon yourself to talk to the people that need to hear your message in a way that they can actually use it. Do your research, provide detailed data and get in front of the individuals who can help.

While I was writing this chapter and pulling emails I had written as examples, I realized that the Facebook Group, Revitalize Port Angeles, was the perfect example of Taking a Stand. It was started by Leslie Robertson, a mother of two, who left Port Angeles for Los Angeles in 1985 and moved back in 2007. On October 6, 2014, Leslie wrote a post on her personal FB page. This was the last sentence. *Why does our little town look so very different from every other picturesque seaside town I've ever been to? What are we missing?* Three days later about twenty-five individuals met at the library and the rest is history. This was the beginning of a grass-roots community involvement movement spawning a number of groups that got their genesis through the Revitalize page. Groups like PA Can, Port Angeles Rocks, Healthy Eats for Kids, the Port Angeles Food Co-Op and many others all started with a conversation on Revitalize. Those who were interested had the confidence to know that it would be possible to form a community group that could actually make a difference.

Here are a few of my examples. Our community was promoting a Buy Local Campaign that today is important to all communities with local businesses up against chain stores and, of course, Amazon. This is an article I wrote for the local newspaper.

. . . I Long for Yesterday
To Remain Local, Is To Be Local

Driving home from the winery the other day I found myself listening to a very familiar song, "Yesterday" by the Beatles. We've all heard this tune a thousand times before but a phrase kept ringing in my ears and had me longing for yesterday.

That afternoon I had talked with a colleague in Seattle who owns a very successful wine brand (and also helped me market our Working Girl Wines). She was on a real rant, upset that another opportunity to get market exposure had been canceled. She kept saying, "It's harder and harder any more to be the small guy." In this case, our distributor had cancelled a holiday trade show, the one event where we're on equal footing with the *big boys* in the wine business.

Still thinking about our conversation, when I got home I looked up the lyrics to the song. That's when another phrase caught my attention, the one about believing in yesterday.

How many times have we thought life was better or simpler when we were young? We all long to recapture that time when life seemed less demanding, slower, and not so chaotic.

Like me, maybe you moved from urban sprawl to this gorgeous Olympic Peninsula, captured by a rural landscape, unmatched scenery, fresh food, temperate climate and open land to build a home without postage size yards.

Or perhaps you grew up here, even part of multi-generations. For you the loss of farmland, rising home prices and the influx of box chain stores may have saddened you, and possibly changed your way of life.

We all know that change and growth are inevitable. We can't live in the past. Even tucked away here, we're all part of a global economy whether we like it or not. It's a question of the right balance between yesterday, today, and tomorrow.

Somehow we must find that proverbial common thread that ties us all together, that special something that caused us to stay or gravitate here in the first place.

Me? Oh, I'm guilty too. After moving here six years ago I often find myself feeling, "Now that I live here, don't let it change!"

But I straddle a line. See, I own a small business. And for it to not only survive, but also thrive, there needs to be a robust Peninsula economy with tourists flocking to our shores.

And I need an equal chance to serve you as a customer.

That's why lots of questions keep running through my head. Can a small business really be successful next to a chain store? Can a small community keep its unique persona without its family-run businesses, boutiques, galleries and restaurants? Can we keep our quality of life and still grow? Can we be small yet think big? Do we even have enough small businesses left to attract tourists ... *Longing for Yesterday?*

I think we all believe in <u>Yesterday.</u>

We want small town life but big city conveniences. *And please don't put me in a box, addicted to consumption, with invasive marketing, that invents wants I don't need* (Whew! I needed to get that off my chest).

Here's the thing: the reality and success of chain stores is 'homogeny' and 'economies of scale.' Corporations buy in large scale for huge stores. The stores are told where and how to display the same products. *Robotic Merchandising* has us buying the same products, wearing the same clothes, eating the same food. There's no individualism or decision making required!

But... the price is often right. And that's where our struggles usually begin... and where, I think, they need to end.

See, if we want our community to *remain local*, then I think there is a shared responsibility to *be local*.

As small business owners we have a responsibility to you, our customer. Sure, it's harder to be the small guy but we can't use that as a crutch. We know we have to earn your loyalty. We have to provide a quality product, convenience, and customer service: no different from chain stores.

But when you enter a small, local business it's different. It should be different. Call it 'personal,' if you will, as individual as each of us who own our businesses. We live the American Dream (but I'll tell you... it's way harder than any corporate job I've ever held). When we have a *good day* there's no higher high. When we're asked to contribute to the many worthy causes, it's hard for us to say no. Because it IS personal. It's our community.

Still, it's a fact. We can rarely compete on price. But what we can do is provide a *local* experience that's personal, heartfelt, and appreciated. It's the *local spirit* you carry home with you in your bag. It's what gives you reason to smile and know you ARE an individual and important to us.

Now, here's how I see it: if you don't find that experience at a local business, then you have every right and obligation to buy from the big guys next door. We can't expect handouts just because we're small and local.

But when you do find it, then, even if it costs a bit more, I think you must consider BUYING LOCAL.

BUY LOCAL is a decision to support a local economy, to support this spectacular place you chose to make your home.

If all of us, both individuals and businesses, don't choose to spend a portion of our hard-earned dollars BUYING LOCAL when our trust has been earned then _Yesterday_ will fade like the setting sun into an all-too-familiar distant memory.

Tourists visit our community every day and especially during the summer months. We want them to have a great experience and go home and tell their friends and family. What happened in downtown Sequim one afternoon got me so mad that I went straight home and wrote this letter to the editor. It was published and residents knew who I was. Letters to the editor are popular with those who read the paper regularly. I just hope the man that I wrote about it saw this.

Road Rage... or Just Extreme BAD Manners?

Sequim, WA
Tuesday, July 3, 1:30 p.m.
(Sent to the Sequim Gazette)

Standing on the corner of Sequim Ave and Washington, I found myself enjoying the sunshine, having forgotten to hit the button to trigger a light change that would allow me to cross the street. The man directing traffic called out with a friendly reminder to hit the button. Three ladies came up behind me. Their conversation clearly indicated they were visiting our community.

Light turned green and cars started moving south on Sequim Avenue. A non-descript white car goes through the intersection with driver window down. The driver yells out his window at the man directing traffic, "You've really f ... d it up this time," while displaying corresponding hand gestures.

Speechless for a second and equally embarrassed given the comments of the tourists behind me, I hear the "traffic man" say, "Third time this week," then shrug his shoulders. And, it was only Tuesday, midday.

OK, we know what is going on in downtown Sequim. The crosswalks are being repainted, I think for the third time. Traffic is being rerouted and there are longer than usual delays.

We may not be thrilled with the crosswalks but let's get really honest. We had a choice. Get involved. Try to understand the issues. Make input into the decision process.

It is much easier, though, to complain and throw out *educated* opinions over coffee, casual conversations, and encounters on the street.

The real folks out there *doing* the job did not make the decision. They are just doing their job. Yet they're treated with disdain.

Unidentified man in white car: Your conduct was inexcusable and you brought shame to our community.

I'm a local small business owner. Communities of small business owners are challenged daily to survive and thrive in our global economy. It takes a lot of work, partnerships, community involvement and, most of all, *customers*. All expect our businesses to provide excellent service.

What we forget is each of us, every day, represent our community. Our actions speak volumes to visitors.

Do we convey warm hospitality and a great place to live or just another impatient, over-stressed, don't-care, not-my-problem society?

Respectively,
Kathy Charlton
Olympic Cellars Winery

I guess by now you've noticed I can't keep my mouth shut when I have something to say. I've learned to think about it first, write it and then re-read it before submitting an article to the paper, sending an email, posting to Facebook and linking to my Blog.

When the economy collapsed in 2008 our income dropped 25%. Folks weren't traveling or spending money. Everyone was impacted in one way or another. Some businesses went under.

I was really ranting at home and was on a tirade about the economy, Congress and used the phrase "they need Brass Balls" frequently. My husband, unbeknownst to me, ordered two brass balls, which were really heavy and solid brass. When he unpacked the box and put them in my hand he said, "Kathy, enough talk. Do something. Go write an email." The balls still sit in my office as a symbol – don't just complain, get involved.

I took Ralph's advice and wrote an email and sent it to my entire list. Did this email start conversations? Yes. Did it effect change? Not directly, but there definitely was a movement afoot. There was a realization that change starts with each of us. Acting locally but thinking globally was more than a belief or the latest slogan, it was a rule for action that got a lot of notice.

This email was a little too much for a winery email list that didn't expect or want my political rants. Had I known I would get the push back, negative emails from customers and unsubscribes that followed, I think I would have still sent it out.

Congress Needs BRASS BALLS!

As a citizen and now a small business owner I'm outraged at the gross lack of leadership in our members of Congress.

Stories are prolific on the Internet but two statements jumped out as demonstrating again **POLITICS AT IT'S MOST SELFISH BEST** regarding the financial bailout plan.

"Not enough members were willing to take the political risk just five weeks before an election."

"Congress has been trying to adjourn so that its members can go out and campaign."

With a United States and Global financial meltdown potentially eminent, how could any elected official worry about his/her campaign or their states' constituents? May sound harsh, but what good is shortsighted pork belly politics if the entire country is driven into a depression.

We need LEADERS who can think, ask questions and make the hard decisions under pressure in the BEST INTEREST OF THE UNITED STATES!

Senators and Congress ... delete the party initial and the state you represent from behind your name and replace it with ... *J. A. Congressman*, United States Leader

And, if you need a pair of **Brass Balls** to help, I'm sure there are a number of citizens who would order a pair delivered straight to your office. Maybe you need a New Symbol of Leadership, Responsibility and Action.

Kathy Charlton
Private Citizen and Business Owner

CHAPTER 28

Fight for What is Right

As a small business owner, you don't always know when and how you're going to get hit from left field. This one certainly took me by surprise.

On September 11, 2007, Olympic Cellars received a cease and desist letter from the United States Olympic Committee (USOC) for being in violation of the Ted Stevens Act of 1998, in which Congress gave the USOC exclusive commercial control of the word *Olympic*.

At first when I saw the return address I flippantly said, "Maybe the Olympic Committee is soliciting sponsors for the upcoming games." Ha, I knew you had to pay big bucks to be a sponsor, but it was fun to think about for the 30 seconds it took me to open the envelope and read the jaw-dropping letter. I couldn't keep my mouth shut and I started ranting a bit too loud. Nancy Yeatman, working the tasting room part-time, came back to the office to shush me as we had customers.

Turns out, since the 2010 Winter Olympics were in Vancouver, B.C., the USOC was checking out all the businesses with "Olympic" in their name in our neck of the woods. The federal law grants an exception to businesses here on the Olympic Peninsula. They can use the O-word when marketing themselves – but only in Washington west of the Cascade Mountains. This comprises basically about a fourth of the state, but includes Seattle and surrounding cities. And since Olympic Cellars had a website (OlympicCellars.com), and since Working Girl wines were shipped across the U.S along with Internet sales, the winery sold and marketed itself far beyond Western Washington.

In the original letter the USOC suggested we might consider changing our name to *Olympia* Winery. Obviously, they had not checked out a map. Olympia is over 2 hours *south* of the winery and the capital of Washington State. Just a little confusing for our customers, to say the least. In a later USOC conciliatory response they offered that the winery could continue to sell wine to current customers regardless of where they lived, but if a *new* customer wanted to buy wine outside of Western Washington after 12/31/2007 we would have to turn the order down. Obviously, we didn't agree on either point but continued the discussion.

Regarding our URL, what the USOC failed to take into account is Olympic Cellars was already operating under an agreement with the USOC and that our presence on the Internet at the Olympic Cellars

URL address had been approved by USOC's outside trademark counsel, Jim Bikoff. This approval was granted in 1999 in writing after Mr. Bikoff determined that "Olympic Cellars" and "Olympic Cellars Winery," used then the same way we use it now, would not be likely to cause confusion or falsely suggest a connection with the USOC or the Olympic Games. The reach and impact of the Internet was well known at the time of approval.

But this fact didn't seem to change anything, and we went into serious and sometimes heated negotiations. Word got around town and our local newspaper, Peninsula Daily News (PDN), asked if they could do an article. At first I said no but then as I got really frustrated with negotiations going nowhere. Thought maybe a little media support might help. What I didn't realize was how much negative sentiment surrounded the USOC. The PDN's article went somewhat viral: **"U.S. Olympic Committee pops its cork over a certain peninsula's vintner and the 'O' word."**

We also received hundreds of emails from our customers and the article was picked up by bloggers, other media and other 'Olympic' businesses sharing their stories. We even got a political cartoon published in "WashingtonCEO" by Milt Priggee. (I purchased the original and today it sits in my office.)

Some bloggers didn't hold any punches, one even calling the USOC

lawyer I was dealing with a "douchebag." Well, you can only imagine the phone call I received from the lawyer the next day.

After the story published, we sent an email to Olympic Cellars customers updating them on the situation and letting them know we wouldn't give up the fight and wouldn't give up our name. Many asked about writing our Congressman and/or Senators or signing a petition. One had to find some humor in this ordeal and I had a devilish thought that I shared via an email I titled, "What if you sent your letter in an empty Olympic Cellars wine bottle?"

One USOC stipulation we complied with during the negotiation – we added disclaimers to all of our website pages stating that we had no connection or affiliation to the U.S. Olympic Committee, the U.S. Olympic Team or Olympic Movement. In addition, we also added a one-step "click thru" capability at the top of our home page to a geographic map providing directions and identifying our location.

As I said, we got hundreds of emails, but this one changed the tide in our favor.

"I visited your winery in March of last year and thought it was really wonderful, so this is especially disturbing to me. I have a friend who's a trademark lawyer and he's offered to help. Do you have a direct email address I could pass on to him so he can contact you; I'll make the introduction via email."

An iconic Seattle company provided Olympic Cellars with pro bono legal support. I would write a response to the latest epistle from the USOC and the lawyer would edit in legalese ... back and forth until we got the language just right. After numerous calls with the USOC lawyer and edits to our final settlement agreement, on June 3 we had an agreement we both approved. I held off signing it till my birthday on June 24, 2008. Then I wrote a letter to the editor, which was published as an article. I was honored when the Seattle Post-Intelligencer also published it on July 31 and named me as Guest Columnist.

I learned a valuable lesson throughout this ordeal. I mentioned that Nancy Yeatman had to leave the tasting bar and shush me in the office. Totally embarrassed and still mad as hell, I lowered my voice and spit out the details.

Nancy put a hand on my shoulder and looked me straight in the eyes. "Kathy," she said, <u>"You have two choices when life throws you a curve. You can let it control you or you can take control and do the best job you can while working with the people you have to."</u>

Nancy worked for us that summer season and had cancer. She was living her life to the fullest, her way. All of us at the winery learned so much from her and were grateful that we could share that summer and celebrate ... La Dolce Vida with her.

Letter to the Editor from Kathy Charlton
Owner, Olympic Cellars Winery
July 29, 2008

Running afoul of the Olympics ... and Surviving

As the owner of the Olympic Cellars Winery I'd like to let everyone who has supported me in my conflict with the United States Olympic Committee (USOC) know that we've finally reached an agreement regarding the commercial use of our business name and the framework under which we can continue to operate.

Nine months of negotiation took place from the date we received the USOC's first letter citing us for violation of the 1998 Ted Stevens Act, which gives the USOC near exclusive rights to the name "Olympic" and its derivations. The timeframe is ironic considering I could have birthed a baby during that time, but also could have lost my baby ... a winery that is part of the heritage of the North Olympic Peninsula. In the end, I feel that the agreement meets both parties' key objectives.

I appreciate the USOC's understanding that my business was very important to me and to the employees who count on it for their livelihood. At the end of the day, I was the one who needed to know I had done my due diligence. I read the law, asked the questions and considered my options. I didn't sign the first, second, or even third drafts of the agreement. My detailed attention to every word in that agreement was critical to the final resolution.

While my settlement with the USOC cannot be made public, in summary I can still operate as Olympic Cellars, sell wine via the Internet, keep my website URL and sell to my wine club as long as my sales and marketing of "Olympic Cellars" branded wines beyond my local area are not deemed "substantial."

Bottom line: I can't significantly grow a brand that uses the winery name, Olympic Cellars. The winery will be forced to remain small even though the term OLYMPIC is our birthright and heritage, where we live, and part of our local culture. My Working Girl Wine® brand was exempted from all restrictions.

Even though I understand the funding and sponsorship intent behind the legislation that gives the USOC total control of the commercial use of the word OLYMPIC, I believe Congress must amend the 1998 Ted Stevens Act to comprehend the dramatic changes in both electronic commerce (the internet) and our flattened, global economy.

By forcing Olympic Peninsula businesses to be *local in nature* and restricting sales to the Olympic Peninsula, it unjustly limits our ability to grow, be competitive and survive. Sure, we could change our business names. It certainly would be easier, cheaper, and less hassle. But that means shedding our heritage as well; basically giving in and giving up. And we just can't do that.

It makes far more sense for the USOC to simply limit its investigation to companies outside the Olympic Peninsula using the mark OLYMPIC, and sue those who would try to create an association with, or trade upon the goodwill of the USOC, the U.S. Olympic Team or the Olympic Games for commercial purposes.

Unfortunately, the bigger picture has been lost.

Contrary to what the USOC claims, there is no confusion as to whether the name "Olympic" refers to one of our businesses, the Peninsula where we're located, or the Olympic Games themselves. When you hear the name "Olympic Cellars Winery," is your first thought of a swimmer racing across the pool at the Olympic Games? I don't think so.

The only way one of our *local* businesses could ever escape the harassment of the USOC is to become a giant like the Olympic Game sponsors, AT&T, VISA, McDonalds, Nike, Bank of America, or Anheuser-Busch and actually help sponsor the Olympics! And it would have to do that without national recognition or basic use of the Internet. When someone pulls that off, I'll be the first to raise a glass of vino.

Kathy Charlton
Owner, Olympic Cellars Winery

CHAPTER 29

Women Supporting Women

We started celebrating March 8, International Women's Day (IWD), at the winery in 2004. In previous years, a small group of women would gather at Hollywood Beach in Port Angeles to commemorate the day. Nancy Newman who coordinated that event reached out to me because the weather generally sucked in March and she was looking for a warm, dry place to meet.

The first year we promoted the event it was like a stampede of women converged on the winery. Our press release headline read *All women are working women – so take the night off and join us.* I guess the long, cold, and gloomy winter was getting to everyone. It was a perfect opportunity to get out and see friends.

That night the roar of conversations and laughter couldn't be dimmed even when I announced that we had a special musical performance, Sherry Flanigan, who was going to sing featured songs from her CD, Wild-Hearted Woman. Sherry moved from the tasting room, and then to the gathering room, and finally to the cellar, but music was just not on the ladies' minds that night. She finally put away her guitar and we poured her a glass of wine.

Across the country, Code Pink, Gather the Women, and other organizations coordinated 2004 events. "Stop the world and change it" and "Invest in caring, not killing" were the slogans of the Global Women's Strike, an International Women's Day event held in more than 60 nations. I honestly don't know if I ever really thought about what International Women's Day was all about until this year. Over the years this new event got me to research, read, and especially think what this day meant to me.

In 2005, we had a very small turnout and ended up in our Gathering Room all sitting around the feet of Clara Carlson, a long-time Port Angeles resident who worked passionately to inform and involve women in the political process. Her relentless advocacy for women's rights continued until her death on Jan. 10, 2009, at the age of 102. Clara talked about voting, which was one place where women have a real equal opportunity to make their voices heard. Clara said, "To inform oneself, and to exercise the voting privilege, is the very basis of freedom, the foundation of good government."

Each year I would start writing my press release and opening comments in February. I would Google that year's IWD theme and focus to find a local connection. I needed to personally dig deep as this wasn't one of my fun stories of winery escapades. A theme of women helping women began to evolve.

After the first few years we partnered with Womanfest, a local non-profit that has been empowering women of the Olympic Peninsula for more than twenty years, to put on each year's event. Tasks were doled out and when we opened the doors on the day, guests could smell the evening's buffet; a dozen homemade soups, breads, cookies, and of course, sip wines. We took donations at the door and also donated half of the wine sales to one local and one international non-profit each year.

When I look back at the non-profits supported by this event a quote by Margaret Mead probably says it best, "Never doubt that a small group of thoughtful, committed citizens can change the world: indeed it's the only thing that ever has."

I've included below my opening comments for the 100th Anniversary of International Women's Day Celebrations. (Also sent this as email to list.) I always try to find meaningful connections to our heritage, to the winery, to women, while still keeping it interesting. To me the winery became more than a business. The Working Girls welcomed Working Women – Women Supporting Women is our legacy to support for years to come.

March 8, 2011

100th Anniversary - International Women's Day
I want to start out tonight talking about our Rosé wine. And, if you bear with me a bit there really is a link to tonight's celebration of International Women's Day.

Most of you know we have a new winemaker, Virginie Bourgue. (Benoit moved back to France in 2010 and Virginie contracted to make our wine until we could find a new full-time winemaker). We are going to release her first Olympic Cellars wine during the July 4th weekend. It's a beautiful 2010 Lemberger Rosé known to all as Rosé the Riveter and affectionately known as Rosie.

So my first thought – how best to distinguish her wines from Benoit's, market and celebrate Virginie's first Olympic Cellars wine release?

Lisa came up with the answer: bring back the Dungeness Rosé label that I retired years ago as the Working Girl Wines evolved. Then retire Rosie.

A perfect solution. Made perfect sense. You know we tend to go back to our roots in life and, for us, our winery heritage.

Then I started thinking. Big Mistake. How can you <u>just</u> retire Rosie, our iconic label? Many a time I've looked at her poster in the cellar and muttered to myself when facing wine production madness – We Can Do It. Yes, We CAN Do It, <u>Too!</u> (I muttered it so many times I felt like Dorothy in Oz: I want to go home, I want to go home.)

For those of you that know me, you know my brain may be miss-wired. I think there is a ping pong ball inside my head. As a thought or idea starts to form, it bounces precariously around. If I described the path a decision takes through my brain you would definitely label me certifiable.

But if I'm going to explain the path of one idea, Rosie is the perfect example.

The work issue: We want to sell out our current Rosé in time to release the 2010 vintage. How best to do this?

First, the marketing side of me kicks in. Well, we'll just announce that the Rosie label is off to the "Cellar" Vault just like Disney. As you know, the studio simply places a moratorium on a film and halts production until the timing is right for a re-release. Issue solved. Rosie will be featured, sold out, not to return until the time is right.

Then I got to thinking about Geraldine Hoff Doyle, the face of Rosie that inspired the well-known poster by J. Howard Miller. Sadly, Geraldine passed away on December 30, 2010.

Now I'm thinking. Is this a sign? Shouldn't I retire our Rosie label for good?

Next ping pong ball bounce. It's the 100th Anniversary of International Women's Day. Pretty momentous occasion. This day honors the work of so many, celebrates women's success, and reminds us of inequities still to be redressed. That why we're here tonight.

Oh Lord, the ball is bouncing back and I'm thinking, Rosie is part of this 100th Anniversary of Accomplishments. She changed the workplace for women. We can't retire Rosie.

But, are we past the slogan "We Can Do It?" Didn't We Do It? Haven't We Done It?

We've Come a Long Way Baby floated through my mind.

Then I gagged. Wasn't that the tag line for the Virginia Slims cigarette commercial? Actually, it was *You've* Come a Long Way Baby. (To me that is so condescending.) This hideous reminder was quickly cooled by the recollection that Loretta Lynn also wrote a song titled, "We've Come a Long Way Baby." Okay, I'm feeling Much Better.

As <u>women</u>, we've made monumental strides in every arena of life around the world. And we all know that there is so much more that needs to be done.

Dang, I still don't know what to do with Rosie? So, I Googled her and watched A Library of Congress Rosie video seven times.

What stood out in the video is another war slogan that I've never seen before: The More Women at Work the Sooner We Win.

This slogan obviously refers to WWII. But I'm thinking, isn't this more applicable and urgent today?

War is everywhere but not here. Hunger is here but not so visible. Education is lacking but we have schools. Violence happens but not in our neighborhood. I could continue but you get the picture.

Women have always gathered and solved problems. It's in our genetic makeup. So tonight, the 100th Anniversary of IWD, I'm personally asking each of you to get involved in something that is core to you and to your roots – where your passion lies.

It takes a village and be it a 100 years ago or today, we still have work to do.

Rosie's fate? She's headed to the "Cellar" Vault. Stay tuned. She will return, maybe reincarnated.

For now, drink her wine. And consider the possibilities of The More Women at Work the Sooner We Win.

Another year has come and gone. 2012 is the 101th anniversary of International Women's Day, which to me is even more symbolic. Why? Because women never stop making a difference, day after day, year after year in their community, within their family, for their girlfriends, extending a helping hand, mentoring a young girl.

One of those women is Pamela Hastings, whose doll making classes can be a healing process. Doll makers create symbols of an emotion, a feeling, a sensation, a struggle or a celebration. The first time I saw one of Pamela Hastings artistic creations – *her signature Hot Flash Doll* – I was hooked. This doll conjured up so many images, feelings, experiences . . . good days, bad days, hope, sorrow, reality and just plain joy.

This year Pamela has challenged herself to photograph and paint 100 HOT FLASH WOMEN of all ages. She also wrote in her blog that she was nearing retirement age (what is that anymore) and wanted to gather 'older women' together to discover the *potential* inherent in our age (notice I use the word "our" liberally) and celebrate what we've done, the skills and energy we possess.

When she sent out her email about this project, I held on to it. I knew it had something to do with this year's International Women's Day Celebration but wasn't sure why.

Then I read the theme for International Women's Day – CONNECTING GIRLS, INSPIRING FUTURES.

Before I continue, I'm deleting the reference to 'older women' because Pamela has definitely redefined the term HOT FLASH, giving new meaning to the term "Power Surge!"

Doesn't matter our age… we can do anything we put our minds to.

In 1983 Clara Carlson attended her first Womanfest Fall Retreat at the age of 77 years. In 2006 at the age of 100, Clara wrote a poem about the annual Womanfest Fall Retreat.

A Special Place

I know a place,
A Special place,
A peopled place,
A place peopled with women.

In 2007, Kellee Bradley performed at our IWD celebration and wrote her own lyrics to one my favorite songs, I am Woman, by Helen Reddy. While this was also linked to our Working Girl Wines, it is also a Hot Flash, a Place Peopled with Women.

I am Woman Hear me Pour
In numbers too big to ignore
and I won't stop until my glass is full

I am strong and I am brave
and I've never been afraid
to ask for what I want and to be thankful

oh yes, I am red
I'm full-bodied and I'm proud
Yes, I've found my voice
I'm not afraid to say it loud

If I have to, I can do anything
I am strong
I am invincible
I am woman

Chapter 30

Managing Business Downturns

What happens when your ride to the top starts suddenly rolling downhill?

The winery was making steading gains like a gondola rising to the top of a ski slope with some exhilarating, heart pounding, swishing back and forth downhill runs in fresh snow-white powder.

Life was good.

Then, need I whisper out loud, 2008, for you to get a visual of me tumbling head over heels, landing on my back, spread-eagled with skis pointing East and West.

All our businesses experience downturns for many reasons. Hopefully we see it coming and plan ahead. But if not, we dust ourselves off, adjust our business models, modify our operations and then get back to work. That's why a rainy-day fund is so important, to tide you through the downturns.

But the 2008 economic collapse hit us and everyone else like a ton of bricks. Winery income dropped 25% it seemed just over night. There were very few folks crossing our threshold or buying online and tourism was down. Folks only spent money on what they had to, the necessities of life, saving where they could, not knowing when the next crash could occur.

It helped that the necessities of life included wine and beer, maybe just a less expensive brand. We kept our prices as low as we could afford. We had a hard time selling our premium wines because of the price tag, so there were a lot of specials to entice. Visitors to the winery loved tasting Benoit's beautiful red wines but when it came to what they purchased; well let's just say the Working Girls helped save our bacon again, being our lower priced wines.

We worked hard to not sink further but couldn't scratch our way back to pre-2008 levels.

Guess I'm into analogies but we were sitting right smack in the eye of the Perfect Storm.

Market changes were brewing in our own industry that caught me by surprise. And, who would have thought it would come with the name Coors-Miller.

A bit of background. Alaska Distributing, long-time family owned business located in Seattle, distributed Working Girl Wines. They distributed WG wines throughout Washington, Oregon, Idaho, and Alaska. One of my best days EVER was getting a call from the secretary to the VP of the Alaska wine division to schedule an appointment. I was asked to bring samples of WG Wines to the meeting. When I arrived and was escorted into the conference room I noticed a copy of "Wine Spectator" on the table. It was the issue that featured the Working Girls' story and our wines.

I tried to remain calm as I uncorked the wines, hoping I would remove the cork with one professional looking tug. I can't tell you how many times I've begun to pull a cork just to realize I needed more leverage, so I would just bend over putting the wine on the floor and pull - with my butt in the air. Not an image I wanted to leave with them.

Samples were poured and I launched into my Working Girl spiel. When I finally shut up and looked around the table there were smiles. We got the gig and Alaska chose to represent our wines.

But in 2008, Coors/Miller beers merged and left Alaska for another distributor. This was a major hit to Alaska. When a distributor loads their trucks for delivery, it is mostly filled with beer and then back-filled with wine. Losing these two iconic beer brands required them to sell out to a new joint venture, Southern Wine & Spirits of America, Inc., the nation's leading wine and spirits distributor, and Odom Corporation.

I had already experienced the impact of Southern moving into states where Working Girl Wines were distributed mostly by smaller and often family owned businesses. Many of these distributors lost key persons to Southern, were bought out or closed their doors, unable to compete. We also wrote off a few bad debts from our previous distributors during this time.

This was my wake-up call. It felt like the wine industry was finally thrust into the 21st century and was trying to catch up. I was re-living my corporate career again; more women in leadership positions (technical/management), consolidation in the market, fast paced technology changes and an emerging global economy. But, going through it as a small local business, though, was a totally different experience.

Maybe I had just been riding the good wave and not paying attention to the changing current. Market place consolidation hit us even worse than the economic collapse. Consolidation included larger wine conglomerates buying out brands and wineries. Just to put this in perspective; there are approximately 8,700 wineries in the US and the top thirty U.S. wine producers represent nearly 90 percent of the domestic wine sold annually. Bear in mind, though, that the top three companies just by themselves represent more than half of U.S. case sales.

Initially, our wines remained under the Southern/Odom portfolio but there wasn't much energy around it. We lasted a few more years but the Working Girl Brand was just too small and we couldn't compete on pricing. No longer were we distributed in the Pacific Northwest and national distribution receded with the ongoing industry consolidation.

OK, no more whining. I needed to put my big girl panties on and make a plan.

National distribution of a small brand like Working Girl was a thing of the past. We needed to promote in our own back yard, regionally in the Pacific Northwest. At least I wasn't on the road constantly, Ralph had his wife back, and it felt really good to be back at the winery and just not calling in. And traveling sucks.

Our inventory was out of balance with the beautiful, premium wines gracefully aging in the cellar. Although we promoted with discount specials, we needed these wines to promote the winery in a different way.

First, we changed our spiel to our customers. Our conversation at the tasting bar changed to a more traditional discussion of vineyards, the wine making process, Benoit's French-American wine style, our wine awards, etc. Then we would intersperse a few of the WG stories and antics just to keep the conversation lively.

I also changed the way I promoted the wines outside the winery. I didn't pour WG wines much anymore, changing my focus to pushing our premium wines for wine shops, chefs and restaurants. Prior to our meetings, I would visit their shop checking out the wines for sale or study the restaurant's menu. Now I carried the 'wine bag' filled with our premium wines that I would pour for owners and chefs. In my spiel to them, of course, I'd weave in how well our different wines were paired with their delicious entrees or why Olympic Cellars on their shelf would sell. My strategy? To get featured on the restaurant's wine list and get invited to pour my wines at a wine shop customer tasting.

Restaurants bought wines in smaller quantities directly from the winery so we generally had to do our own deliveries. We identified local and regional restaurants that promoted small, artisan wineries and asked if we could talk to the wait staff about the wines. I told stories about the winery as we tasted the wines, giving them educational, interesting and fun sound bites they could share with their customers. Think about it. If you were contemplating four Merlots on a wine list and you asked your waiter for a recommendation and he/she briefly shared a story about one of the wines, well, stories sell. We knew if the wines were enjoyed at a restaurant, customers would generally seek out the winery.

Back to the eye of the Perfect Storm.

There was one more major change in Washington State via Initiative 1183, dubbed the Costco initiative, which was on the November 8, 2011, statewide ballot. It was passed and the measure called for closing state liquor stores and allowing state licensing of private parties. Privately owned stores were required to have at least 10,000 square feet of retail space to sell and distribute liquor. This was a slap in the face to smaller businesses that would have liked to supplement their beer and wine sales with spirits.

In our industry, many were opposed to 1183 because it eliminated uniform pricing, which supported the small wineries. But frankly, do you know of another industry that enforces pricing – so regardless of your business size all pricing is the same? That goes against free enterprise. Why would somebody innovate? Hard for me to say as a small business, but it is a free marketplace.

What did this mean for us locally?

Let's take our local Safeway, a grocery store chain, as an example. Prior to Initiative 1183 only wine and beer adorned their shelves. Now the same space must include twenty-two flavors of vodka or whatever the "corporate" approved list of spirits were. Shelf space was at a premium and wines were cut from their approved list based on volume sold.

Will the chains value small producers? I believe so, even if on a small scale. Consumers still want it. Safeway sure did. Nora Bush, the wine steward at Sequim Safeway, is an ardent supporter of local wineries. She made it her mission to get shelf space for local wineries, including Olympic Cellars. And she did. We have "primo, prime" end cap shelf space.

2008 thru 2012 – yes to me it was mind-blowing time of change. And yes, we were back to our roots when I started the winery but not bankrupt anymore. We'd rebuilt our infrastructure, had a quality cellar, strong local support, a vibrant tourist season and a growing wine club. The summer concert series and tourism kept us on our toes between bottling and harvest.

Did I have all the answers back then? Not entirely. But, with any challenge, there are opportunities.

I own a small business. I am a Working Girl. It's sounds cool to say I work for myself . . . but in truth I work for my customer. <u>And, my customer is "the new consumer."</u>

Well, I'm also the new consumer. What attracts me to a business? How do I adapt my business to reach out? Emails, yes, but so much more. First question, do I have a mobile website? Jeez, no. Now top of my list.

Bottom-line, I can't do it alone as a small business. On the Peninsula and communities all around our country, there was a collaborative model of small businesses working together in conjunction with their Chambers of Commerce, tourism-focused organizations, downtown associations and private groups supporting the economic backbone of their community. We are creating the "experience," telling our story. Yes, it continues to still work the tourism business model, but these new collaborative types of businesses create the personality of a community and that "vibrancy" helps draw new businesses to a community and keeps families here working and playing.

While the retail model has shifted to the ease of purchasing on-line, that's not all there is to life. As important as effective the use of technology can be, never let yourself lose sight of the fundamentals of business. <u>It is always a human interaction.</u> It starts with "*How Can I Help You?*" be it in person or via on-line live chat. *Then the conversation begins.*

CHAPTER 31

Life Doesn't Stop Just Because You Own Your business

Life happens every day. And just because you own a business doesn't mean you don't have a life. Well, maybe sometimes, during peak seasons of your business or an on-line product launch.

I'm writing this chapter about 7:30 p.m., which is my wine time with my computer. I did get out today; I walked Harley and got some groceries before we starved. But, I'm not the best person to talk about work-life balance. In fact, I really don't like those three words, work-life balance, because to me it implies a 50-50 balance, which I just can't do more than I care to admit.

But when it's a FAMILY crisis, you have to know where your priorities lie.

I'm thinking back to Sunday, January 7, 2007, when the caregivers who took care of Ralph's Dad in Ellensburg, Washington contacted us. (Ralph's Dad and his mother had been divorced for many years and she had since remarried and lived in Sequim.)

We got some very disturbing news that required us to immediately drop everything and head to Ellensburg the next day. What we found out was every family's worst nightmare. It's not necessary to go into the details, but suffice it to say, for the next three months all we could focus on was ensuring Ralph's Dad would live out his life in a loving and caring environment.

While we could have hired professionals to lift some of this burden from our shoulders, we felt that it was important for us to take on this task for Ralph's Dad and the entire family This was our skill set - get to the bottom of an issue, analyze it and then find a solution. I know this isn't a business problem so w*hy do I even tell you this? Because life does not stop just because you own your business. Though I couldn't neglect the business, I also couldn't neglect family. The days just got longer.*

If it wasn't for a strong team that had my back during the worst of times we would have never made it. My husband and I owe Molly, Libby, Benoit, and Kathy Kidwell a huge debt of gratitude for carrying the load during our months in Ellensburg.

Fast forward two years and life happens again.

I found out that I had extensive basal skin cancer on my nose and I scheduled surgery for early December 2009. A new nose grafted to the skin from my forehead, a couple of surgeries later, and I was stuck at the house recuperating. I checked in with the winery team by phone, but for a while I couldn't even wear my glasses. Thank goodness this happened in December – no bottling, the harvest was complete and the new wines were bedded down in barrels for the next few months. Just the tasting room and wine shipment responsibilities. The team had it well in hand.

At first all I could really do is watch TV. Feeling a little (well maybe a lot) sorry for myself that I couldn't do all the normal holiday activities, I thought watching the Christmas shows on the Hallmark channel would get me in the Christmas spirit. I even ordered a new, brightly colored scarf to wear on the couch.

Do you know how many holiday movies are aired in December? I tried to count and then started listing all the titles of the movies – I hit thirty-seven and was still finding new ones. I still couldn't wear my glasses for the honking bandage on my nose, so I had a pen and a yellow pad at hand and would scribble the titles out in big letters so I could read them.

Then I got this bright idea (too much time on my hands) that if I could combine the **titles (in bold below)** in the right way, the titles would write a story that could rival the best country ballad. I tried to use thirty-one but twenty-nine will have to do.

Hallmark gave me back the Christmas spirit and also was the inspiration for a new holiday email. (I didn't need Google this time.) Although after reading this, I'm sure some of my friends just shook their heads wondering what the heck. One friend even asked if I was certifiable, i.e. maybe just a bit crazy.

My *Hallmark* Christmas Tale

Christmas is **THE MOST WONDERFUL TIME OF THE YEAR** ... truly **A SEASON OF MIRACLES**!

I've had quite a dry spell without someone in my life so all I wanted this year was a **BOYFRIEND FOR CHRISTMAS**. Putting a plan in action I auditioned for the Bachelorette reality show and won! Now I have the television famed **12 MEN OF CHRISTMAS** to pick from.

It's a hard job but someone has to do it.

When I met **MR. ST NICK**, # 12, I knew he was the one. Must have been the name and being quite superstitions I knew this was also a *sign*. During the finale show on Christmas Eve, #12 swept me off my feet with the most beautiful **CHRISTMAS PROPOSAL** and the promise of **OUR FIRST CHRISTMAS** in his family's **CHRISTMAS COTTAGE**.

Mr. St. Nick said his best Christmas memory was a **FAMILY HOLIDAY** when all his brothers and sisters were able to come **HOME FOR CHRISTMAS** to their hometown. Till this day that **TWIN PINES CHRISTMAS** brings tears to his eyes. (*I so like a big strong man that can express his feelings.*)

Well, after all the interviews and paparazzi questions, Mr. St. Nick and I had very little time to get **HOME BY CHRISTMAS**. The drive to Twin Pines was a true **RECIPE FOR A PERFECT CHRISTMAS** with snow on the ground, **MOONLIGHT AND MISTLETOE,** and the car loaded down with presents.

You know when you find your true love on a television show; you probably should ask a few more questions before setting off to visit his family. I thought I knew everything about Mr. St. Nick because after all, I met him on a reality show! And this year I was going to be part of a real family.

The rest of the story ...

See, I don't have any family of my own as I am an orphan. I was born **A CHRISTMAS CHILD** and was abandoned under the **NATIONAL CHRISTMAS TREE** on the White House Lawn in Washington, D. C. Miracles do happen especially **WHEN ANGELS COME TO TOWN** in the form of a White House guard who found me under the tree. He wrapped me in his coat and took me home and laid me in the arms of his wife, Eve, who could never have children. I was truly **EVE'S CHRISTMAS** present. Eventually I had to be turned over to the authorities but just for a few days I had my own Grandma and **GRANDPA FOR CHRISTMAS.**

Back to Mr. St. Nick. When we arrived there was a **SPECIAL DELIVERY** envelope waiting for him. He quickly tore it open, read the stack of papers and then motioned to me that he needed to talk to me in private. He told me he worked for the FBI and that he had another reason for coming back to Twin Pines... it was an **UNDERCOVER CHRISTMAS** assignment. OMG!

There was a group of thieves operating in the area who were also magicians by day. They used their special talents to steal jewelry and replace it with fake paste pieces right under people's noses. These sneaky thieves pulled off a perfect **HOLIDAY SWITCH** just before the jewelry was to be auctioned off for the Children's Hospital Fund at a fancy **HOLIDAY AFFAIR**. To make a long story short, Mr. St. Nick tracked down the thieves and they will be spending their **HOLIDAY IN HANDCUFFS**.

Mr. St. Nick, his family, and I were about to sit down for Christmas dinner when we heard the local **CHRISTMAS CHOIR** singing carols outside the front door. We rushed to give them refreshments and listen to a new song, **CHRISTMAS IN CARTAAN,** by Achy Breaky Heart-famed country legend, Billy Rae Cyrus.

One of the carolers bent down and retrieved an obvious looking Christmas card that had fallen from the mailbox. It had a Washington D.C. return address. Apparently, the guard who found me so many years ago tracked me down after watching the Bachelorette show and reading all the stories in the tabloids. (Orphaned on Christmas at our country's capital, bachelor's home at Twin Pines, etc.)

Now to finish this Hallmark Tale, we're off to Washington DC. **"I'LL BE HOME FOR CHRISTMAS"** for **OUR MAGIC CHRISTMAS** to **MEET THE SANTA** of my dreams!!!!

Chapter 32

Times Are A Changing...

My husband, Ralph, and I have been making our bi-annual pilgrimage to recharge to a small fishing village, Sayulita, north of Puerto Vallarta for the last five years. The place we stay is rustic but boasts fast wireless and good food. I worry about the speed of the Internet and have the staff check it prior to arriving. I may be a little OCD, but my other priority is good wine, which is checked with my luggage. So I'm not totally a lost cause.

Billed as a working vacation, we pack up two laptops, two iPads, two iPhones (now on the Mexican phone plan), and six inches of working files, yellow pads, and pens. Then if there's room, we add some clothes.

I'm the worst – it takes me about four days to slow down and stop checking email every hour. I'm anxious... waiting for my creative marketing streak to kick-in because by November each year I'm brain dead. And by April I need to charge up for bottling and summer tourist season. Finally, though, the music of the surf has me relaxed enough to count lizards on the ceiling

I have to say, 2012 was a year of major change in my life. Ralph and I own our respective businesses, or, as they say, the businesses own us. But anyhow, both past the age of 62++, we always said we wanted to work together instead of just working together in the same office.

At the time, he was dealing with a death in his team. Vonnie McClean, a long-time employee and right-hand lady to Ralph, passed away from cancer in September 2011. The last time I saw Vonnie she was wheeled into the winery covered in blankets to attend an August concert so she could hear the Beatles Tribute Band, Crème Tangerine, which she loved. Her face lit up listening to the music and I remember her smiles.

In early 2012 I took over the operations part-time of Target Focus Training (TFT). Ralph's partner, Tim Larkin, is the founder and creator of this very effective Self-Protection Training and Ralph does all the marketing. The business was growing and from an operations standpoint the business needed their own customer service team. Previously, they had outsourced it. In addition, the day-to-day operations needed reviewing and processes defined. This I could do with my eyes closed, but I wasn't terribly excited about the work; it was just a job. To me, initially it had no soul. I couldn't find my passion.

For me to divide my time between two businesses wasn't going to work. I needed to get out of the day to day of the winery. Lisa started learning the ropes of the winery and managing its operations. While not in the tasting room much anymore, I still had my feet in the grapes, so to speak, with wine production, marketing, and events.

Instead of enjoying a glass of wine at day's end with the Working Girls in the tasting room, I toasted my computer with wine each evening, Harley, the winery dog in training, my constant companion.

The next year, 2013, turned out to be another year of life changes for this Working Girl.

Although, I'm not the retiring type, I had hoped that by getting things under control from an operations standpoint, Ralph's workload would be reduced and we would have more time together.

But the self-defense industry was growing at a rapid rate. If you think back a few years, the mass shootings seemed to be never-ending, starting with the attacks at the Aurora movie theater and Newtown elementary school in 2012. There were forty-five terrorist-spawned and related incidents in the US after 9/11 to February 2017. People were anxious, afraid, and looking for answers to protect themselves and their loved ones. http://www.johnstonsarchive.net/terrorism/wrjp255a.html

Terrorism isn't the only violence we face today. Just as life threatening are the home invasions, drug induced crimes, and attacks against women. The bottom line is that all of us are at risk every day. This was the focus of TFT training. The calls to our customer service team increased from individuals searching for self-defense training. And, calls from women seeking help increased, changing my whole focus.

I was miserable in 2012. I was working two businesses, one that I love with all my heart, Olympic Cellars, and Target Focus Training? Well, it was a job.

I really couldn't do both well so I chose my husband over the winery and Lisa took over full operations and management responsibilities. Once I committed and wasn't standing in both camps I began to find TFT's soul and my passion.

In the summer of 2013 I spearheaded the launch of Tim Larkin's new NY Times bestseller book, Survive the Unthinkable, A Total Guide to Women's Self-Protection.

I read his book more than once, with highlights and notes all over the pages. Researching further and facing the cold hard stats: annually 1.9 million women are physically assaulted, every two minutes someone is sexually assaulted and 1 in 6 women are raped in the U.S. – and that's only the ones that are reported. Women have the right not to live in fear of being targeted for assault, rape, and murder simply because of their gender.

TFT had the opportunity to pre-sale the book to their customers. We also conducted a survey of the buyers and discovered that 84% of books were purchased by men who wanted to get the information and training to the women in their lives.

What we heard from these men was that the women in their lives simply weren't interested, for a myriad of reasons. They didn't think violence would happen to them; they were too busy to do the training; they feared that they were incapable of defending themselves, and, because of their moral code – they couldn't imagine hurting another human being. To address the last one; if you ask a woman if she would defend her child if a predator was hurting him or her, the answer was a resounding YES. So, taking it one step further, if you asked, "Would you defend yourself and disable your attacker if necessary so you would not leave your child without a mother?" The answer was a thoughtful, YES.

Addressing the first three reasons. (1) No one is safe today. (2) Training can be done in a weekend. (3) Self-defense books and classes still advocated cooperating or screaming – not attacking as the form of self-defense. Women were conditioned to NOT fight back, made to believe they were the weaker sex, told to capitulate and not to make the predator mad.

Which is a bald face lie. Women regardless of their age, size or physical condition can defeat the bigger, faster, stronger predator. This book, "Survive the Unthinkable," provided women with the knowledge about how predators think, taught women how to spot them, outsmart them and stop them in their tracks.

I am so thankful that I had the opportunity to a be a part of this book launch and to know from firsthand accounts how the book and TFT training helped so many women. "*I felt like it opened something up inside of me. Looking back, I understand what that something was, permission to defend myself.*" While this is one women's comment, we had hundreds that said the same thing in different words.

I've worked for a corporation. I've owned a small business. The difference between TFT and my last two careers was the fact TFT training can save lives. The TFT team was on a mission to combat Violence Against

Women. I was proud to be a part of it.

I will never regret my decision to leave the day-to-day of Olympic Cellars to Lisa and work with my husband. But after almost two years with TFT I needed to make a decision. Lisa and her husband Tom were very interested in buying the winery; it was their American Dream. They also owned a brewery, Fathom and League, and the combo of the two would be dynamite. Beer and wine, giving customers more choices.

So, in the summer of 2014, we shook hands and started drawing up the papers, which we signed in October of that year. I consulted for another year easing myself out of the business I felt we had all rebirthed.

I used to say semiconductors to grapes was not a natural career path. Now add in self-defense and the only common attribute among all three was my glass of wine at day's end. Cheers.

This was the last email I wrote to my winery customers. By now, you've read many of my emails and know there is usually a story behind them.

Bottom line, I'm still a Working Girl. Proud to continue supporting Women and their families.

Working Girl goes far beyond the wines. It stands for what we did as a team and as a business. I still get on rants and have been know, to blurt out, *Hey, I am Woman, Hear me Roar. And don't you forget it.* (Yep, now had to change *Pour* to *Roar*)

Boys [Girls] in the Boat
June 30, 2015

Hi, Kathy here,

I haven't emailed in a very long time because it was too sad to send a good-bye or even an *Au revoir* email when I sold the winery last year. My excuse ... I'm still doing some training ... sooo I'm still a <u>Working Girl</u> and, of course, loving our wines.

However I did have another reason for writing today. It seems all I can think about is the Working Girls as I read the book, *Boys in the Boat*, this amazing true story about beating the odds, finding hope in the most desperate of times, the nine young Americans and their epic quest for Rowing Gold at the 1936 Berlin Olympics.

Now I'm sure you're beginning to wonder where I'm going with this and

What IS the link to the Working Girls?

Of course the Boys in the Boat team rowed at the University of Washington in Seattle and yes, one of the main characters had lived in Sequim just about nine miles from the winery.

But did you know there is a boat named "Working Girl" in the Sequim Museum and Arts Center. This racing shell was built by *the* George Y. Pocock, internationally known for designing and handcrafting the best and swiftest racing shells in the world of crew racing. He built the boat, *Husky Clipper*, for the 1936 Olympic Team – The Boys in the Boat.

So say again, Kathy what does this have to do with the Working Girls (Neilu, Molly, Kerrie, Kathy, Lisa, Kristi, Cathe, Randi, Libby, Cally, Rosemary and Nancy) and the boat?

The boat was built in 1947, originally christened the *City of Naches* and was rowed immediately by Al Ulbrickson crews (retuning GI's) at UofW. Later the boat became part of Western's new rowing program and ended up as surplus in 1997 by the Everett Rowing club. She survived being sold to TGI Friday's to become a s*alad bar* and was rescued by the Orcas Island Rowing again with another new name, *NACHO*.

In 2009 the Olympic Peninsula Rowing Team in Port Angeles purchased and restored her and Olympic Cellars shortly thereafter sponsored their inter-generational team, hence the name change to *Working Girl*.

As I continue reading *Boys in the Boat*, I find myself pondering George Pocock's quiet, intuitive insight to coaching, along with his quotes on life through rowing liberally interlaced throughout the book.

That's when I thought about the Working Girls and our *Handyme*n the most. Rebuilding the winery, whatever it took, many long hours, successes and failures . . . but we kept focused with a single goal. And, we worked as a team.

"Great crews may have men or women of exceptional talent or strength; they may have outstanding coxswains or stroke oars or bowmen; but they have no stars. The team effort— the perfectly synchronized flow of muscle, oars, boat, and water; the single, whole, unified, and beautiful symphony that a crew in motion becomes — is all that matters. Not the individual, not the self." George Pocock Daniel James Brown, The Boys in the Boat: Nine Americans and Their Epic Quest for Gold at the 1936 Berlin Olympics

Au revoir,
Kathy, Former Owner of Olympic Cellars and still a Working Girl

PS. One last connection to this story and the Working Girls. It may be a stretch but I kept thinking about the women after the war ... the GI's _came_ home, and the Rosie the Riveters _went_ home.

And then a different kind of struggle begins ...

Women had achieved much during World War II in professions that had been closed to them for years. Many women didn't want to stop working when the war ended. There were those who needed the extra income to help support family members who had been disabled. Others simply enjoyed the freedom of pursuing what had been a male occupation.

During the war, women had proven that they could do a "man's job." Having taken the step forward, they weren't prepared to go back. Women had learned to fight for their rights during World War II, and it was a battle that didn't end with the war.

"It doesn't matter how many times you get knocked down," he told his daughter, Marilynn. "What matters is how many times you get up."
George Pocock
- Daniel James Brown, The Boys in the Boat: Nine Americans and Their Epic Quest for Gold at the 1936 Berlin Olympics

Chapter 33

The Circle Is Still Unbroken

Sharing the winery's story and history with you through this book has been a joy and an honor.

A few years ago, I wrote the "The Unbroken Circle." There were so many incredible connections to the origins of the winery, the founder, our home and our wines it was almost eerie, as if we were following a destiny of sorts. This final winery email is a compilation of our heritage, my fifteen years owning the winery, and its future.

Olympic Cellars is a premium blend of old and new. We never stood still and always worked together to grow the winery and in that we also grew personally.

If you own a business, I know you understand. It's like raising our kids. There is so much love, a few ups and downs, hard decisions but in the end an immense amount of pride at day's end.

For me my product was wine and it is like life ... full of possibilities, ever changing and aging gracefully!

The Unbroken Circle

Back in the late 70's, Gene Neuharth, a grape grower from California, retired and moved to Sequim. He immediately planted a *vineyard* from cuttings from his California vineyard and started a winery, the first on Washington's Olympic Peninsula. The winery's home was an old *dairy barn*.

While the vineyard didn't thrive, *Neuharth Winery* did. Gene's best-known creation, his *Dungeness Red* and *Dungeness White* wine series, was one of the early *"fanciful"* brand names in the industry.

At Gene's *death* in 1992, assistant winemaker, Dan Caudill, took the winery reins, eventually changing its name to *Olympic Cellars*. Forced to move because of a highway bypass around Sequim, Dan chose a century old *dairy barn*, originally known as *Wayside Farm* just east of Port Angeles.

In 1999 I purchased the winery, taking over operations in 2001. Joined by Molly Rivard and Libby Sweetser, the three of us took the winery in a new direction, always careful to preserve its *heritage*.

We released *Working Girl Wines* in 2003. With "*fanciful*" labels depicting the personality of each owner, the wines struck an emotional cord with Olympic Cellars customers. "*Created* by women, *In Support* of women," the wines underwrote our commitment to philanthropic giving.

I began fundraising in late 2005 to commission a Micro-Climate study designed to identify areas on the Olympic Peninsula warm enough to grow cool weather varieties of grapes. If climate and soils prove suitable for cool weather grape growing, the establishment of *vineyards* will help enhance the Peninsula's *historically* rich *agricultural heritage*.

Last year we removed plywood covering the cupolas towering above the barn, replacing it with playful stained glass. As we lit the cupolas for the first time in 2006, I guess we can call it "*barn nouveau*." I like to think it is *smiling*!

Harvest 2006 was a year of celebration. Libby and I picked the first local grapes ever used in an Olympic Cellars' wine! *Dungeness Bay Vineyard* (owned by Tom Miller of Sequim) was the source and our winemaker, Benoit Murat, created from them our first *local Le Vin Nouveau* wine.

Dungeness Bay Vineyard is located across the road from the *Dungeness Cemetery* where Gene Neuharth is buried. I know Gene is proud, a "*smiling*" papa, as he looks down on his dream come true . . . *vineyards* in the Dungeness Valley.

Benoit planted Olympic Cellars' first "La Petite" vineyard in March of that year. Continuing with the original farm's heritage, we dedicated it "*Wayside Vineyard*." Future vintages from each of our local wines will be labeled under our *heritage Dungeness* series label.

Looking back now on the history of the winery, the community and the owners, there does seem a *plan* for us all to carry out: shortly after Benoit planted the vineyard a mother Killdeer laid her eggs in row #3.

<u>*Life* starts again! *The Circle Is Unbroken.*</u>

Life does go on.

Lisa, Molly and Randi are now the women of Olympic Cellars. Working Girl is no longer its persona but part of its heritage. It is now a family-owned winery writing their own story.

Molly still is the face of the tasting room. Without Molly, my sister through the grapes, the winery wouldn't be what it is today. Thank you from the bottom of my heart.

Randi Corcoran took over the financial, state and federal reporting from Kathy Kidwell in 2012 amongst her other WG duties.

Kristi Knowles joined the tasting room team in 2011 and retired to her many art and gardening projects in December 2015.

Michael Smith, our beloved Handyman, always had our backs. If we needed help he was there ... ALWAYS - Anytime - Anywhere.

Greg Vogtritter sold his winery, Sun River Vintners, in Eastern Washington and moved West. He joined the Olympic Cellars Team as winemaker in 2013.

I handed Olympic Cellars and all our dreams and accomplishments to Lisa and her husband, Tom.

This is now their American Dream ... The Circle is STILL Unbroken

Thank you for reading,
Kathy, A Working Girl

Appendix

Olympic Cellars Winery and Working Girl Wines

Website http://www.olympiccellars.com/

Facebook https://www.facebook.com/OlympicCellars

Kathy Charlton, Facebook: https://www.facebook.com/Kathy.Charlton.Working.Girl/

Kathy Charlton, Blog: http://blog.kathycharlton.com/

Olympic Peninsula Wineries and Tourism

Marrowstone Vineyards http://www.marrowstonevineyards.com/

Alpenfire Cider https://alpenfirecider.com/

Camaraderie Cellars http://camaraderiecellars.com/

Eaglemount Wine & Cider https://eaglemountwinery.com/

FairWinds Winery http://www.fairwindswinery.com/

Finnriver Farm & Cidery http://www.finnriver.com/

Harbinger Winery https://www.harbingerwinery.com/

Marrowstone Vineyards http://www.marrowstonevineyards.com/

Wind Rose http://www.windrosecellars.com/

Olympic Culinary Loop http://www.olympicculinaryloop.com/

Olympic Peninsula Wineries Association http://www.olympicpeninsulawineries.org/

Olympic Peninsula Washington State http://www.olympicpeninsula.org/

Wine Bites

Wine and Moods Pairing http://www.bettertastingwine.com/wine_moods.html

Canoe Ridge Vineyard and Winery http://canoeridgevineyard.com/winery

Chateau Ste. Michelle https://www.ste-michelle.com/

JaM Cellars http://www.jamcellars.com/

Pasek Cellars http://www.pasekcellars.com/

Robert Mondavi Private Selection https://www.robertmondaviprivateselection.com/

Rombauer Vineyards http://www.rombauer.com/

Saviah Cellars, The Jack Series http://www.saviahcellars.com/wine/the-jack/

Treveri Cellars http://www.trevericellars.com/

Waterbrook http://waterbrook.com/

Woodward Canyon https://www.woodwardcanyon.com/woody-way/

Credits

Bella Italia Restaurant http://www.bellaitaliapa.com/

Best Friend Nutrition https://www.bestfriendnutrition.com/

Captain Joseph House Foundation http://captainjosephhousefoundation.org/

Christopher Enges https://www.facebook.com/christopher.enges

Daniel James Brown, The Boys in the Boat: Nine Americans and Their Epic Quest for Gold at the 1936 Berlin Olympics

Fathom & League Hop Yard Brewery http://www.fathomandleaguebrewery.com/

Kathy Womack Gallery https://www.kwomack.com/

LeRoy Bell http://leroybell.com/

Lucy and Ethel wrap chocolates https://www.youtube.com/watch?v=W-mAwcMNxGqM

Molly, Libby and me re-enact the Chocolate Factory https://www.facebook.com/Kathy.Charlton.Working.Girl/

Melissa Klein http://www.melissaklein.com/

Olympic Peninsula Humane Society https://ophumanesociety.org/

Pamela Hastings https://www.pamelahastings.com/

Target Focus Training https://targetfocustraining.com/

The Fat Chance Band https://www.facebook.com/thefatchanceband/

Willis Chambers Barn and home to Olympic Cellars Winery http://archive.peninsuladailynews.com/article/20110123/news/301239983/clallam-barns-reminders-of-farming-past

Womanfest www.womanfest.org

Women for WineSense http://www.womenforwinesense.org/

Made in the USA
Columbia, SC
12 June 2018